Where Did That Member Go?

Rediscovering the Lost Art of Member Service

Thomas Plummer

ISBN: 978-1-60679-101-1
Library of Congress Control Number: 2010922934
Cover design: Brenden Murphy
Book layout: Deb Oldenburg
Front cover photo: Stockbyte

Healthy Learning
P.O. Box 1828
Monterey, CA 93942
www.healthylearning.com

This book is dedicated to Susan and her children, Jill and CJ, and our granddaughter, Madison. I was late to this family dance. I never expected or dreamed that I would ever have a family of my own, but you have changed my life, and I am grateful for all of you and all the love that you bring. Things like this remind you that if you ever want to make God laugh until the thunder rolls, just show him your plans for your life, and then He will show you where you are really going to go.

Dedication

Acknowledgments

I have promised myself, and have proclaimed loudly to many friends, that each coming year will always be my last in this industry. Now, it's 30 years later, and the journey still continues. It seems that maybe God is not done with me just yet, and there is more work yet to do.

Last year, a participant in a workshop came up after we had finished to thank me for the two days of fun and education. I thanked him for coming and thanked him for taking the time away from his business. I hadn't realized it at first, but he had been in a workshop a number of years earlier, and I simply didn't recognize him. There was a day that I could remember almost everyone who passed through a seminar, but after well over 50,000 participants it all sort of runs together these days. I apologized for not remembering and thanked him again for the faith and support through the years.

He was with his wife, and they smiled, shook my hand, and turned to go. They got about 10 feet away, and the wife turned and came back. She was crying and gave me a hug, as I stood there bewildered. She told me that they were down to their last few dollars when they first came to the seminar and were very close to losing their club, and perhaps their house as well.

After that first seminar, they went home and made changes as I suggested during their first two days. She told me that I was the only reason that they were still in business and that they would have failed if they had not found me when they did those five years earlier. They left after a number of hugs and tears and with the belief that I had changed their life.

I owe my life to these people and everyone like them who has ever passed through a workshop. The guests in our workshops have done more to change my life than I have ever done for them, and I am thankful and grateful for every single one who has ever sat in a chair for a day or two and who has listened to me rant and rave about how to run a successful fitness business.

I have no idea when this will end. Sooner or later, another door will open, and this one will close, and that will be that for me in this industry. Until that time, I remain true to the original mission: you can make money ethically in this business, and every owner who tries deserves respect and a fair chance. We strive to continue to change this industry for the better, one owner at a time, and my thanks to everyone that has allowed me to do this as my life's work.

Contents

Introduction

The fitness industry is an industry of mistakes, failures, and over 60 years of history of doing the wrong thing for our clients. We have mastered the art of the adversarial membership sale, we have advocated equipment and training that is both harmful and ineffective, and the member has never been anything more than a sales number recorded on a daily tracking sheet—easily replaceable by the next new sale tomorrow.

Even today, there are still thousands of club owners, including most of the largest chains in the country, that still believe they are in the membership business, not the retention-through-client-success business, and that we will always have an endless stream of new clients to replace the ones we continue to fail.

The fitness business should be a business of trust. We take money in exchange for the client's belief—and trust—that we can help him change his life through our leadership and guidance. In reality, in most mainstream clubs, unless this person can ante up the necessary money to declare himself elite and, therefore, buy leadership through personal training, the member is left to seek fitness on his own through magazines or help from other lost members.

The members believe we will help them, but we set them up with antiquated circuit training, including the giant workout card, that will fail them after a few weeks, and then ignore them until we need them again at the end of their membership. If a member wants to get in shape in these clubs, he has to damn well work hard on his own because the club simply can't, or won't, provide the leadership and help he needs to be successful over time.

We have in essence created a culture of failure in our clubs. We run insulting advertising, pressure hard on the first visit, and only give a couple of workouts with a disinterested trainer, unless the person has a wad of cash sticking out of his pocket, and then we love this member. For everyone else, we default to 1970s training philosophy that every major fitness guru in the industry has declared not to be effective in getting people into shape and keeping them there once they do arrive. Everything we do is for the simple sake of selling memberships, which is the way it has been since the dawning of the modern fitness era in 1945.

This coming decade will be remembered forever as the decade of change in the fitness business. The industry has changed more in the last several years than it has in the previous 60. Maturing markets—defined as more clubs in your competitive area, new breakthroughs in training theory, the advent of functional training that allows an owner to generate big money in less space, the shift in the economy that will end the ability to build endless big-box clubs and a more sophisticated owner—all combined at this point in history to force a new, harsh reality on the way things have to be done if you want to continue to make money in this industry.

What has become apparent from this collision of factors is that the member is now becoming more important. Competition prevents endlessly replacing the ones you do get. The consumer is brighter and better read about fitness, bringing new demands on how he wants to be trained. Most traditional marketing sources are no longer valid to create leads for the clubs. Most importantly, everyone is now realizing that it just costs too much to acquire new members as opposed to simply keeping the ones you have already purchased.

The foundation for keeping your members is customer service. We have never, ever in this industry practiced anything but the most primitive basics of customer service. We don't know how to teach it, we don't know what it looks like, we don't have the right people to deliver it, and we don't have any systems in place to track the ultimate goal of good service, which is member retention.

Customer service is the mastery of many small things, such as the ability to handle complaints or create systems that individualize the member's experience no matter how large your club is. When it comes to developing a customer-service image for your business, most owners are starting at the bottom of the ladder with nowhere to go but up. And no matter how good you think your service might be, if you haven't trained your counter team for at least four hours last week, and every week, in creating and delivering customer service, then you too are at the bottom.

Service can be taught. Systems can be created that any owner can apply to his business. This book is about rediscovering the lost art of member service and then implementing it in your business. It is also about where we have failed the member, and how we should respect his commitment to our businesses.

Your goal with this book is to move away from the culture of failure where we have let down the people who have trusted us with their time and money and move toward building a business that retains its clients through the creation of legendary customer service.

NOTE TO THE READER

Use this material at your own risk. Much of what is written here is based upon my own opinion, derived from my own research and experience in this industry. All the material included in this book is offered as a simple starting point for an owner or manager to use to begin building a better customer-service image for his business.

In all cases, and especially in legal issues concerning your business, such as staffing, you are advised to seek the advice of qualified professionals that support your business locally, including accountants, attorneys, and other business professionals who may know your business and your situation on a more intimate level.

Neither the author, nor publisher, nor any party related to the information and development of this book assumes any responsibility or liability for the consequences, whether good or bad, of your application of this material.

Also please note that some examples or bits of information are repeated in several different chapters in this book. Many of the readers of the earlier books have reported that they read this material by choosing specific chapters that are relevant to their interest or business problem at hand and don't always read the book straight through in order.

These owners and managers also report that they often assign specific chapters for their staff training without necessarily requiring that the staff read the entire book. This necessitates that some information may be repeated where needed to enable the chapters to stand alone.

IMAGINING LEGENDARY CUSTOMER SERVICE IN YOUR BUSINESS

IT Stock

Section One

Searching for legendary service ...
why service matters.

The most important asset in your company—and the hardest thing for any competitor to copy—is a well-trained staff.

Fitness trends come and go, but a quality, professional staff is something so rare that it gives any owner who has the drive and patience to build one an almost insurmountable competitive edge in the market.

The definer for this staff is the commitment to delivering legendary service to the members who have trusted that business with their money, faith, and time. In most markets, people interested in becoming a member of a fitness facility have an almost unlimited choice in today's marketplace.

The people who become your members and support your business deserve more than just the insulting service that most people have come to expect from all fitness businesses in this country.

Delivering legendary service should be your goal every day you are in business, because these people had a choice, and they chose you and your facility as their own. Legendary service can be defined as exceeding the member's expectations in relationship to what he pays—and what he gets in exchange—from your business.

Members expect a great deal in this exchange for the hard-earned money they spend with you each month, but exceeding that level of expected service is what will separate you from all the other pretenders in your market.

Good service is defining for your business the sense that your image in the market is based upon a solid reputation of taking care of your members, but creating legendary service ensures that your business will be a financial success for the years to come by setting you apart from all other fitness businesses.

1

We Treat Our Friends Better Than We Do the People Who Pay Us as Members in Our Businesses

My house. My guests.

If you are coming to my house as a guest, I will treat you with respect. I will be courteous. I will dress for the occasion to show respect for my guests.

If it is a big party and there is a caterer, or perhaps someone parking cars, those people will respect the guests of the house, be courteous, and dress nicely for the guests.

The guests are always more important than the people working the party, and if you are rude or disrespectful to the guests in any way, I will always choose the guest over you because the guests are more important than you are. You are here to serve and take care of the needs of our guests, and you can be replaced if you disrespect or dishonor the guests of this house.

The previous illustration is your analogy for what service should be in your club, and "My house, my guests" is perhaps the most powerful way there is to convey your expectations to your staff of what level of service is expected in your business.

When you throw a party at your home, you always make sure your guests are well taken care of beginning when they arrive. Each one is greeted at the door as a welcome friend, and all your guests are attended to with care and respect throughout the duration of their stay.

Even you weekend savages that equate a party with 50 drunks in your backyard, drinking beer and barbequing, at least get enough beer and food to sustain the group and to make sure everyone has a good time. If we throw a party, we instinctively try to take care of our friends and guests and make sure they all feel appreciated and special.

Perhaps the better analogy is the family holiday party. If you invite family and friends to your home over the holidays, most folks spend a great deal more time making sure the house is perfect, the food is well thought out and planned perfectly, and that everyone dresses up a little because your mother or in-laws are coming to visit, and you understand the concept of showing respect for others during this time of year.

Where we fail in most businesses—especially if we have been in that business for a long time—is that we forget who is paying the bills. The intense nature of constantly delivering customer service in any small business ultimately leads to customer fatigue. At some point (and it will happen to everyone who has ever worked in a fitness business and who has to deal with member problems on a daily basis), you begin to hate the people who provide your living.

This anger usually arises when we forget the importance of the people who support our businesses and what they actually want from us on a daily basis. Why did the member choose us over our competition? What are their expectations from my business? And most importantly, we forget that since they are the ones paying us for service, their expectations are always higher that we are willing to match. Why are these people here, and what do they want from us?

Start your drive to become a more successful owner by building your business around the "My house, my guests" mind-set. You will make better decisions in your business because the members are no longer numbers or faceless revenue on a billing report, but honored guests who will stay longer and pay longer if we remember to treat them with the respect they deserve.

We Should Strive to Make Our Fitness Business the Third Place in Their Life

This overworked line is so overused that it has become an almost meaningless throwaway phrase used by every customer-service speaker in the world, but it has a basic truth to it that is worth exploring one more time in the context of creating customer service in a fitness business.

We often repeat this tired statement to our staff without taking the time to explain its hidden power or give any hints as to how to implement it within our businesses. We also hear it from new speakers at industry trade shows who want to share their limited (usually to the one club they have managed in their three years in business) customer-service experience to the point of being nauseated. We hear the tired service messages repeated so often that we don't hear the true meaning anymore.

Those of you married for 10 years or longer can probably relate. How many things do you have between you and your spouse that have been repeated so often that the words have no effect any longer? If you think about it, you can only hear "Put the toilet seat down" about a hundred times or so, and then the brain just locks the words out of your sensory inputs.

Comstock

Explained simply, *we should strive to make our fitness business the third place in their life,* meaning that we strive to establish our business at the same level of importance as their family and their business/job. In other words, we want to achieve family/work/fitness as the holy trilogy of owning a fitness business of any kind.

This adage fails in direct application, however, because we always depend on the hope that fitness alone will become the central focus in their lives. We get hope when we get a few members that get so excited by fitness that they become freaks, lose 100 pounds, and virtually live at the gym six days a week. These limited success stories ruin us mentally because now we think every member coming through the door is going to drink the Kool-Aid® and join the fitness cult, but most members have other, and much simpler, expectations about their new membership.

Many owners have lost their way in understanding the essence of fitness over the last few decades or so. We have simply lost the power of coaching and teaching people to get fit, and replaced this hands-on support with a dependency on machines as tools to provide service. It has become much easier for many owners to just buy six new pieces of the latest and greatest from a trade show than it is to properly train their staff to provide service.

We have through the years become machine convenient rather than people-oriented, and this subservience to the machine circuit has cost us millions of dollars in lost revenue through members who fail in the club and leave without achieving their goals, because going around in a circle, holding a large workout card to get in shape, only works for about six weeks. After six weeks, you need help and personal guidance to continue to benefit from a fitness program, which most clubs only offer to the elite few who can afford personal training.

What is the real product we sell in this business? The three most common misconceptions are:

- We sell memberships (the memberships become the products).

- We rent equipment and expect the equipment to provide the service (the product is the amount of stuff we have compared to other clubs in our market).

- We sell fitness/getting in shape (the product is you getting into shape).

All three of these concepts represent a failing business plan for most clubs. Membership clubs—such as some of the big chains that have failed during the last decade—put all of their emphasis on crushing potential members at point of sale. The marketing, the first experience, and the lack of service after the sale all point to a club that only exists to sell memberships and not sustain members over time. In this model, every member is replaceable, and success in the business today is measured by units sold today.

This model worked in the past because of lack of competition and lack of choice in the market. As markets mature, meaning a higher density of clubs in your five-mile member zone around your club, this type of membership-driven model fails. Even the low-priced/value clubs that offer memberships in the $9 to $19 range will at some point often burn up their market because there just aren't enough new members out there to replace all the ones you will lose.

Keep in mind that about 85 to 90 percent of your entire membership only comes from about a 12-minute drive time around your club, and that eventually you run out of potential members if all you do is count on driving high volume each month.

Most owners who are in the equipment-rental business don't even know that they are in the equipment-rental business. There are a number of clubs in the Northeast, for example, which are beautiful facilities, costing often $4,000,000 and more to build and ran by talented owners. These owners often charge between $49 and $69 per-month-per-member, and many have been in business for a number of years.

These same owners become furious, however, when a low-price/volume competitor opens in their market for about $10 per month. The owners with the top-end clubs can't believe that they lose members to these low-priced guys, but most ignore the reality of what they truly own and have built.

If you don't provide any leadership or service, and merely sign up members who come to use your treadmills and other equipment and then get ignored, the members are going to be much happier only paying $10 a month to rent the same brand tread these guys are charging $49 per month or higher for each month. These owners thought they were in the people business, but the low-priced guys down the street proved that they were actually in the equipment-rental business and are even overcharging for the right to use that treadmill.

Fitness is also not a saleable product. If someone just wants to get in shape, all they really have to do is just open the front door and go for a walk, which is more than most of our fat citizens do anyway each day. Fitness can be done in a small space at home, and cheaply, too, if you know what you are doing. No one needs a fitness facility to get in shape, so why do people continue to join one year after year?

What we really sell—and what people pay for—is the "you time" factor. Yes, this does mean that if the member pays you money, it is indeed all about him and what he wants from you and your business.

"You time" relates to people joining clubs for personal reasons that relate to their life and needs beyond just plain getting in shape. What do people really want from your business, from you, and from your staff, and what are the simple expectations that many members carry with them when they become a client of a fitness business?

- *Someone to design a program for them so they don't waste time:* Time is everyone's most precious asset these days. In the past, we have built failure into our members from their first experience by painting unrealistic pictures of what it takes to get and stay fit. It was not unusual in this industry just a few years ago for a trainer to lay out a program that might take more than an hour a day, five or six days a week, and give it to the member as their minimum workout. The member knew the second he saw the workout sheet that he would fail because of existing kid issues, work issues, and other obligations. Members want the most bang for the buck spent, and that means teach me to get in, get it done, and get out so I don't waste a minute doing something I don't need to be doing.

- *Private time without the spouse or kids*: Just one hour with no phones, no kids, no boss, no spouse, and none of life's intruding hassles. Just me, all by myself, for one hour, hiding in your business. Why do you think men sit in bathrooms reading sports magazines for an hour at a time and women go get their nails done once a week? My time, without intrusions and the other stressful issues that ruin my time.

- *Leadership and guidance to enhance the fitness journey*: We sell leadership. Fitness and eating well is confusing and even most fitness professionals can't agree on what to do or what to eat. The people seeking your help are looking for guidance on their fitness journey, and the best clubs are willing to provide the structure that the members are seeking.

- *Social atmosphere and the power of group dynamics*: Most of the good things in life are done in groups. Ski trips, rafting, parties, going to games, and even sports as a kid or in high school are all done in a group setting; yet, as fitness business owners, we try over and over again to turn fitness into a solitary sport. Fitness is social, and we are social beings going all the way back to the cavemen who hunted in packs and then went to the hot springs for a beer and hot tub after the big hunt. During the last decade or so, the trend has been to isolate the member in the club. Training is either done solo, using your own workout, or one-on-one with a trainer. Cardio is done with your own headset, watching your individual television screen. Except for group exercise, everything else in a commercial fitness business has been designed to only support one person at a time, which goes against the main reason most people come to a club. People want to interact, and an intelligently designed club would design that into its plan.

- *Weight loss and weight management*: No one comes in a club to buy a membership; they come to buy a solution. I am fat; sell me the solution to become skinnier. Formalized weight management is good service that many club owners haven't yet embraced, and it's also good money for the club.

- *A strong service experience in relationship to the money spent by the client*: You can also think of a visit to the club that day by a member as a short visit to a hotel. He spends money for a room for the night and expects good service for the money spent. Why is coming to your club any different than that hotel stay? He pays for expected service, but because we see him every day, we treat him as a regular and forget that, in his mind, his one hour with us is the same as a mini-vacation at a hotel. He pays for the experience with all the same expectations of service that he has with any other type of exchange of money for time spent.

The amazing thing to people in the industry is that clients will spend money to buy what they want, if we understand and sell what they are looking for when they come through the door. If we truly understood "you time," then we would run our businesses much more differently.

For example, if you understand "you time," and if you realize that if the client pays you, he then has the expectation that his service experience will be all about him during each visit, you would run your business from a different perspective.

If it really is about the member experience in your business, you might hire an older, and better-trained, front counter staff to provide a higher level of member/staff contact. You would also dress your staff in nicer uniforms, because the staff now understands that the clients expect a higher level of service from the club and its staff since they are the ones paying you to come to your club. Also, remember that the member is a guest at our house, and we always dress for our guests.

You might also be more concerned about the total member experience in the club each day, no matter how big or small the club is, since the client considers the quality of the daily experience as one of the reasons he joined your business. Other things in the business, such as locker rooms and group rooms, become more important since it really is all about the client who pays us each month for the privilege of coming to the club and then spending more money while he is there.

Because the client has lost guest status in our house, and has now become another pain in the ass along with all the rest of the members that are forgotten once they buy that membership, he leaves us. By the way, by this time, we no longer refer to the person as a client or guest. He has by now become "the meathead," the "cheap bitch in the 1980s leotard," "the smelly fat jerk," or we simply lump them all together as the "animals." It is hard to get your staff to respect the guests of the house if the owners and managers refer to the paying members as animals or worse during the normal workday.

Why We Lose Customers

In his book *The Ultimate Marketing Plan*, Dan Kennedy cites why businesses lose customers. His research offers a direct insight as to why many clubs fail despite having an endless sea of equipment or the most skilled salesperson. According to Kennedy:

- 1 percent of your customers die, although in the fitness business we might be able to actually affect that number if we can keep the member coming on a regular basis and pursuing a healthier lifestyle.

- 3 percent move away. This number is actually higher for the fitness industry. The typical club will lose about 1 percent per month, or 12 percent annually, through people who move over 25 miles from their business, resulting in a forced cancellation by most states.

- 5 percent follow a friend's or relative's advice and switch to that friend's preferred merchant.

- 9 percent switch due to price or a better product.

- 14 percent switch due to product or service dissatisfaction.

Add all of these up and you only come up with 32 percent. The strongest point Kennedy makes is what happens to the other 68 percent?

- 68 percent switch because of what they perceive and describe as indifference from the merchant (insert club here) or someone in the merchant's organization (insert the name of any of your poorly trained staff here). Kennedy says, "In other words, they felt unappreciated, unimportant, taken for granted. That's not my theory, remember—that's what actual customers have said."

The 1 Percent Group

Let's look at these numbers more closely and directly apply them to your business. First of all, we can't do anything about dead, although if the person might have started at the club earlier, he might not have died sooner than he hoped.

The 3 Percent Group

We also can't do anything about the people who move away from the club. The states usually dictate, and it is a fair law, that we must cancel anyone who moves over 25 miles from the club with proof of move. While you can't do anything about them moving, you should spend more time on the proof part.

The only acceptable proof is a utility bill from their new home. You can fake everything else easily but the utility bill is the hardest one to come up with if you are trying to lie your way out of a club membership. "I would be happy to cancel your membership, sir. Simply send a copy of one of your new utility bills from your new address, and I will cancel your membership immediately."

We actually have more control over the rest of these categories than most businesses, but we fail to recognize why people leave and then we compound the error by failing to act. Remember, the club industry is changing, and your emphasis should be on acquisition of new members *and* retention as opposed to just going for the highest number of new members you can get each month with the belief that all members are replaceable in your market. Severe competition has forced us to realize that the old adage where a member lost can always be replaced next month is the path to failure in today's fitness business.

The 5 Percent Group

Next, look at the 5 percent that get dragged away because a friend or relative gave them a strong reference about a new club they found. There is a lot of psychology at work here you need to think about because you can have an effect on the outcome.

Start with considering that there is always a certain percentage of people who like to be the one in their social circle who is always the hipster, defined as the friend who always has the newest phone, computer, trendy car, or is the first at the trendiest bar or vacation spot. This is the guy who loves to "turn his friends on" to the something he discovered that they—the poor, uninformed, socially inept circle of friends—are missing.

What makes us unique in this business is that we build relationships with people on an almost daily basis, which should be the foundational truth of your customer-service training. If we are successful with our service program and achieve a relationship with our customer, we are much less likely to lose him to a casual referral. Think about your relationship with your accountant or family dentist. If you have one of those professionals you enjoy working with, then it would be pretty hard to pry you away just because your friend brags about his newest accountant.

This assumes, of course, that your accountant or family dentist has done her job. Does she take the time to know you personally? Does she contact you on a regular basis? Has she taken time to get to know you beyond just being a customer? If you don't have a relationship with this person, and especially if you have even the slightest dissatisfaction at the moment, then you are easily swayed and can be talked into something new.

Building relationships through a planned attack based upon solid customer service protects your membership from the casual referral about the hottest new club in town. You still might lose a few, but you can lower the five percent by fighting for the members you do have.

There is also a side issue that is important. You and your club should be leading the change in the market as to what is hot and what is current in fitness. Members in this category are often easy to pry away because their club is years out of date when it comes to programming and equipment.

For example, when the movie *The 300* came out about the Spartans and their epic battle against overwhelming forces, the DVD version also came with a disc on the training that the actors did to prepare for the movie, which involved kettle bells, rope training, and other current and effective functional training ideas. Sadly, when the guys who bought the movie and watched the training disk got excited and wanted to go train at a club with this equipment, they were out of luck in the large majority of mainstream fitness facilities.

Small training clubs had already embraced this type of training, but mainstream fitness facilities—even at the date this book was published—hadn't yet adapted this type of training. If you were already a member in a club, you realized your club didn't have the information or tools to deliver this service. How many people left their clubs, and often ended up paying much more for service and the chance to work with trainers armed with these new tools in parks and garages, because the typical fitness club simply didn't "get it"?

Leaving for price is a hard issue to define. During recent years, there has been an advent of the low-price/value clubs entering the market. These clubs simply eliminate many of the moving parts that a typical club offers, such as childcare or group exercise, and then offer a cheap price that is the equivalent of renting a treadmill for $9 per month.

What is interesting is how competitors react when these new clubs enter the market. Some—especially the ones who have been negligent with staff training, upgrading programming, and reinvesting in their businesses, and who have arrogantly taken money for years without putting much back into the business—usually fail quickly and disappear within a year of the low-price club entering the market.

On the other hand, some clubs thrive when a low-price competitor enters the market. These clubs practice strong differentiation and usually have the strongest customer-service team in the market.

For example, these survivor clubs might have a solid group-exercise program offered in a three-room configuration, an advanced childcare program, and a personal coaching department based upon a small percentage of one-on-one training, semi-private training, and an extended group personal training. This same club would also be totally focused on building a functional training culture throughout the club, which again differentiates it from a low-priced competitor that does nothing more than rent a large floor of equipment at a cheap price.

This club could do quite well in the market over time because it offers an alternative to the low-price club. In other words, the low-price guy has a plan and serves a specific clientele in the marketplace, and the other, full-service club also targets a specific market and does well. Both businesses survive, both make money, and both are needed in most marketplaces.

The hard part to deal with if you are the owner of the full-service club, and if you happened to be in the market first, is that you will still lose a certain percentage of your members to a low-price competitor no matter what you do. For example, if you own the full-service club and sell memberships at $49 per month, and your competitor offers memberships at $10 per month, you will lose a small, but painful, percentage of your members who simply want or need a lower price.

This number, in most cases, is still less than 10 percent of your membership, depending on how good your service is and how strong your relationships are with your membership. Price matters to some people, but not to as many as you think. People who are on tight budgets will leave you. People who are in between are reluctant to leave if they have a tie to the club. And some people will stay at the higher price club because they don't like a lot of people around or they want programming or services the low-price club doesn't offer.

The key thought is that it isn't always price when someone leaves you for a new club. If you have failed to develop a relationship with the member, and all he is doing is renting a treadmill, then he might as well go to the lowest-price club, which probably has the same treadmill or better, and just use it at a lower price.

iStockphoto/Thinkstock

One of the biggest mistakes an owner makes is that he has a constant urge to overreact to market conditions. "Overreactive" is when you respond to competition, or to market factors, too extremely instead of applying the appropriate response that would protect your business. Too much too soon can often weaken the business instead of providing the stability and protection you are seeking.

There is another old saying that is very important to consider: your perceived fears are usually worse than what actually happens. Put another way, the more you think about how bad it could be seldom matches the reality because your mind almost always comes up with the worst-case scenario. An owner especially magnifies the possible horror when he starts using absolutes, such as, "That new guy will take *all* of my business," or "If I rewrite my memberships and adjust the price, I will lose money because *everyone* will want to do that."

Someone usually overreacts to a situation when he is running the business in a totally reactive mode instead of driving the business to dominate the market. For example, if you constantly react to a competitor's moves in the marketplace, you will make mistakes. Reacting to his plan, rather than trying to run your own business dictated by running your own business plan, forces you to make short-term reactive decisions based upon something that is happening today, rather than trying to set your business in motion over time to weather anything that might come your way, such as the entry of a low-priced competitor into your town.

For example, one owner who is a very sophisticated businessperson in other businesses, but runs his club in a totally reactive mode, was hit hard with a number of lower-priced competitors in his market that all arrived in a very short period of time. When he encountered this first wave of new competition, he immediately lowered his price to meet theirs. At first, this seems to make sense, but in reality you have now changed your business plan to match theirs, and in this particular case, the owner's facility and type of club didn't warrant the overreaction to the changing market conditions.

In this case, this owner had a multi-million-dollar club that could have withstood the onslaught, but in anticipation of bad things happening, not based upon actual results yet felt in the business, he jumped first and jumped too far by matching their low prices.

Keep in mind that price is the last thing you should adjust, but it's usually the first thing to change for owners who don't have a tight plan in place to grow the business. If all you do is worry about maintaining your business, then you make mistakes because every decision is based upon doing what you can to not lose business. If you focus on growth as the core of your plan, you make decisions based upon constantly trying to increase market share and keep competitors locked into their own niches and out of yours.

If you are running a proactive business, you may still get rocked temporarily by a new competitor, but the damage is usually less significant and, most importantly, you have time to react without panic.

Proactive business management is defined as building a plan, and then driving revenue and the business every single day based upon that plan. For example, if you have a four-million-dollar investment in your club, you should be running that business very aggressively. Aggressively means you are marketing every week, you continually work to develop the club's money zones, you adjust the prices as needed every two years, you train and develop staff daily, and, in other words, you run your business as a business driving the market rather than reacting to others in the market.

Most owners don't do any of these things and then seem shocked that they get their ass kicked by a new player in their game. *Staffing and customer service may be the biggest indicator of how you will fare in a price attack.* Most owners pay too little for desk staff (therefore attracting idiots), try to use too many part-timers instead of trying to hire a few skilled full-time people, and then only train their team a few hours a month.

Let's see: you hire stupid kids, pay them at the poverty level, offer them part-time hours because you think you are beating the tax and benefit system, all resulting in your team having little real loyalty to your business, and then you don't train them in customer service. Then let's complain a lot about how unfair it is when a low-price guy moves in and takes your members.

Proactive assumes there is always a competitor coming, and that he will be good. Preparing your staff to retain your members is a fundamental truth of business. Hiring idiots and not training them is what you do when you want your members to leave you.

Miss your spouse's birthday a few times and blow off your anniversary to go out with your friends, and you'll see first-hand what happens when you don't work on retention in a relationship, which is what a club is all about if your price is $39 a month or higher. Why should a member stay with your business when you offer weak service and rent the same brand of treadmill for $30 more a month than the guy down the street?

You can't compete on fields of equipment based upon price. You can run a proactive business and dominate a market based upon differentiation, constant service, and a better club, but it is harder, which is probably why most owners prefer to endlessly complain about how easy it was in the early days and how hard it is now to make money in today's marketplace. These owners are right; it is harder, but that is the new reality that drives the current market.

The 14 Percent Group

The members in the 14 percent group, or those who leave due to product or service dissatisfaction, are usually the ones we simply drive away through mistakes that we never rectify. You will make mistakes; it's how you handle these mistakes that separates you from the rest in the customer-service world.

Most owners never realize how many mistakes and how much damage they do each day to their membership. For example, a trainer late for an appointment, a front counter person on her cell phone who doesn't acknowledge a member when he checks in, a billing mistake on a membership payment, and a group-exercise instructor who can't teach today because the music system is down are all errors on our part and all represent a chance to drive a member away from the club and into the arms of the owner down the street.

We forget that these are mistakes that need to be rectified, because after a few years in the business, we simply accept all of these things as "$#!+ happens," and it's part of a normal day in the fitness business. We should have, however, given the training client a free session, fired the counter person, or at least retrained her, immediately corrected the billing problem, or at least got an answer, now, while the member is in the club, and given everyone in the group class a free smoothie.

Mistakes happen, but if you don't acknowledge and deal with these issues as they occur, then you are driving a member away from your business because you simply didn't value the relationship. If a member pays you for a service, then that member has an expectation that they will be valued in the business. Not fixing the problem devalues the relationship and the member as a person. Remember, again, "My house, my guest," and we always honor and respect the guests in our house.

The 68 Percent Group

The 68 percent group, of course, is the members you can fight for and keep if you have a plan in place. Remember, this group is defined as the ones who classify themselves as unappreciated, unimportant, or taken for granted.

We don't lose these people because of tough competition, economic concerns, or friends that drag them to the newest club in town. We lose these people because we drive them away due to poor service and lack of caring. We simply put more of our time and effort into chasing new sales rather than putting energy and thought into what it takes to make a customer who has already trusted us once feel appreciated in our businesses.

Customer service is the solution to this category of losses. These losses are, for the most part, controllable by an owner willing to fight for his membership and who understands the importance of retention in today's market. How to fight for this group is what the rest of this book is all about.

Do These Things Now

- Learn the "My house, my guests" analogy, and make it yours. This is the strongest way you can start to reshape your thinking about what customer service should be in your business.

- Understand that the members want more from you than just fitness. They want a place to escape each day to seek their time and their space. Make the club the third important thing in their life after work and home.

- Stop isolating people in your business. Anyone can get in shape at home without you. These people come to the club seeking the group experience. Design your club with socialization areas, stretching areas, sports bars, group training, and other design features that allow the members to interact.

- Work on the 68 percent of the members who leave us because they feel the club ownership is indifferent to their membership. Customer service builds relationships, and people who have a bond with your business will stay longer and pay longer.

- Run a proactive business designed to create fresh revenue each day and to keep as many of the members you already have in your system connected to the club for a longer period of time. Fight for your business, and stop worrying about what the other competitors are doing.

Customer service is as simple as …
saying "Thank you."

We often tend to view customer service as something that is hard to define, or as something so soft and esoteric that no one understands what it means or can find a way to teach it to our staff.

Sometimes, the best approaches to being successful in business are the most simple. The words "Thank you for your business" may be some of the most powerful words we can use with our members, and for member retention, but sadly, these are often words that we use too infrequently or without any real sincerity.

If you have been in business for any length of time, and this is your only income, be thankful for all the members who pay their membership each month, which ultimately becomes the money that allows you to pay your bills, send your kids to school, or just to buy food and shelter for your family. For most people who make their living in this industry, everything you have in your life started out as a member who believes in what you do and who writes you a check each month.

Be grateful to the people who make your life possible, and say, "Thank you for your business" a little more often each day.

2

The Most Important Reason to Master Customer Service Is Retention

The modern fitness era began at the end of World War II with the creation of the commercial health-club market. The first large-scale clubs opened on the coasts and centered on the "physical culture" life and the desire to produce the first modern generation of fit bodies.

Obviously, at that time, there were only a few clubs trying to create markets in a population that hadn't yet embraced fitness as a lifestyle. These clubs only had one goal: spread the passion, and get new members to embrace the physically fit life.

There also weren't many professional fitness people yet in the market and few real business systems that could be applied to the growing club market. Without a proven, established formula to make money in this industry, most owners at the time reached out to other industries for sales and marketing ideas. Most of the business systems upon which the fitness industry was founded came from insurance sales, dance studios, traditional door-to-door sales techniques—still a viable business opportunity at the time—and other businesses that put a premium on aggressive sales techniques to move a product.

The important point to learn as an owner today is that the industry was started in an aggressive acquisition mode, meaning everyone who worked in the clubs at that time focused on just adding as many new members as possible since the market was virtually untapped. The industry did grow over the first 60 years or so by being totally focused on only developing systems that were centered on acquiring as many new members as possible in the shortest time possible.

Retention of existing members really wasn't an issue at the time since untapped markets and unlimited new sales didn't force an owner to spend too much time worrying about keeping the members he had already acquired. Every member lost was easily replaceable with two more since there were fewer clubs than demand for membership. In those days, there were actually entire states with only one or two fitness facilities, and owners often had access to easy capital based upon early presale numbers—something almost impossible to do in today's market.

*In today's mature markets, with often too many clubs for
the number of active consumers, the rules have to change
or the clubs will perish.*

We no longer have the advantage, or perhaps the arrogance, of thinking we can just sign up new members and ignore them until they leave, knowing that two more are waiting to take their place. The market has changed, and our business model has to shift from one focused on just acquisition to a more balanced model that couples new sales with a strong, dynamic retention program.

Most owners claim that they do understand retention, but under careful analysis these claims don't hold up. For example, many owners talk about retention but still build their businesses on old tools from the last century designed to get as many leads through the door and in front of the salesperson as cheaply as possible. If the person chooses not to become a member, he is eliminated quickly, and the club is ready for the next prospect. For example:

- Most clubs have a dedicated sales team, but few have any dedicated member-retention people.

- Most clubs still pay heavy commissions for new sales and little money for keeping the members already in the system. For example, a club might pay a salesperson $25 for a new sale, but only $10 for a renewal even though the renewal is a cheaper acquisition and better for the club's overall bottom line.

- Most clubs still only offer three workouts as a new member, and then you are on your own. Fitness has become more complicated, although much more effective, as club owners move from typical circuit-driven workouts on single-joint, fixed-plane equipment to function-driven workouts. When you give a new member just three workouts on a circuit written on an old, 1980s workout card, and then ignore him from that point forward, you are guaranteeing he will fail and leave the club. The entire training system most clubs practice is actually geared toward failure since the member is never set up properly during his first 30 days and doesn't have a chance to get real results after his first six weeks. Almost any fitness program works for six weeks, but what happens when the new member has gone around the circuit circle too many times, but then finds getting new information, in the form of a new workout, is too expensive.

• Most clubs still only offer one-on-one training as their only coaching option, as opposed to semi-private training and even group personal training done in groups of up to 10 people with a trainer (personal coach). These clubs can't afford to help the client because it costs too much to deliver one-on-one and the member can't always afford one-on-one, so he doesn't get help and eventually fails on his fitness journey.

Chris Clinton

- Most clubs offer no trial membership of any kind, and many still won't let you try a single workout before becoming a member. This is one of the oldest pieces of sales nonsense still left from the early days. Salespeople are asking the person for $400 to $500 for a membership in many cases, but won't let the person try it first to see if he will like the club. In the early days, you didn't have to let the person try anything since there were no other choices. Today, simply drive another mile or so down the road, and someone with another fitness business will let you try a workout and experience their club.

- The majority of clubs also still use marketing that puts all the emphasis on getting a person to make a decision to buy now, today, and without getting any chance to try the facility. Typical ads in this category are the ones that offer huge discounts if you come in and sign up now, such as 50 percent off of the membership fee. These ads might have worked in the 1960s when the consumer was far less sales jaded than he is today, but in the modern market, how many people really believe that they are getting an actual 50 percent discount on anything? If the guy does believe he is receiving an actual discount, then he might be too stupid to actually be your member.

- There is still a high percentage of clubs, estimated to be at least 70 percent, which still drop-close the member during the first visit. Drop-closing is defined as a salesperson showing one higher price to get started, but if you are willing to make up your mind today and today only, then he will knock off money as an incentive for the person to get going today. For example, a salesperson might show a $149 startup fee, but if you are willing to get started today, he will slash that amount to only $49 and you will save $100, but if you don't sign today and come back tomorrow you will pay the $149. Again, this worked in the prehistoric days of the fitness industry, but only a very unsophisticated client who has spent the last 10 years locked in a closet would actually believe this today.

None of these techniques were designed to get and keep members, only to get as many new members as possible signed up today. All of these techniques and business practices work against a club owner trying to make money in today's market, since the owner using these techniques assumes that he still can get a lot of volume (unlimited lead potential) to play with in his town.

The Case for Customer Service and Retention

Maturing markets change the focus from volume to retention.

There are a number of reasons that retention is the business plan of the future. First of all, maturing markets, defined as how many competitors you have in your three- to five-mile service area, are forcing good owners to move away from fighting for just constant volume.

Few clubs get hit hard by a major competitor if they are running tight businesses. Sadly, the ones hit hardest by a new competitor are often the ones that deserve it the most. These are the owners who fail to reinvest in the club, who have dated equipment and programming, treat their members with little respect, and if they can get by with it, hire the cheapest and dumbest staff on the market.

Small business is very Darwinian in nature. Only the strongest survive, and if you aren't constantly improving your business, then a new competitor will come and take your members away from you.

Most clubs that lose ground in their markets due to new competitors do so by just slowly leaking their membership away over a period of years. For example, that little club that opened in the strip plaza a mile from you didn't take all your members. It did, however, take about 50. And then there was the mixed-martial-arts guy who opened that took about 20 of your free-weight guys. Oh, wait, and there was that church that put some weight equipment in their basement, and that cost you about 30 members. Volume used to be easy, but now it is a struggle to fight for members against a dozen different business concepts all targeting the same small percentage of potential fitness clients. Death in business today is not a major blow to your business; it is sort of like being slowly pecked to death by a thousand hungry chickens.

In mature markets, retention might be the only tool you have to survive over time; because good clubs will have to learn to make more money internally, through the addition of multiple sources of revenue, and by learning to run a business focused on keeping the largest amount of members you can staying longer and paying longer.

There is an important side note to consider. As of the date of this book, only about 16 percent of the people in this country actually belong to a fitness facility of any type. Each year, new clubs are being added faster than new members. One of the biggest issues for an owner to understand is that you need to stop fighting over the same small market of people who actually understand fitness and start working on developing new markets for your business.

If you grasp the number previously discussed, only 16 percent of the population belongs to a club, which means that 84 percent of the people in this country don't belong to a fitness facility of any type. Direct your marketing, and build your brand, by targeting the 84 percent who have yet to experience what happens in the fitness world.

Marketing is more costly and less effective.

If you stand at the finish line of a large marathon race, you see streams of people crossing the line who are just thrilled to survive. Those that run for the purpose of pure accomplishment often finish in four hours and longer. If you were standing at that finish line selling bottles of ice-cold water, you wouldn't keep your stock very long. Four or five hours of slow running, sipping out of the occasional cup, makes a runner very thirsty, and everyone is looking for their own bottle of the coldest water they can get. If you have a cold beer available, so much the better for anyone celebrating the feat of completing something special.

Marketing for fitness centers used to be like free bottles of ice water for parched runners. Any ad would work, and every club owner thought he was a genius in marketing. The secret, of course, is that marketing is easy if you have a limited product sought after by a large number of people, which is the way the business was in the early days.

Marketing today is tough and expensive. Every day, the consumer is overloaded by messages far beyond what anyone experienced even 10 years ago. Going back for a single 10-year period, there was no electronic social networking, such as Twitter™, no instant access through your handheld crackberry, few personal Web pages, no Facebook, and even your television had fewer choices.

All these images fluttering around a person's head—combined with radio, satellite radio, newspapers, instant news access on the computer, and a huge pile of direct mail in his mailbox—leads to a potential client that is almost immune to marketing and advertising. Everyone is chasing this guy, but the sheer number of images he has to process just to get through his average day makes it hard to get his attention.

The cost of marketing is also much higher and the choices are much wider for an owner to deal with when putting together a marketing plan. Simple direct mail will cost you at least $3000 or $4000 per month. Web pages start at $4000 or more for something simple and go up from there. Flyer inserts in newspapers, once the cheapest way to get your message out and maybe still the best buy for most clubs, seem to increase every six months as newspapers try to stop the hemorrhaging in their operations.

> *Both of these points, too many competing images*
> *chasing the same person and the increased cost of*
> *consistent marketing, build an even stronger case*
> *to keep the members you already have in the system*
> *for a longer period of time.*

In the old days, you could run a cheap ad in the paper, based upon a stupid price discount, and talk to leads tomorrow. Today, you can run thousands of dollars worth of ads a month and see your leads decline because there are seven other competitors in the same market area chasing the same potential members.

The cost of acquisition

The cost of acquiring new members has also been rising through the years. Besides the higher cost of marketing to get a new member, we also have higher initial costs to get the person started. For example, we might have a $25 commission paid to a salesperson for making the sale, as well as a direct cost of labor during the first 30 days to get the person set up with a trainer. Many clubs also give away small gifts as a means of validating the buying decision, and these items need to be factored in as well.

Let's assume that this facility charges its members as follows: $59 to get started, and $49 per month for 12 months. The following is a typical expense flow needed to start a new member.

Marketing

- $4000 monthly marketing expense generates 80 new leads for the business.

- The club gets 48 new members out of the 80 leads (60 percent closing rate).

- $4000/48 = $83 ($83 per sale in marketing expense)

Sales

- The club pays $25 commission for the sale.

Labor

Labor costs can be dramatically reduced if the club understands semi-private and group personal training and uses group orientations to get new members started. The clubs that don't use these tools incur a much higher initial cost because everything is done using one-on-one, which is simply too costly.

Because of the high cost in the old one-on-one system, most clubs limit their help for a new member to only about three workouts, and then you are on your own. This simple mistake is very costly in retention because the new member was never set up properly during his first 30 days, meaning he will leave earlier in his membership, and this type of member will leave more often because he never got any results from his efforts.

- One-on-one labor costs in the traditional system based upon three workouts = $60 (three workouts at $20 per session for the trainer)

Group personal training and semi-private training would reduce this to less than $25 per club per initial 30 days because a larger number of people are sharing a trainer.

Stuff

Validating the buying decision through gifts and other incentives at time of sale is very important in competitive markets. These gifts not only start the new member off with a strong sense of being appreciated by the club for the given business, but also set a nice standard of member service. *Validating the sale*, which means simply proving to the consumer that he made the right choice joining your facility, also leads to higher retention because the buyer doesn't start the relationship with doubts about what he just bought.

Most clubs just let the member leave with a copy of the membership agreement and a few pieces of paper. If your new client leaves with a gym bag, a tee shirt, and other small gifts, you have proven to him he made the right choice with you and that you appreciate the business. If you are simply cheap, at least give your new client a tee shirt with a small club logo on the sleeve and a motivational saying, such as, "Sweat: The perfume of the skinny" on the front.

Based upon a $49 monthly fee, we would give this new member a gym bag, water bottle, and tee shirt with a few munchie bars and some other samples from the club's profit centers. Hard cost for this loot bag would be about $25.

Total startup cost for this member:

- Marketing cost = $83

- Commission = $25

- Labor cost = $60

- Sales incentives = $25

- **Total cost of acquisition = $193**

In this example, the club is actually not showing any profit on this member until he goes into his third month at the club (income to club is $59 + $49 + $49 = $157/over startup and first two months). This is an aggressive example, but most club owners have higher acquisition costs than they realize and don't always calculate the true cost of starting someone new.

Keeping the Members You Do Have, and What It Can Mean to Your Business Over Time

Keeping members is cheaper than getting new ones. Ask any person who has gone through a nasty divorce, and they can validate the theme that it would have been much cheaper to keep the one you have than to replace that person with a newer, younger model.

In our business, keeping the person eliminates many of the direct costs of the acquisition. For example, keeping a person eliminates the marketing expense, as well as the startup labor to get the person into the system. It also cuts the administration expense of adding a new person and can lower the sales expense as well, especially if you are using any type of program that allows members to automatically extend their memberships.

There are other auxiliary costs, of course, that have to be considered in developing a retention program. Following are a few other things that add cost to the operation, but also lead to a higher retention percentage.

Clean clubs keep members longer and are a direct reflection of customer service.

Most clubs are not as clean as the owner believes they are. Members associate clutter and dirt with an owner who no longer gives a damn about them or the business, and most members take a dirty club as an invitation to leave. Females especially are harsh when it comes to club cleanliness, as they should be, and often just quietly disappear when a club falls below a certain standard.

Following are a few things you can do to not only increase your perception of customer service, but also help your retention numbers climb higher over time. Some of these factors will be discussed in-depth later in the book.

It is clean if I see you clean it.

Get the club serviced during the day when the members can see it. Hire a retired person or special person, dress that person in a club jumpsuit, and let them clean the club while it is open and members are present. They can pick up trash, wipe equipment, check locker rooms, and do other small things that members appreciate, but that don't interrupt the flow and atmosphere. The only thing you shouldn't do during the day is vacuum. How clean is it? I just watched your retired guy wipe it down, so it must be really clean.

Load the person up the first 30 days.

Offer master group orientations, semi-private training, and group personal training. Group dynamics sell, and the members want to make friends and gain a broader experience in your business. Offer introductions to training (called fundamentals) at least four times per week, and teach functional skills, such as a walking lunge, body weight squats, or kettlebell swings. It is important in the fundamental groups to teach people how to work out, not to simply give them a workout. Also include teaching cardio in your fundamental groups so you can avoid the member just walking on a tread for an hour while watching television and not getting any results.

Offer unlimited semi-private training during the first 30 days for the new members who have some fitness experience. Get your new folks into group exercise if you can. If you set the people up correctly within the first 30 days, you are demonstrating advanced customer service compared to your competitors and you will drive a higher retention number because clients who start right will stay longer and pay longer.

Keep equipment and offerings up to date.

Most clubs have equipment and offerings that are years behind what the client sees in the magazines. Training clubs are the early adapters in our business and are the ones who recognize the newest training trends and equipment before the mainstream fitness clubs. For example, there were small training facilities on either coast using kettlebells, 50-foot ropes, and full-body functional training at least 10 years before mainstream fitness owners even knew what was happening in the markets. Most clubs are years out of date in their fixed equipment and programming, and members leave because other clubs offer things you don't but should. Stay in tune, attend training seminars, read the popular fitness magazines, and start with the premise that good customer service is offering the client what he wants.

Hemera/Thinkstock

Reinvest.

Paint, social nodes (defined as socialization areas in the club such as stretch areas, low tables and chairs, and sports bars/juice bars), design, and layout are all factors of retention and service. Cheap owners who take all the money and run lose members to newer, fresher physical plants. Rudy Fabiano, perhaps the best architect of all time in our business, said, "Design and color is not only part of the acquisition process, but it is also part of the retention process. Good design attracts, and fresh paint and reinvestment keeps them."

How often should you upgrade and add to your business? Plan your budget so you can add something new, such as paint, locker room upgrades, equipment replacements, or new programming monthly. Showing constant reinvestment shows you care and that you value your members' support of your business.

Touch the members weekly.

There is retention power and customer service in touching your members electronically weekly, but never remind people they are not working out. Your website should offer 30-minute workouts the member can do at home or on the road without equipment. The members should also get an email per week with a motivational theme to keep them excited about working out.

Training clients should get a tweet (a Twitter message that might be old news by the time this is published) a couple times per week with food or motivational tips. Group exercise people should get invited to special workouts not listed on the club schedule (make them feel like insiders), and you can always offer in-house secret sales only offered electronically. Try to touch each of the members once a week with a reason to keep fitness in their lives, but again, stay away from any negative touches, such as "We miss you" cards that remind people they aren't using the club, but are still paying.

Time is the scarcest commodity we have in our lives.

Rebuild your training department to understand the power of short, but intense, workouts. No one can possibly stick to two-hour workouts these days, and very few people want to try. While most of those in the industry thought the circuit clubs were vile, horrible creations, there are many things we can learn from them.

First of all, while the circuit only works for a few weeks and then plateaus, the concept of short, full-body workouts proved to be a powerful sales tool for this style of club. Get in, get done, and out the door in 30 minutes is a hard concept to argue with from the consumer's viewpoint. We can learn to do this in commercial operations by embracing advanced training concepts, such as HIIT (high-intensity interval training) and full-body functional workouts.

Pioneers such as Alwyn Cosgrove, Mike Boyle, J.C. Santana, and Todd Durkin have been advocating shorter, more intense, full-body workouts for years, and we can learn from these people. The consumer wants to get in shape, but only on his terms, and those terms are get me in, get it done, and get me out.

Remember that if someone works out about eight times per month, they are more likely to stay longer and pay longer, and from the customer service viewpoint, people pay for results versus time spent in the club, so embracing a training philosophy that drives serious results in the shortest period of time means everyone wins.

What Can Retention Mean to Your Business?

In John McCarthy's landmark publication, *IHRSA's Guide to Member Retention*, he talks about the power of just extending the average lost member by just one month. For example:

- The club has 2000 members.

- The club loses 40 percent per year in attrition.

- The club charges just $39 per month per member.

- 2000 x .40 = 800

- 800 x $39 = $31,200

If this club kept these 800 members just one more month, it would increase its revenue by $31,200. If the club's owners and team master customer service, therefore increasing its retention rate and cutting the attrition rate, it could add an additional $62,400 by just keeping people happy and paying for two more months.

The power behind this, according to McCarthy, is that once a club has reached the break-even point, 75 percent or more of every subsequent dollar drops to the bottom line. Another way to look at this is that we are a fixed-cost business similar to a ski area. If a ski area has a break-even of 5000 skiers for the day, every skier on the hill after that point is mostly profit because the cost of operation only goes up slightly for things such as food costs or labor in specialty areas, or in lessons, where the increased cost is offset by a direct pay.

It is the same in the fitness world. Once we hit the break-even point, everyone after that adds to the bottom line with only a slight increase in expenses, such as food costs at the sports bar or labor in the training department, which again is offset by direct pay from the member for the service.

Customer Service Is Member Retention

There is no retention without customer service. Building relationships between your staff and the members, and within the members themselves, gives your clients reasons to stay longer and pay longer. Anyone can rent equipment, but equipment is only a tool to create fitness and is not the source of the relationship that members seek and value for their money. In competitive markets, your long-term edge is your ability to keep existing members in the system longer than your competitors, because keeping them is simply cheaper than replacing them.

Do These Things Now

- Switch your business from just a model based upon new-member acquisition to a more functional concept based upon a balance of new-member acquisition and member retention.

- Analyze your startup costs for a new member, and compare that cost to what it costs to keep someone you already have in the system.

- Review all of your current systems. Much of what most owners do is based upon leftover concepts from the early days of the industry that were designed to only get new members and ignored any type of retention plan.

- Put more effort in the first 30 days of a new person's membership. Get them involved in some type of group activity. Learn how to implement low-cost ideas—such as group orientations, semi-private training, and group personal training—into your business. People will stay longer and pay longer if they get started with a better grounding in fitness.

- Customer service is the foundation for retention. Start training your staff now, and forever, at least four hours a week in service.

- Track and learn the average length of a membership in your club, and then try to extend that by just one month over the next year.

Customer service is as simple as ...

being on time.

When you value someone's time, you are really placing a value on that person. Being late for an engagement devalues the person, and the relationship you have with him, because by being late you made a statement that it just isn't worth it to you to make the effort to show up as promised.

In the fitness business, honoring set times sends a direct message on the value you place on your members. Trainers who walk in a few minutes before a training appointment, for example, are sending the client a message that they had better things to do than to make the effort to get to the club and get prepared before the client arrived.

In a service-based business, which is what the fitness business is really about, there is no greater insult than to abuse the time of someone who is paying you for service. The rule is that the member's time is always the most important thing for you to protect, and that there is absolutely no excuse for abusing a paying client by being late for an appointment.

This rule also applies to all other aspects of the business. Group exercise classes that begin a few minutes late send a clear message to the members that the instructor and her time is more important than the people who pay her wages. Instructors who keep the class for an extra five minutes are not providing great service. The people who have other commitments, such as picking up a child, don't see the extra time running over as a service benefit, but as another stressful situation that is going to make them late for what they have to do in their lives. And don't forget that the next class now starts late, which hurts the club's image with all of its members.

Do exactly as you promised when you promise it, and you are already laying a solid foundation for customer service. On time for any appointment, or for any situation in the club such as a class, is 15 minutes early. If you say the class begins at 7:00, then customer service dictates that the class begins as promised, and ends as scheduled, each and every time.

Valuing your members' time sends the message that we want them to hear: that we respect them as people, and we respect the obligations they have in their own lives.

3

Your Nice—but Poorly Trained—Staff May Be Hurting Your Business More Than Your Competitors

Everyone has the "kid" working for you in the club. The kid might be that sweet counter person, who has been with you for a few years, is always on time, and does whatever you want, but is a little shy and quiet at the front desk. Or you might have that energetic young guy, who puts in the hours, and works cheap, but is so young that he has a hard time really talking to your members.

Both cover hours well, are loyal to you, and both of them should be fired Monday because they are killing you. Why? Because they are too young to communicate with your members, too undertrained to deliver effective customer service, and too inexperienced to build relationships in the club. They both fill slots, but they don't—and probably can't—build relationships with the members or understand the importance of delivering legendary customer service.

Even worse is that all your staff, except for the occasional random salesperson, is probably undertrained for their role in your business. We hire too young in our industry and then fail to train the ones we do have: a fatal combination that leads to lousy customer service and eventually lost members.

There are many definitions of customer service, but the one that should be ingrained in your brain is the following:

Customer service is the ability to build and maintain a positive relationship with your clients.

Relationships revolve around the ability to communicate. In any relationship between a business and a client, this communication is based upon your ability to make and keep the client happy by solving problems, anticipating needs, and making the client feel appreciated for the money he gives you each month.

All of these are daily issues in your business that affect your ability to deliver customer service, but you can teach a willing staff to handle every one of these situations. For example, the following are the more common ones a club team might encounter.

How to solve problems a typical member might have during a visit

- Handling billing issues

- Scheduling conflicts

- A bad class or training experience

- Conflicts with other members

- A cleanliness issue

- Handling phone calls, waiting policies, and transferring guests to salespeople

Anticipating the problems that occur regularly in your business

- Getting rid of weak instructors

- Covering for late or no-show trainers

- Getting information to inquiries about your business in a timely manner

- Responding to weather problems that affect the club

Making the client feel appreciated

- Greeting the client by name every time he enters the club

- Thanking the client as he leaves and for any money spent in the business

- Using common courtesy, such as "Please" and "Thank you," with each transaction

- Having the group instructors standing by the door to welcome each participant, and again standing by the door after class, to thank everyone and invite them to the next class

Every one of these things can be scripted and taught, but two foundational concepts have to exist first:

- Did you hire people who can carry out service once they are taught?

- Are you willing to spend the time, and create the systems, it takes to build good employees?

The answer to these basic management questions for most clubs is "No," as dictated by the common denominator in most clubs of young, worthless employees who only get an hour or so of training per month. Nothing is more futile and draining for an owner than hiring wrong and then not training that person. You are doomed to fail, and to fail quickly.

What Does It Take to Be a Good Employee Who Can Deliver Customer Service?

Many of the people typically hired by a club simply can't deliver customer service. These people are too young, too dumb, too shy, have no prior people experience, or simply suffer from the lack of basic communication skills. We get these people because our model is to get someone/anyone to cover a shift or fill a slot without the consideration of how this new hire fits into the club culture, or if this person can deliver the service we need to retain our members over time.

One of the first considerations when it comes to staff is whether the person matches the club's demographic. Understanding this concept means you have to understand the club's target market.

Your target market is usually defined as the demographics of your core 80 percent of members. This group also usually consists of no more than two generations limited by the factor that likes attract likes.

For example, a club might have a target market of the 24- to 40-year-old demographic. This means that 80 percent of the club's members will usually fall into this age group. Yes, you may have older members who like the energy from being around a younger crowd, or who work out during the day, and you might have younger members who want to feel like they belong to this age group, but mostly your club's members will all look alike and be close to the same age and income level minus the extremes on either end.

If you remember that the basic element of customer service is the ability to build relationships, then the key element of hiring should be to find people close in age and economic status to the demographic that populates the club.

Every new hire should reflect
the population that he is serving.

The typical failure occurs in mainstream fitness facilities. These clubs, for example, might have a target membership of 30- to 50-year-olds; yet, they hire

19-year-old counter kids because the club can get these employees cheaply. The disconnect happens because these employees have nothing in common with an older, more mature membership; therefore, they fail as staff to build the relationships necessary to build a solid customer-service program. Simply put, the young staff just can't relate to the people who are paying to come to the club each day.

If the club wants to build a program that sets the standard in the market, then it needs to view employees as part of the equation, and the first line of that equation is that every employee should be as close to the club's target market as possible. This means that if your target market is 24 to 40, and 80 percent of your members fall into this age demographic, then every employee you hire should be in that age group as close as possible.

The issue for most owners is that they are unwilling to pay enough to get an older employee. This is where the two-dollar rule comes into play.

Most markets have their own version of minimum wage. In this case, we aren't talking about the legal minimum wage set by the government. True minimum wage, or local minimum wage, is set by how much you have to pay to get a front counter person to show up. If you are in a northern state, and you have to pay $10 per hour to get a counter person to take the job, then your local minimum wage is $10.

The two-dollar rule states that if you pay about two dollars more, or $12 in this example, you will attract a better, more efficient class of employee. The difference is between getting someone to fill a shift at $10 in that market and someone who can produce revenue and is more effective that works for you because you're offering $12 in a market that thinks $10 is the standard.

This difference of two dollars is about $340 per month in pay, or about half of a membership or a small training package. The real difference, however, is that for a couple of bucks more you get talent versus a warm body with just a pulse and a bad attitude.

Getting people who are close in age to the ones who pay to be members usually means that you have folks who can relate to your members and who might be equals outside the club. Your new-hire housewife who wants 30 hours a week because her kids are getting older is probably in the same church as some of your members, has kids who have gone through the same schools, and whose husband does business with the woman in the club who owns the insurance agency or with the guy who works at the bank she uses.

We're a Business Driven by Contact Points

Service businesses of any type—and always remember that we are in the service business not the fitness business—are driven by a simple concept ruled by contact points.

Contact points occur all day, every day, in most service businesses and can be defined as any interaction between your business and a client or potential client.

For example, your advertising is a contact point because, in essence, you are sending out a representation of your business miles from your club to a potential member. His only contact with the club, and his only impression about who you are and what you do, comes from what is in the piece.

Most of the time, however, contact points are more intimate. Every time the phone rings in the club, a contact point occurs between the staff person and whoever is on the other end of the line. When a member checks in at the front counter, it's a contact point. When a staff person walks through the club, there will be a number of contact points as your staff encounters your members.

How you handle contact points defines how you deliver customer service. Successful customer service businesses train their staff to handle the anticipated contact points throughout the day.

To the consumer, contact points only have two outcomes: the contact is either great, and personally satisfactory, or, on the other hand, you really suck as a business and your staff is nothing more than a bunch of rocks with tee shirts. In the consumer's mind, there is no average or okay; you're either great or horrible, and there is nothing in between.

If you look at a good hotel, you can usually see the mastery of the contact points. Good service begins outside the business, and a good hotel makes sure you are greeted warmly and welcomed to the hotel when you just get out of the cab. Next, you should be warmly greeted as you approach the desk. The lobby, another controllable contact point, should be exceptionally clean and soothing to anyone who has spent the day on a plane getting there. The W Hotels, for example, often use hundreds of candles at night to light the lobbies, and they turn down the regular lighting, making for a relaxing arrival if you are stressed and tired.

Good hotels also have the great towels, classic beds, oversized televisions, and nice amenities in the bath. Every one of those small things is a contact point, and every one is either really good or really bad to the consumer.

Clubs are no different. When a member, or potential member, pulls into your lot, the games begin. If your entrance is poorly lit or marked, you lose the point. If your front desk is cluttered or cheap, you lose that point as well. If your front counter person is on the phone and makes the potential member just stand there for three or four minutes without at least acknowledging him, then you not only lost the point, but probably the sale as well.

There are literally hundreds of contact points in a typical fitness business, and the bigger the business, the more contact points you have to worry about each day. Good owners anticipate those points since working for a positive on each and every point sets the tone for customer service, and also for retention, because if the overall experience in your business is good, members will simply stay longer and pay longer, and your sales will be easier as well.

Contact points are also why clubs with mediocre physical plants can often survive and thrive in crowded markets. Customer service builds loyalty, and even a club that is on a somewhat of a downward slide can still make money, and take on newer and fresher players, because customer service in an average club still beats poor service in a new club.

If these contact points are so important to a club's success, then why do we continually hire people who aren't capable of building positive experiences with our members? Start your thinking by imagining the typical hires a club makes. These are stereotypical, but the stereotypes do hold up across way too many clubs in our industry.

First of all, start with the front counter person. Her average age might be around 20, she has limited (if any) work experience, and she might be working part time. Her training has consisted of several hours of where things are and how things work at the counter, and after that she becomes a fresh face at the counter each day. Because she was bought at the cheapest rate the market would bear, she is seldom committed to the club. She is in at one minute before 9:00 when her shift begins, and she leaves one minute prior to 4:00 when the shift ends.

Her day is basic. She talks on her cell phone, answers the phone as if it is a nuisance in her life, answers questions from members by just getting someone further up the food chain to come to the desk, and really can't explain much in the club because she probably hasn't done much in the way of experiencing what the club has to offer.

Most importantly, she has absolute zero customer-service training from the club or from any prior job she might have had that pertains to a high-volume, service-driven business (such as a club), limited phone training beyond how to answer, and probably no training on how to handle member complaints or solve problems. Also, due to age and experience level, she has little in common with the club's members, which makes her weak in her ability to build relationships.

All the transactions that involve her are negative contact points because the club hasn't ever taught her basic common courtesy, something also neglected by her parents as well. One of your solid members hands her a five-dollar bill for a two-dollar water, and she shoves the change across the desk with a "There you go." No "Thank you." No "We appreciate your business." All the member gets is just a rude statement that in her world, again because she has never been taught any different, this is her version of customer service.

Next up is a typical trainer. He is hired by the pound, is proud of his body, and dresses to show it. His clothing is too tight, he trains virtually everyone the same way, although he claims everyone is on an individual program, and he trains women and anyone over 50 as second-class citizens. Males are trained hard as athletes, and women and older folks go around the circuit with a big card, because he only believes in one way to train—and that is bodybuilding.

Assuming the club keeps him busy, he spends 8 to 10 hours a day with clients, but he has never been taught about sexual-harassment issues, making conversation, nor has he had any sales training, although we do expect him to resell his own clients.

Most importantly, for our young trainer, he has also never had any customer-service experience. We have not taught him how to shake hands, send thank-you cards to the regular members, to be grateful for the business he does get, or to carry on a conversation with our guests. He may be able to train, but he has never been taught to retain.

Finally, there is our manager. She started as a salesperson, sold a lot of memberships, and was moved up to the management position, although secretly, she is nothing more than a salesperson with a cool title since her primary duty is to still sell memberships all day.

During the day, she sits in her office trying to do her manager work, and once prime time happens, she is out selling. She is never, ever standing behind the counter, training staff and greeting members, because all she has ever been taught is how to sell and do some basic manager paperwork.

Following the theme from the previous examples, if you went back through the five years she has worked for the club, you'll find that all of her customer-service training has been things such as: smile, be nice, be happy behind the desk, be positive, answer the phone with a smile, and be helpful. She has, however, had an immense amount of sales training and can cover every objection ever thrown, but no one has spent more than a few hours in five years talking about service and retention.

We hire the counter person because she is young and will work cheap. We hire the trainer because he looks like a trainer and maybe has a certification. We hire the manager because she can sell, and we worry about the volume of new sales and never about keeping the members we have.

None of these people were hired because they have customer-service experience, customer-service training, or because they are great communicators who can build relationships within the club's culture. They were all hired because of the wrong reasons and, therefore, service will remain a language not spoken in this club.

When you hire folks for your business, the first things you should look for should be whether they are communicators and if they are "people" people. These are traits, or things the person brings from the culture they were raised in, or are natural things they were born with and are part of their personality. These are also the people who will prove to be able to turn a daily contact into an outrageously positive experience for the client.

The mistake we make is we hire skills thinking skilled people will eliminate the need for us to train and develop the person. What happens it that yes, the guy you hired does have three years of sales experience, but when you put him into your business, his sales tactics are too aggressive, and it becomes more of challenge to retrain him than it would have been to hire a great communicator and an in-your-face people person, and then train that person in sales.

Pre-existing skills are almost always a false savings when it comes to hiring for a manager's job or downward. The first question you should always ask before you hire is: "Will this person be able to deliver legendary customer service in my business?" It will amaze you when you look at your existing base and realize that very few of the people that work for you on a day-to-day basis would rate a yes for this question. Most were hired because they were available, you were desperate, and they had a little vague experience somewhere else. Very few were ever hired because you started with the assumption that this person would turn your business into a customer-service heaven.

Based on all of this, here is where to start when you look for people who can deliver customer service in your business:

- Does the person have an outgoing, almost in-your-face personality?

- Has he ever worked in an environment that required him to do a lot of interaction with a large number of people? How did he like the job if he did have one that required that interaction?

- What are his communication skills?

- Can she ask for money? Has she ever worked in any kind of sales situations, even a minor one such as working the front counter in a fast-food restaurant?

- Does she lean forward during your interview and ask you questions, or did she lean back in the chair and wait for you to ask? If she is shy in your office, it won't be any different at the desk.

- How old was he when he had his first job? This is a legitimate question you can ask in an interview and gives you insight into long-term work experience. If the person had a paper route or worked at a fast-food joint when he was young, then you have work experience in the real world, doing a job that required people skills. If the person is 21, just finished school, and has never worked a day in his life, then do not hire this person. You never want to be anyone's first job, because you will spend most of your time teaching the person how to show up on time rather than how to produce revenue for your business.

- Does the person act and dress professionally? Older clients are by nature more conservative and are used to dealing with a more professional person, such as their doctor, accountant, or perhaps banker. Staff people who dress poorly and have ugly personal grooming habits don't establish relationships with older clients. Remember, everyone on your staff should be as close to your target market as possible, because likes attract likes, but different generations usually terrify each other when they interact.

Are You Willing to Spend the Time and Do the Work to Create Good Service Employees?

An employee may bring the traits you need to build a service business, such as being a people person, but that doesn't mean that employee is ready to stand at the counter and service your most valuable asset, meaning your members.

Legendary service employees are created through consistent training and don't just spontaneously combust from dust bunnies under the front desk. Good, efficient staff is a reflection of consistent training of the fundamentals. Later in this book, we will address some of the specifics needed to train a good staff, but in this chapter we will lay out a few ideas as to how you should approach your staff training.

Start with customer service training first.

The first three hours of any new staff person's training should be on customer-service training. If this is the most important thing in your business, and it is, then make it the first thing the person learns. Are sales more important? Sales are easier if the guest was greatly warmly and was handed over to a salesperson professionally. Are procedures more important? Greeting the guest and members, answering the phones, dressing for success, keeping the club clean for our members, and learning to thank every member every time that person leaves the club is customer service, and if you get these things right, everything else you do will get a lot easier.

Train for the customer-service basics.

Master the basics through repetitive training. The basics for us are the phone, greetings, dress, handling problems for the members, and ensuring we offer a quality experience for the member through keeping a clean club and common courtesy. These are all examples of fundamental customer-service skills that can be taught virtually every week to every person on the staff who interacts with your members.

The real businesses train for hours per week, not just hours per month.

You simply don't put enough time into your people to develop them into capable service people. When asked why the staff was so efficient at an area Starbucks, the manager stated, "We train our people about four hours per week on all the basics of good service and in delivering a quality product." Most club owners and managers are lucky if they train their people four hours per month, and for some owners, four hours of training might take four months.

One of the easiest things you can do is to block out Friday afternoon from noon to four and make it staff training time every week. Put your mama or your out-of-work brother-in-law at the front desk, get your people together, and train them on things in the business that lead to better service, a better experience for the members and better sales, and do this every week until the powers of the universe drag you out of your business by your feet with your hands wrapped around the largest dumbbell you own.

Yes, you should pay the staff for this training. In most states, you can offer training pay you set in your employee manual for anyone who comes in off shift to train. For example, if you are paying the person $9 per hour, but she comes in for training, you can pay her a $7 an hour training pay, if that is established in your employee manual when she is hired. You have to pay them if you ask them to show up. If the person would normally be on the clock for those hours anyway, then pay him the regular hourly he would get for his work. Check with your attorney before you establish this policy.

Break the training into smaller segments, such as one hour per topic, and make sure you review the basics several times a month, including answering the phones, greeting members, using names, and thanking people for their business.

Master spot training.

We'll cover the exact techniques of this later, but the subject is worth mentioning now as well. Most club owners shy away from training because they always think it has to be something formal involving tables, white boards, and handouts; therefore, unless it becomes a major production, no one on the staff is ever trained.

Spot training is training done in 5- to 10-minute segments, whenever there is a break in the day or someone is just standing around staring at you. The tool we use for spot training is the simple index card.

There is a common happening in the clubs, mentioned in other books in this series, which absolutely drives members insane. For example, a member walks up to a staff person, who is walking by on the floor, and asks about the new yoga class the club is offering. The staff person, who happens to work at the club full time, shrugs and says, "I don't really know anything about the class. Yoga just isn't my thing."

The member is confused but tries another staff person near the front counter: "Say, can you give me a little information about the new yoga class?" The staff person turns to the member with her eyes glistening and breathing heavy in excitement: "Oh yeah, I can tell you about yoga. It is the freakin' best thing any human being can do. It changed my life, and sometimes when I am at home I do yoga poses naked in the backyard to tap the inner soul and focus my chi-chi energy. You just have to try this class because yoga will change your life."

The member, eyes wide in fear, wanders to the locker room, thinking about checking out the treadmills on sale at Sears that weekend and getting out of this crazy club. One full-time person has never even tried the class and another is a freak that is the equivalent of an old bodybuilder that thinks fitness is getting everyone in the club huge. Sadly, both of these employees had a chance to deliver customer service by helping a member with a common question, yet neither was prepared to properly help our guest.

One component of spot training is to develop sales talk. Sales talk means that everyone in the club can explain every program and offering pretty much the same way.

In the case of the yoga class, each employee would have been given a stack of 5x7 index cards with the name of each club offering on the front. In this example, the card would have simply had the word "Yoga" on the front. On the back of the card would have been three or four sentences describing the yoga class by using the benefits, or what's in it for the member. For example:

Yoga is a safe and simple way to tone muscles, increase core strength, fight stress, and develop a more athletic body. Certified instructors, who have years of experience, teach our classes, and the club offers every member a chance to try the classes first before signing up for the program. If you decide to take part in the program, it is only an extra $15 per month. May I help you get into your first class?

The staff people would memorize this card and use the words if someone asked about yoga and the club's program. Spot training means the owner or manager would use a down time in the business to grab the employee, pull out his cards, and read the front word. The manager says, "Yoga," and the staff person then should be able to explain the program using the approximate words on the card. In this case, we have developed a common language in the club of service, where every staff can help every member with consistent and accurate information.

Later in the book, we will give more examples of how spot training works and how you can adapt it to your business.

The best training is side-by-side and on the floor.

In our business, training done in an office is usually boring and not nearly as effective as training a staff person live on the job. There is some training, of course, that requires you to use an office or classroom, but most basic customer-service training is often done better at the desk or on the floor.

Let's use your front counter person as an example. She is new and has gone through her first three hours of customer-service training and has spent a few hours learning front counter procedures. The best way to train this person is to learn by doing.

The manager or owner would stand right next to her at the front desk and teach correct action by demonstrating correct action. For example, let's say we are trying to teach the proper club greeting and how you want it done as club owner.

When the door opens, you greet the arriving member with a strong, "We're having a great day at the Workout Company" followed by a "Good to see you, Bryan. Thanks for stopping by today. And by the way, this is Kaitlin, our new counter person, in case you two haven't met."

Your new staff person shakes hands and says, "It is a pleasure to meet you, Bryan. Please come find me if there is anything I can do to help you while you're in the club."

She says these exact words because you told her to say those exact words. She is courteous, she used his name, and she is establishing herself as the person who can help deliver service in the club.

When the next member approaches the door, the owner tells her to handle this one on her own. She practices the greeting that was demonstrated by the owner, uses the member's name if she knows him, or introduces herself if she doesn't, and then works the member's name back into the conversation and introduction. If she is slightly off or misses a few words, the owner quietly and discreetly corrects her after the member heads on into the club and she tries again when the next member comes through the door.

There is power in this type of training. It is immediate, it is timely, and you as the owner can see exactly what you hired. You can also correct behavior as it occurs, which will help your new hire get the desired action much more quickly than an hour lecture in a classroom.

This type of training also works for the phone and almost any other customer-service action. Start in the classroom, but use the floor and counter to hammer home your point and to check for understanding.

Offsite Training

One of the oldest staff reality rules in management is:

What if I train my staff and they leave?
But what if you don't train them and they stay?

Staff training accomplishes two things, which is why you should go fast and furious when you hire anyone. First of all, even a small amount of training makes a very large difference in your business in a short period of time. Secondly, training is actually considered a motivator by most of your staff.

The phone, for example, is perhaps the easiest tool in the club to prove that small amounts of training make a big difference. Locking up your staff for three hours and focusing on answering techniques, explaining the trial membership options to increase inquires showing in the club, screening techniques, handling customer problems, and handing off a call to a salesperson—all of which will be discussed later in the book—can all be addressed in-depth in a few hours of intense training.

Good phone training will make an immediate difference in your business tomorrow because member calls will be handled with better service, and inquiries would be more likely to visit the club if they were treated professionally on the phone, especially compared to other club businesses in your market that they might call first and where they might have a much nastier phone experience.

Taking your staff offsite for training is actually considered a reward by most staff. If you're an owner, it is sometimes expensive and a pain to be away from your business for a few days, but if you're a young staff person, offsite training becomes a "business trip" and has status and the ring of an adventure.

Good owners don't waste a second of time while on these trips. This is your chance to get to know your staff on a deeper level, determine their strengths and weaknesses, and most importantly, it gives the owner a chance to use the breaks in the workshop and other free time to write a business action plan based upon the new information you are gathering at the seminar.

In this case, you don't have to come home and try to translate what you learned. Instead, you come home with a plan to implement on Monday and a motivated staff ready to make change and move the business ahead.

There are a lot of owners, however, who refuse to spend money investing in staff training. Perhaps the stupidest thing ever heard on the phone by a person calling to fill a workshop was: "I don't attend workshops. I have been in business for 20 years, and there is nothing anyone can teach me about this business I don't already know."

Business legends, such as Bill Gates and Jack Welch, are often quoted in their writings as saying (paraphrasing here): "It isn't what you know that makes you successful. It's the ability to continually ask good questions that makes a great leader."

Businesses are like people. When a new business is born, it needs time to grow the first few years and get healthy. Later, it hits its strong growth years and matures. If a business is treated well, meaning it is constantly fed a new stream of ideas that keeps it relevant and growing, a new business can go on forever. Stop the new ideas, however, and the business will die from lack of food, just like a real person.

You have to take the risk and train your staff. Your business needs new ideas to grow and your staff needs new challenges to help them grow as well. You should obviously cover yourself with non-solicitation agreements and other legal tools, but you have to be prepared to take the risk of investing in training and making your business more effective as opposed to not training your people and having them stay for years just going through the motions and working at a very ineffective level.

Training Is Different From Staff Meetings

Staff meetings, which should be held weekly, are tools to keep staff informed and focused on making the numbers the business needs that week. Staff meetings should be no more than 30 minutes and should ideally be held every Tuesday. If you have a large business with a large staff, you will need to repeat the meeting early and late in that day.

Staff training is focused on doing nothing more than learning techniques that will make your staff more effective in your business. Staff training is positive (we never use a staff training to chastise people), focused on set topics, and should have a small exam or expected outcome that validates what your team learned. If you want to make money, you have to block out rigid times each week to train your team and you have to do it every week forever. Remember, the difference between your club and your competitor's is always going to come down to whom has the best trained staff.

Customer service is nothing more than staff training. There is no customer service, and therefore no retention, without a consistent training approach to develop your staff. But training is deliberate and planned and has to be done daily to work. The best-trained and most efficient staffs are the ones that are reminded daily through their training as to why they are there and what they are trying to accomplish as a team.

Do These Things Now

- Learn that customer service is the ability to build a relationship between a business and its clients. Most clubs hire people who aren't capable of getting this done. Look at the people working in your club, and slowly start replacing the ones you have that can't deliver service with people who can deliver legendary customer service.

- Replace your existing people with staff that reflects the age and demographics of your club's membership.

- Make lists of the contact points in your business that occur between your members and your staff. How many of these would you consider extremely positive on a daily basis?

- Start blocking out a set four-hour period each week, preferably Friday afternoon, to start the ongoing training with your team you will need to build a legendary customer-service business that can acquire and retain the largest number of members.

- Couple formal training with the most effective training: standing side-by-side with a staff person, and showing him exactly how to get it done.

Customer service is as simple as …
answering the phone live.

Fitness businesses are very intimate people businesses. People pay for help and guidance, and we provide it in exchange for that money.

The fitness business is also somewhat wacky in that we service our guests when they are wearing funny clothes, or are wearing almost nothing compared to their normal day clothes. We laugh together, sweat together, and work together on the path of improved health and fitness. This makes us an informal business far removed from the image of a company that doesn't know you or care about you as a person.

We are also not a huge, soulless corporation that has thousands of employees at one location who can hide behind that mass of sheer numbers. We are a simple business that depends on each guest receiving the service and attention they expect in exchange for their monthly fee.

What does all this mean? It means that you have to answer the phone when it rings, live, within three rings, and with a happy attitude that lets the caller know that we are really happy he called us today.

The phone is often the first line of customer service for potential members. Our callers are often nervous about fitness, embarrassed about their fitness level and weight, and don't even know what to ask on the phone except for, "What does it cost?"

What this person does not need to hear when the phone is answered is a machine-generated voice that says, "For billing questions, press 1; for sales, press 2. Hold please, and I will ring that extension. I am sorry, but no one is answering that number. Please leave a message at the tone, and when naked sumo wrestlers dance in heaven, someone will call you back. Thank you for calling, and have a great day."

We should always answer live, which is our chance to demonstrate our great customer service, and we should also use a powerful welcoming statement: "Hello, we are having a great day at the Workout Company." Answer live and with energy, and leave voice-mail hell to the credit-card or utility companies.

4

Customer Service Is the Last Great Business Differentiator

*Why would I choose your business or
service over your competitors?*

Most owners have never sat down and contemplated this question, or challenge the mundane responses they might give if they were caught off-guard and forced to respond to this question.

Why would anyone choose your business over a competitor's business down the street? The standard, but weak, answers to this question always include at least a few of the following:

- We have the best equipment in town.

- We have the most free weights.

- We have the most classes.

- We are open 24 hours a day.

- We have the largest facility.

- We have the cheapest price, and no one can beat us.

- We have the best service, and our members love us.

The weird thing about this list is that only one of these is a sustainable differentiator that would work for any type of fitness business. The rest of the list, which are the standard responses an owner gives who doesn't really think deeply about his marketing or place in the market, are not sustainable ways to differentiate your business, because all of these positions can be copied or beaten with a little money or by an aggressive competitor.

Differentiators are *ways you stand out* or are different from everyone else who is chasing the same target market and selling the same product. Differentiators highlight the differences between the businesses in the market, as opposed to trying to get attention by being bigger, having more of something, being cheaper, or staying open longer.

All of these positions in the last paragraph, and all of the previous statements from the list (except customer service) can easily be beaten by a competitor who wants to take those bragging rights away from your business. For example, being the best is not verifiable, and any owner can claim to be the best club in the area since no one claims the opposite position. Everyone says they are the best so often that none of your potential clients really puts any value on the claim, because they have heard this meaningless claim shouted so often, and have read it so many times in advertising, that it has lost all meaning.

If you make a claim of having the most free weights, which is not a benefit to a client, but rather a feature of your business, a new competitor can take that position away from you by simply buying more stuff than you have. The same holds true for claiming you have the most classes, which anyone can beat, or that you are open 24 hours a day, which any club can now match because the technology has become common and cheap. These are not sustainable ways to compete or define your business in the consumer's eyes, since any new or existing owner can simply take the position away from you if they want to add that position to their own business.

Probably the most current trend on the list is the cheapest price position. With the advent of the low-price/value clubs, price is now considered a marketing position by many club owners, but what will stop someone new in the market from dropping his price to $8 per month in order to go after the guy down the street who is offering $10 a month? The $10 guy says, "We're killing everyone now, and no one can match our price," but that is what the first guy who charged $19 said, and it will be what the first guy who charges $8 says, too. If it's all about price, then anyone can play, and someone can always go lower.

The fitness industry is a relatively young industry that has only really existed since the end of World War II. In a sense, the modern industry was born in the late 1940s, quietly grew in the '50s, expanded in the '60s, and blew apart from the '70s through the end of the century.

During that approximately 55-year run, owners could compete and thrive using innovation in technology, or through the exploitation of a series of first events. For example, you could have been the operator who had the first electronic bike, the first motorized treadmill, the first group-exercise program in your market, or the first club to offer a protein shake and nutritional support. All of these were first events that gave that owner a slight edge in the market until someone else matched him.

Even the first clubs that opened at 5:00 in the morning were thought to be cutting-edge radicals who were changing the market by forcing everyone else to match their business plan. If you were the first at almost anything in the early days of fitness, you could often sustain that position for years since there was so little competition, or in fact so few clubs.

Even at the turn of this century, clubs were still listing the most free weights or the most classes in their Yellow Pages ads, though by then everyone was easily matching that business plan. We, as an industry, held on to the practice of having something new or being first for as long as we could, but eventually an industry matures, and everyone getting in can easily take the best practices from the entire industry and build that into an opening plan.

How we compete has changed during the last 10 years compared to how we were able to compete for the first 50 years or so of the modern fitness industry. You can no longer use features—such as number of classes, amount of stuff, or size of your club—to separate yourself from a pack of aggressive competitors. Anyone and everyone can match you and do it before your latest YouTube video is posted highlighting that new class.

Maturing industries, defined as having many more competitors in your marketplace, forces us to grow to another level of play in our marketing and in our operations. When an industry matures, you have to move beyond features and offerings as your method of competing and into advanced techniques, such as niching and specialization.

> *The foundation of a more advanced business plan, and*
> *the signature of a more efficient and business-driven owner*
> *is the delivery system used to sell fitness in your business.*

Niching and specialization can also be defined as targeting smaller segments in your market. For example, a training club might open that only works with women over 50, or another fitness business might open that specializes in sports performance for children. Niching is really nothing more than looking at a broad market and then declaring what segments you want to build your business plan around.

Larger competitors, on the other hand, might try to build a business that focuses on the upscale adult, or perhaps one that goes for a total family atmosphere. Maturing markets force you to move away from competing on features to building your business plan based upon the people you seek in the market.

The key thought to learn is that as an industry matures, the players in that industry almost always move from being generalists to specialists. Almost every service business you can think of has evolved in that manner.

For example, look at a typical attorney. Not too many years ago, attorneys were general practitioners that could help you with almost all aspects of your life and business. Today, most attorneys are very narrowly focused with specialties that might include family law, corporate law, or divorce.

The rule to remember during the next years in the fitness business is:

Generalists are chosen because they are convenient in someone's life. Specialists are sought out because they have skills that people want and desire. That makes the specialist unique in the marketplace, and also helps the specialist separate himself from all the other generalists who are fighting for the same clients.

An owner going after defined target markets, or niches, then builds a business around the needs and wants of that target market. For example, a club based upon upscale adults would hire an older staff, have a higher degree of finish in the club, use more conservative music, and offer different classes and programming than one that is catering to a 24- to 40-year-old market. The target market is narrowly defined and the delivery system has to match the target market.

The delivery system is really the support structure of the business that is built to match the members who will come to the business. The delivery system is comprised of everything from colors and locker-room finish to choice of equipment and types of classes. Choose a target market, and then do everything you can to make them happy in your business by offering the things that match their ages, lifestyle, and demographics.

The Last Great Differentiator Is Going to Be Customer Service

Customer service is the most difficult to create, as well as the most important, of the differentiators. Instead of buying the latest line of Nautilus, which was a brilliant business plan in 1970s, you now have to hire the right staff, develop them to deliver legendary service, and to retain a membership base that can easily leave you tomorrow for a better equipped or bigger club down the street. In other words, you just can't throw stuff at the members to keep them; you actually have to learn to take care of them over time through the implementation of true customer service.

What makes this so difficult is that the only way to prove you have great service is by experiencing that service. Service is something that has little value when you talk about it with someone, or try to explain it to staff, but it has so much value when you are actually experiencing it at the time in a great business.

Perhaps this is the difficulty with customer-service business books. These books, and there are hundreds of them available, discuss in detail how legendary service companies (such as the Four Seasons Hotel chain) train and deliver service. But service is so esoteric and hard to explain in the written word that most of these books fail to convey what service is supposed to be.

Good service is felt through the senses and
never translates by merely reading about it in
an advertisement or book.

For example, an advertisement in a local magazine states: "Come to our restaurant, and experience truly fine customer service," or a fitness business claims in a flyer that they offer the best customer service in the area. How powerful are these claims in driving new business? Who really looks at these ads and says, "Finally, a business that gets customer service"?

Claiming service is like claiming that you offer high quality or cutting-edge technology. All of these, including the word "service," are words that have lost their meaning to the consumer and have become generic fillers that are meaningless in traditional advertising.

Everyone claims to have great service, even the most horrific clubs in your market. In fact, it is likely that the worse the operator, the more loudly he will proclaim he has the best equipment and best service, because he is just too dumb to talk about anything else in his marketing.

But if service is the only sustainable way to compete in the fitness industry in mature and crowed marketplaces, yet advertising great service doesn't really work, then how do you let people know that your people are so much better at service than your competitors?

To Know Me Is to Love Me

One of the most frustratingly ineffective old habits in the industry is our need to close people during the first visit. High-pressure, first-visit sales, or drop-closing, is a false assumption we have carried forward for years, but does it really work?

First-visit closing was built upon the premise that you are going to get only one shot at a person, therefore, you have to do everything possible to close the person now, while he is sitting in that chair across the desk, staring at you in abject fear, because there were no "be backs" in the early days of fitness.

Our solution to the fear that no one would ever come back if they visited a club, but didn't sign immediately, was to show a high upfront fee and then drop-close the person while he is in the club. For example, you might show a start up fee of $150, but if you, our potential members, are willing to sign today, then you only pay $50. Come back tomorrow, and the fee goes back up to $150. In other words, go home to think about it, and you get penalized $100.

The theory behind this concept is that the person was excited and emotional enough to come by the club, either due to his life or an advertisement that drove him through the door, and if the salesperson doesn't get him now, then the potential member will go home, cool off from the emotional high, and never come back again.

Who thinks of crazy ideas like this? There are many things wrong with this premise, especially in today's market. If you review this idea carefully, and actually talk to a potential member, you will find out that this system is the result of a sales system that didn't work; but the salespeople from that era couldn't admit that they might be the problem or the system itself was flawed. Instead of looking internally, we readily blamed the potential client for being a social deviant, since he couldn't commit to a three-year deal 15 minutes after meeting an overly caffeinated salesperson.

Here are some reasons the first-visit pressure close doesn't work anymore, if it really ever did:

- The first-visit sales close is heavily weighted toward the auditory person. This is the person who listens and makes decisions by what is spoken. In other words, he will listen to the salesperson, and then make his decision on what he heard. The problem is that this represents only a third of our business. One third is a visual-oriented group, which wants to read about what they are buying in detail or perhaps spend time watching the club in action. The other third are doers, who make buying decisions based upon their personal experience with a product. This type of person only buys if it feels good.

- The first-visit pressure system is only directed at one third of your potential clients, and, therefore, two thirds have no real chance of signing up the first day. See *Naked Woman at my Door*, the most recent book in the club management series, for a more in-depth discussion of learning styles and how they affect your business.

- Let's say you are emotional about fitness. You just broke up with your significant other, you feel terrible about yourself, and you are going to get in shape and change your life. You try out a gym, do one workout, and now you find yourself sitting in an office getting pressured to sign today. If you think about it, maybe this is the worst time to ask someone to join a club. He has just been beaten by a trainer, feels overwhelmed and that he can't do fitness because everyone looks and acts stupid during their first workout, feels bad about his body, and realizes that this fitness idea is harder than he thought. You want to ask him for money now, when he is at his lowest point? There are exceptions to this, of course. Someone who has a lot of group-exercise experience and tries a class after a layoff might be thrilled at being back in a club and ready to go. Most potential members, however, find themselves dazed and confused after their first experience in your club.

- Why do we assume he is only interested in fitness today? What, he isn't still going to be fat and single tomorrow? Fitness is a more commonly accepted lifestyle choice in today's culture, and he will most likely still be interested in fitness tomorrow and probably the day after tomorrow, as well.

- The price is also too high for most people to impulse buy during the first visit. We want people to commit to memberships that often go $500 per year or higher. At some point, the number has to force the potential client to want to at least think about it for a night. It is just plain stupid to think that real-life adults will impulse a $500 or higher purchase on a regular basis with a young, club salesperson, who is trying to drop-close an adult. The price itself is the limiter on how many first-visit pressure sales you can generate.

- Perhaps the strongest argument that a first-visit drop-close fails is that the general population doesn't believe that percentages off a given price are real. Every questionable business, from furniture guys to car guys, uses the percentage-off tool to get you to buy. How many of you look at those sales and think, "Yeah, the furniture store is offering all their stuff for 50 percent off if I buy this weekend. Yeah, baby, that is a real deal"? Or how many of you see those ads and just laugh because you know the furniture people marked it up to mark it down and that the huge discount is just another marketing lie?

- You also probably think that you have never really seen a furniture store without the sale of the week, and this one is another of an endless stream of never-ending fake sales. Our $100 off at the point of sale is exactly the same thing, and anyone over 15 years old just stares at you whenever you try to whack them with the lower price as if you just insulted their intelligence, which you did by using such a dated tool that insults people's intelligence.

- Modern fitness has too many moving parts to convey in just one visit. As we move as an industry toward functional training and away from fixed plane equipment and going around in a circle through a line of equipment (keep up, you old circuit guys, with the big workout cards kept in a box on the floor), how we train people just doesn't translate in a single workout, or perhaps not even in several workouts. Fitness done correctly is moving away from set workouts on an old Nautilus-style circuit that any young staff person could handle up to a certain level. Now, the trainer is becoming more of a coach, and much more relevant, and it might take several visits for the client to feel the full impact of what fitness can do for him, even with the help of a qualified coach.

- The final reason first-visit pressure tactics fail is that someone finally realized that we are punishing people for doing what we want them to do. For example, someone stops by the club and checks out what we have to offer. He ends up in an office, gets drop-closed with the $100-off today approach, but says no and leaves. If he does come back tomorrow, what are you going to do to him? If you give him the $100 off, you, in essence, lied to him during the first visit, which starts this new relationship off at the bottom, since he is not likely to trust anything you say or do in this business relationship in the future, and there isn't really a reason for him to refer friends either since anyone he refers will be lied to and pressured as he was. The other side, of course, is what happens to the guy who comes back and the club doesn't drop the price, but holds to the $100 penalty (it does happen out there this way occasionally). The powerful thing to think about here is that the guy did come back. Is this not what we wanted him to do? In either of the examples, if the potential member comes back and joins the club, we either lied to him or we hammered him for more money for doing what we wanted him to do, which is come back. This guy was punished for doing what we hoped he would do, which is to think it over and come back to get started.

What all this means is that if we want to bring the largest number of new people into our system, without a reliance on slamming someone during a single visit to the club, then we have to adapt a newer premise to replace the old pressure-now concept.

> *You have to develop a system that has a high chance of closing those potential members ready to sign today, but allows everyone else who tries you to stay connected to the club and become members as they gain confidence and trust in what you do.*

"To Know Me Is to Love Me" Means a Trial Membership Is Your Only Choice

Trial memberships are simple marketing tools you use to attract members to your club in a non-threatening manner. Trials have been discussed endlessly in the other books in this series, but are relevant here because of their use to demonstrate the power of the club's customer service.

We use a trial for the main reason that trials kill risk, which is the biggest barrier to inquiry. Many people out there in your market would like to try fitness, but the first step is simply too big. If you think about it, we're asking people to go from "I never worked out in the last 10 years" to "Sign here today, and now you're a member for two years." What if he signs and doesn't like it? What if it doesn't fit his lifestyle? What if he thinks he is simply so out of shape he can't do it?

Trial memberships offer a half-way step we need, especially if you keep in mind the theory discussed earlier that fitness has just too many moving parts and doesn't translate in only one workout.

The best thing about using trial memberships to attract potential members is that it accomplishes the new premise listed previously: *You have to develop a system that has a high chance of closing those ready to sign today, but allowing everyone else who tries you to stay connected to the club and becoming members as they gain confidence and trust in what you do.*

The trial system uses a strong first-visit incentive package, such as a gym bag and other gifts, but you never mess with the price. Remember, the price is the price is the price, and we don't make deals. If the person is not ready to become a member during his first visit, and only about 30 percent of your new members join the first day (usually buddy referrals), then you offer other, but lesser, incentives anytime during the first half of his trial (by day 15 in a 30-day trial or day 10 in a 21-day trial). For example, we might give you a package worth $400 retail to join today, if you are ready to get started today, but you might only get $250 if you join during the first 10 days of your 21-day trial. Remember, we don't care when the guy joins as long as he does join, so there is no need to force the first visit.

Another important point about the trial is that if he doesn't join the first day, and you haven't come off the price by drop-closing, you still have a reason to stay in contact with the person and keep him in the system. He still has to come back to work out, which gives you a reason to keep calling and emailing. The emphasis is to get the member into the club when he is ready and not force him to join when we want him to be ready.

There are three types of trial memberships a club might use to attract potential members. These are interchangeable, depending on the time of year and the market:

- *The 21-day risk-free trial*: There is no charge for this trial. You simply open your club to the marketplace, with a few restrictions such as age and that he must be a local with a valid ID, and then treat him as any other trial-membership lead by offering an incentive the first visit but also other gifts if he closes by the 10th day of the trial.

- *The 30-day paid trial*: This might be 30 days for $19, for example. This trial usually attracts a different potential member than the risk-free 21-day version. When you use these tools, rotate between this one and the 21-day every 90 days. Paid trials have a higher perceived value, which is important for some people who feel that free is just not worth it.

- *The fixed-time trial*: This trial is for smaller markets where you have more control. In this trial, you might open up your club to the entire community, again with a few restrictions, for an entire month as a sort of long-term open house. The marketing is easy for this one, and you would probably get a local paper or television station to cover this. The premise would be that the club believes so strongly in fitness that it will let everyone in the community come try it for free for the month of May. This would also be a trial that would work in a market where you are trying to do the most damage to your competitors by sucking out all the leads in the market for a month at a time.

Trial memberships are based upon the following concept:

> *We are so proud of our club that we would like you to come try us absolutely free for 21 days with no risk to you or with any obligation. We understand that many of you are nervous about getting started with a fitness program, and we would like you to experience our club and our service before you make up your mind.*

> *We're proud of our club and feel it is the best in town, but talk is cheap. We would like you to come meet our staff, and meet the other members in our club, and try us with a full club membership for 21 days. We will give you all the help, coaching, and support you need to get started before you even consider becoming a member.*

> *At the end of this risk-free trial membership, if we haven't earned your business, then we don't deserve to have you as a member, and you are under no further obligation. Please give us a chance to prove to you that you can be successful with a fitness program and that we're the club that can give you the service and support you need and expect.*

You Use Trials to Prove That You Really Do Have The Best Customer Service in Town

It was mentioned earlier that you can't "get" customer service by reading about it or talking about it. You only understand service by experiencing it for yourself.

The barrier most clubs have is that they base the entire future of their business upon just one short visit by a potential member. Most of these visits, if there isn't a workout involved, usually last less than 30 minutes. Visits this short put all the emphasis on just the salesperson, since the club has only limited chances to demonstrate a caring, supportive, customer-service culture. Do you really want to bet your entire business on just a single encounter between a young salesperson and a nervous, confused potential client?

Assuming that you will learn how to train your staff and build a customer-service culture in your business, the trial membership allows you expose your new potential client to your business slowly over time. If he is greeted by your counter people warmly and strongly each time, welcomed by your sales team, and entertained by your coaching staff, then your chances of getting the sale, and buddy referrals as well, are much stronger. Throw in clean locker rooms, well-lit parking lots, clean cardio, professionally dressed staff, and all the other components that make up great customer service, and new sales and member retention gets a lot easier.

To know you is to love you, and you can only prove how different and good your business is by extended exposure to your people and service.

Trials allow you to demonstrate that it is all about the members and that you're willing to prove it every time the person comes through the door. Keep in mind that during a typical sales encounter at almost any club in the country, everyone is going to be nice to you because you are fresh meat, and they are hungry pit bulls; but after coming to your business for a number of workouts throughout the duration of a trial membership, the potential member eventually learns that being nice and supportive is really what your business is all about.

This is why an average club with a strong customer-service culture can compete and thrive against a newer club that has bet everything on just equipment and that hasn't built the staff and support needed to deliver legendary customer service.

Do These Things Now

- Learn how to differentiate your business in the marketplace.

- Move your business toward a specialization in the market.

- Customer service will be your strongest competitive edge in the coming years. Commit now to building a legendary service culture in your club.

- Eliminate first-visit pressure sales in your club.

- Embrace trial memberships as a way to get more leads and to demonstrate your superior service in your area.

Customer service is as simple as …

a quick greeting.

Everyone who walks through your front door should be acknowledged in four seconds, and your club should be designed to allow this to happen.

Coming to the club should be like coming home to your members. Your goal is to provide such good service that the club becomes that valued third place in their life, behind their home and their work.

We can accomplish this goal by showing appreciation for their support today of the business, demonstrated by how we greet them during their arrival for their daily workout. The person is paying to be a member, so show him we are happy and grateful to see him by extending a greeting, such as the welcome statement, within four seconds.

Four seconds is not a random number. Good restaurants have known for years that the perception of good service begins at the front door. Acknowledging someone quickly, within four seconds, and greeting your guests warmly does a lot to set the tone for the level of service the person can expect from that business. Open strongly, and the rest of the evening is going to be easier.

This rule is also important for the potential members that are coming to see the club. Most new folks will hesitate inside the door and pause for a few seconds to get their bearings. Staff that is trained to a higher level of customer service will recognize that person and call out a warm greeting, "Hello, we're having a great day at the Workout Company. Please come on in."

First impressions are everything in a service business. You are judged by your opening act, which for us in the fitness business begins when that door opens. Use this situation to your advantage to set the tone for expected customer service, and greet your guests within four seconds.

5

Service Begins Where Base Expectations End

How hard do you work for your money?

This seems like such a simple question when you pose it to anyone. Of course, most people think they work exceptionally hard for their money. Long hours, lots of risk, difficult staff issues, and too many competitors are all part of our business in today's market, and anyone who is making money in the industry feels that they earned it by busting butt every day.

The follow-up question, though, is the one that makes people think about their money and how much effort did go into making it. The question is: If you worked so hard making that money, how do you think you should be treated when you spend it at another business?

Think about working hard during an especially brutal week in the club business. The members are in your face, equipment is breaking, and your staff decides this would be a good time to call in sick for a day or two so they can leave town and visit their friends. You might have made money that week, but it was hard, and you feel you earned every dollar in your pocket.

Now imagine going out to dinner that Friday with your significant other at a decent restaurant. You've been there before, and you're looking forward to a nice drink and good meal with the added bonus of someone waiting on you for a change, as opposed to you working so hard for members that fail most of the time to show any appreciation for all that gut-wrenching work.

The service, however, is slow that night; the food is only average, and the experience that you were looking forward to all day is now somewhat of a letdown. Your expectations were high, but the experience just didn't match what you were hoping for that night.

The waiter comes with the check and asks the typical question: "Was everything fine, sir?" You nod, pay the bill, and leave, still a little disappointed and actually somewhat angry. You just paid $90 for a meal, that was at best average, and you swear to never come back to that place again. What just happened in this story, and how does it affect our business?

We All Carry Base Expectations of Service

Every time you enter a business with the intent to spend money, you have a base expectation of how you should be treated. The transaction, if it is a retail business, or experience, if it is a service business such as a restaurant, then either exceeds that expectation or fails to meet your preconceived vision of how you should be treated for the money spent.

Base expectations are the commonalities we expect to take place in every business transaction. For example, when you walk into a big-box store to buy a small camera, you already are expecting certain actions and behaviors to take place.

- You might expect that the store will have a wide range of stock so you can compare.

- You might expect that the person who helps you will greet you with a friendly smile.

- You then would expect that person to be knowledgeable about the cameras and be able to help you, through a series of questions about how you intend to use the product and your level of experience in photography, select the product that is best for you.

- You would also expect the salesperson to be totally focused on you, and not trying to help several other customers at the same time, or to be answering the phone, too.

- When you decide to buy, you would expect the salesperson to explain any other products you need to go with this one so you don't get home and realize you don't have everything you need to get started taking the pictures you want, especially since you bought the new camera to use at your son's birthday tomorrow.

- Obviously, you would also expect the camera you chose to be in stock so you can take it home now.

- When you pay for the camera, you would expect the store to take your money any way you decide to pay, meaning cash, check, or any major credit card.

- Once you purchase, and especially since you just spent $600 for your new toy, you would expect the store to return the item with no questions asked if it has an issue during the first few times you use it.

- As a side note, you might also expect the store to be clean, have restrooms that are nice, and be easy to find your way around.

- Finally, as you pay for your purchase and turn to walk away, you would certainly expect the salesperson to thank you for the money spent at his store.

These are all base expectations that go along with this type of buying experience. After all, the consumer is spending $600 here, which might be a routine transaction for the store, but is a lot of money for the customer. He worked hard for the money, but is willing to spend it if he gets a little help, guidance, and support from friendly people who appreciate his business.

The More You Pay, the More You Expect

Expectations rise as the price goes up, which is easily proven when you look at a typical restaurant. For example, if three restaurants near your house charge these prices for a meal for one, what would your expectations be for each business?

- The first place charges about $12 for an entree and is part of a national chain.

- The second place charges about $22 for an entree and is locally owned.

- The third place charges about $60 per entree, is locally owned, and has the reputation as the best restaurant in town.

Everyone knows what to expect with the first place, since these places are all over the country, and every town has one. We would expect the server to be young, the food to be average, but a lot of it, and that you would be better to go with the beer and stay way from the big, cheap glass of house wine. Huge calories, plain food (and a lot of it) is the theme; but it is consistent, and you get what you pay for when you visit.

The second option is where it gets more interesting. The first question you have to ask yourself is whether $22 for an entree without drinks or desert is a lot of money for you? Depending on your answer, you either have very high expectations and that restaurant represents a big night out on your budget, or you make more money in your life and your expectations for that experience isn't much higher than the chain club; because you are one of those people that feels you get what you pay for when it comes to good food and service.

The final choice, where a meal with wine will probably cost about $100 per person or more, raises everyone's expectations. You are now at the level that the cost carries the burden of leading you to a very high expected standard.

For example, at $100 per head, you would probably expect impeccable service, legendary food, an extended wine list, and a total experience that more than justifies the cost of the meal. This does, by the way, put a heavy burden on the business; because when you charge a higher price, you have to really perform to a higher level or you won't last long. Charge $100 for a meal and deliver a weak experience of service and average food, and you won't be around long enough to see your first ad hit the paper.

Since We Do Work Hard for Our Money, We Always Expect More for What We Pay

Because it is our money and we worked our collective butts off to earn it, we always expect to get the most for what we spend. The $50 the potential member has in his hand and intends to spend in your business may be a routine transaction to you, and may be one of a hundred different small transactions in this store today, but to him that is a hell of a lot of money, and he wants a little respect and courtesy as he spends his cash.

This is where many club owners and managers get into trouble during the daily operation of their businesses. The member thinks his $49 a month is a lot of money, and that he is doing you a favor by choosing your business (which he is, but we take that for granted, too). He expects some big service for that money, and he expects to be treated with a little respect for his contribution to your business.

On the club side, the owner has 2,000 members and not one of them appreciates the $3,000 he spent last month on new water heaters and plumbing repairs in the locker rooms. In fact, there probably aren't even three members in the club who are even aware that this owner spent that money, and out of the three, maybe one said, "Thank you."

The member, who is paying you, brings basic expectations to the business in exchange for his money. The club owner, who does keep the club nice and does reinvest his money, feels that meeting these base expectations is the best form of service he could possibly provide. The owner, in this case, is wrong, and what he is doing is not true customer service.

The way to think about this is that there is an unwritten contract that is exchanged between the member and the owner that far exceeds the written agreement most clubs use for simple memberships. The member is saying: "I chose your club and drove past four others to give you money, and I expect courtesy and respect for that support." The owner says: "We do a good job here of providing classes, keeping the place clean, and taking care of our members. You are only paying me $49, and I go way beyond that in the monthly reinvestment that members don't understand or appreciate anyway."

Both sides are agreeing to do business, but one side—the member's half—is far more loaded with a higher level of expectations. This is why the perception of customer service of most fitness businesses is so low. The club does think it is providing service, while the member doesn't think the owners are even trying at a base level.

What Does the Member Really Expect for His Money?

In exchange for any fee to belong to a club, no matter if the fee is $9 per month for a low-priced/value club or $2,000 per month for an upscale training club, the paying client has certain base expectations that go along with that exchange of money for time in your business.

Following are some of the base expectations that are part of any trade of money for time in our industry:

- The member expects the club to be beyond clean.

- Every member who pays expects you to know his name.

- If the client is paying to come, he expects the counter people to show respect by being courteous and attentive during each visit.

- The clients expect the club staff to be decently dressed, since this is a place of business, and the client is paying each month. Decently dressed is a hotly debated topic, but do you really think cheap tee shirts, jeans, messed-up sports shoes or worn-out, cheap golf shirts show respect for the people who are paying your bills each month?

- The members, again who are paying all of your bills, expect you to do what you promise to do. If you say you open at 5:00, then you need to open at 5:00. If you say the class starts at 7:00, then that class has to start at 7:00 because you promised it would.

- The paying members also expect that all the equipment will work, that you have enough equipment, and that your equipment is fairly current and matches what they see in the fitness magazines and on television.

- Everyone who is a member expects the right of quiet enjoyment. This means that if someone stinks, you will get him out of the club, because stinky members offend the rest of the paying clients. This also means that you will control loud and offensive members, cell-phone idiots, equipment hogs, screamers, the sexual-harassment fools, and anyone else who makes the majority of the paying clients feel bad about coming to and supporting your business.

- The members also expect common courtesy from you and your staff. These members expect to be greeted when they arrive, thanked for any money spent in the business, and thanked for visiting when they leave. If these members go beyond the normal fees, such as spending a lot of money for extra services such as training, then they expect even more from you since they are now paying a great deal more to support your business than the average member.

People who are paying you expect all of these things, and more, from you when they become part of your business. The things on this list are not customer service, but merely base expectations of minimal service in exchange for monies paid. If I pay you $49 each month, then I expect the place to be clean, the staff to be nice to me, and for the equipment to work. These aren't special things you're doing here; these are just things you should be doing as a normal part of being in business. If you did everything on the list, you *are still not providing customer service* in the member's mind, but merely meeting his most basic expectations for the money he gave you to be a member.

Customer Service Begins When You Exceed Base Expectations

Meeting base expectations is part of doing business and is also part of the exchange of money for time. Legendary customer service that will set you apart from all other competitors in your market, and that will keep your members staying longer and paying longer, begins when you learn to exceed the customer's base expectations.

Perhaps the strongest example you can find of exceeding base expectations and arriving at true legendary service is the cleanliness of any given club business. Every owner, even those who are standing in front of you in a stained tee shirt leaning on a cluttered desk in the middle of a smelly club, will swear that his club is the cleanest in that town.

The single biggest negative, based upon 30 years of experience, which drives women away from a fitness business, is the perceived cleanliness of the club. Note the emphasis on the word "perceived."

The old adage that *your perception becomes your reality* has a direct application in this example, although almost all employees under 30 have no idea what this tried-and-true statement really means.

A simple illustration that defines this statement and how it applies to your business is clutter in your club. The older the business, the more clutter it has, since few owners ever throw anything away. New medicine balls are purchased, but the old ones are simply moved to a corner instead of thrown away.

Members bring in piles of magazines for the cardio area (you have to teach your members that if they can read while doing cardio, then the cardio isn't really going to help), but no one ever throws away the piles of old magazines.

The front counter area is the biggest clutter magnet. Club information, boxes of munchie bars, boxes of credit-card applications, check-in computers, and various notices all fight for space all over your front counter. Nothing is removed, but anytime something new is added, the staff simply pushes it all closer together.

The members, and most other folks, equate clutter with being dirty. Those old sweat-wrinkled magazines aren't just magazines after being in the club for months: they become ucky, dirty, nasty junk that automatically proclaims that this business is dirty and disgusting. Clutter is filth, yet we always add to the piles and never subtract.

The perception, due to the piles of stuff that indeed might actually be clean and are just piles, becomes the member's reality in his head that this business is dirty, and that the owner is failing to take care of his business, and therefore, his members. The perception becomes the reality, and members quit because they perceive that your business is dirty and nasty.

Most decent clubs do get cleaned every day in some fashion. The crews come in at night and do a run-through, and the locker rooms are cleaned, and everything else in the club is wiped down, the trash is emptied, litter on the floor is removed, and the club opens the next day clean in the mind of the owner. But is it really clean, and will it stand up to the standards of our members, especially the men and women in the club who know what clean really is?

Most club cleaning crews, and most club staff that help keep the place under control throughout the day, merely *surface wipe*. This means that we grab a rag and a spray bottle and start wiping down that counter or piece of equipment. We use good disinfectant, and the smell of cleaning is in the air. But the place still isn't clean.

Good cleaning is deep cleaning, and most adults who work in real businesses and own their own home know that wiping stuff down is not the same as moving stuff, turning stuff over, removing all cleaning obstacles and occasionally shutting down for a few days and really cleaning stuff to the roots. There is cleaning, and there is really deep-down clean, which few clubs ever achieve because, for most young male owners, clean is good enough.

The point is that cleaning a club every day with a crew is good customer service, but legendary customer service begins when you start to understand that you have to change the member's perception to change his reality. After all, aren't we all chasing the title of "Cleanest Club in Town"?

It's Clean if I Watch You Clean It

It has to be clean if I stand there and watch you clean it. This simple statement illustrates the power of creating the next level above service, which is legendary service that sets you apart from all others.

Service is always about perception. Average coffee always taste better if the person who sold it to you, and poured it for you in a nice, big, white ceramic coffee mug, is happy, clean, courteous, and thanks you for your business. That same coffee will always taste worse if you bought it at an airport from an employee at a small kiosk who has the face of someone serving a life sentence of menial labor, grunts when you order, pours the coffee in a crappy paper cup, and lays your change on the counter and slides it across without even eye contact.

The perception is that the coffee tastes better because the experience was better. How we perceive our world dictates how we judge our world, and a membership at your club is that member's world several days a week.

If we want to create the perception that we have legendary service in a market filled with competitors that are at best barely surviving, then we need to consider the perception we try to create with every contact point between our members and the business.

Using the cleaning example, if we want to create the perception that we are the cleanest business in the market, we need to put on a show for the members, and that show is based upon the premise that we will prove to you that we are the cleanest by having someone actually continually clean while you the member are in the club.

This cleanliness show can be as simple as hiring a retired couple, putting them in a club jumpsuit or uniform, and turning them loose in the club during normal business hours. They clean, move things and clean more, wipe mirrors, touch the locker rooms every 30 minutes, keep sweat marks off the cardio, hit the benches, and do whatever it takes to not only keep the business really clean, but to prove to the members we have the cleanest club by continually cleaning it in front of them during most of our busiest hours. Clean is clean, but a cleaning show is more powerful and builds your reputation.

In this example, we have exceeded the member's base expectations. She expects the club to be clean, and it is, but we also want to exceed those expectations by creating a perception in her head that we care so much about our members and our reputation of having the cleanest club in town that we will have a cleaning team in the business during all busy hours keeping the place spotless just for you.

Don't think this is important? Imagine this woman dropping by the club for a little cardio. While she is on her favorite treadmill, she sees your crew wipe all the other cardio pieces, wipe down the benches, pick up the occasional piece of litter, wipe the drinking fountain, and empty all the trash. That night when she arrives home, she has a renewal notice from the club, or perhaps she notices the monthly draft on her bank statement. What would you want in her head when she compares the cost of being a member with her perception of how she is treated and valued by the business?

Another simple and brief example of exceeding base expectations is apparent in most of the decent hotel chains. Just a few years ago, some of the better chains, such as a Marriott® or a top-end Sheraton®, began to invest in extremely nice beds. When you are paying $150 a night or more for a room, you expect to have a quality bed, but the hotels learned to exceed your expectations, and to actually delight the customers, by offering beds that were often better than the consumer had at home, or had ever experienced anywhere else. Good beds were the base expectation; but the perception that these beds were heaven sent and unavailable to even a home buyer established a higher reality of legendary service.

Your job as an owner is to first understand the base expectations a member brings to your business. Next, you have to understand that meeting those base expectations is important, but merely meeting them is not customer service. Customer service that leads to higher retention numbers and stronger sales is only achieved by learning to exceed the base expectations we all carry with us in the normal exchange of payment for time.

Every Action Has to Have an Expected Outcome

There shouldn't be many random actions in your business. For example, a front counter person who was hired quickly, given three or four hours of training, and then thrown into a 40-hour workweek with limited supervision will improvise and fill the void. In other words, if you haven't taught her the proper technique to greet a member, handle a problem, answer the phone, or even exacting standards as to how you want her to dress for the job each day, then she will establish her own rules and techniques to get her through the day.

She can, of course, check people into the club, process basic paperwork, answer the phone, and take care of other front counter basics that keeps the members moving and the club open, but is her own self-imposed method adding to your business or costing you members?

This lack of structure in one of the key positions in your business, meaning a job that has the highest contact with all of your members and potential members, devalues the perceived value of the club since no one has really taught this employee what she is trying to accomplish. Put simply, there is action, but no expected outcome.

What Does It Look Like When It Is Perfect?

If you can see it in your head, you can teach it. If you can visualize a front counter person delivering legendary service, then you can indeed train that person to get it done each day she is at work.

Most service is weak in our industry because the owners don't know where they are going and where any of their training is going to lead. Every job, and every action an employee takes while doing that job, should be built upon a few of these key concepts:

- Does the job or action create legendary service?

- Are there other ways to do this job that would set me apart from my competitors?

- If this person was perfect, and she delivered the perfect service to my members, how would she do the job, how would she be dressed, and what would the employee say to my members?

- What is the basic expectation by my members for this job, and how do I exceed that expectation every day?

Jupiterimages

If you train an employee to answer the phone for an inquiry call, for example, how would that call lead to increasing your service image, what would the staff person say, or how would she act to set you apart from other clubs, and how do you train her to exceed your potential member's base expectations with each and every call she takes? In other words, what does perfect look and sound like?

Before we define perfect, let's define typical first. Typical is how you might be answering the phone now and undoubtedly is how your competitors are answering their phones:

- No energy is displayed at the pick-up, and the person answering always sounds stressed.

- The phone will often ring five or six times or more before being answered.

- Often, no real person ever answers the phone, and you are thrown into voice-mail hell.

- The person answering the phone has to get someone else to give out any information.

- The person answering the phone will click you to hold in the middle of a question.

- No one ever thanks you for calling that club.

- No one will give you any real information unless you make an appointment and come down in person.

- The front counter person takes your number, and no one calls you back for an hour or more.

- You have a real feeling that the person answering the phone is really young and has about an hour of training if that much.

- Your perception of service and the help you can expect at that business is very low based upon the quality of that call and you move on to check another club.

First of all, you spend thousands of dollars a month for advertising, all designed to get the phone to ring more often, yet you only train your counter people who answer that phone an hour or so a month. The success of all this money invested in building your brand is often destroyed with a five-minute phone call handled by a young, undertrained counter dummy working because you got her cheap and she shows up regularly.

Knowing all that is bad with these calls, let's look at what should happen if you sit in a chair, close your eyes, and imagine your phone being answered perfectly each and every time it rings in your business:

- All employees that answer the phone in your business receive at least several hours *per week* training on all aspects of customer service and basic sales skills so you know that each call will be handled by a trained staff person and not someone who has only had one or two hours of phone training in the last six months she has worked for you.

- The call is answered quickly within three rings and answered live and never with a machine.

- The person answering the phone brings energy, enthusiasm, and courtesy to the call, and always begins with a strong energy statement. For example, "We're having a great day at the Workout Company."

- If no one on the sales team is available to take the inquiry, the counter person has been trained to completely answer all basic questions and to invite the caller to come and try the club's trial membership–the only guaranteed way to increase the conversion rate of calls to actual leads in the club.

- The person begins the call with, "Thank you for calling us today. We appreciate the chance to tell you about our club." She says this each and every time because she has practiced this opening hundreds of times in her training. She says it so smoothly that it sounds natural, and not part of her training, because that is what good training does for you and your team.

She then follows her opening statement with, "By the way, have you ever been in our club before?" The client might answer, "No, I just moved here, and thought I would check you out."

She follows with, "Welcome to the area. I think you are really going to like living here. How did you hear about us, if I may ask?" Can you feel the courtesy just oozing out of this call, which is a major separator from you and your competitors? And she is courteous because she was taught to be that way through her training, and because in your head you want the expected outcome of this call to be that the caller is so impressed by the service on the phone that they just know the club is going to treat them right.

After asking two leading questions, she now says, "Oh, please, let me apologize. I didn't even introduce myself. We are really busy today, and I just started talking. My name is Sarah, and you are…?" Sarah was trained to get the caller's name discreetly and with courtesy rather than bluntness.

If there were a salesperson available that could better answer questions about the club than Sarah, she would transfer the call using this line: "Thank you for calling the club today. We appreciate a chance to tell you about our business. The person you need to talk with is Ben. May I put you on hold for second while I transfer your call?" Courtesy sells, can be taught, and establishes service immediately with your guests.

This could go on, but the point is that if you sat in a chair and imagined great service and an effective phone inquiry, it would probably play out something like the partial script outlined in the previous section. Everything that Sarah did in this call can be scripted and trained. Everything she is doing can be practiced in staff training to the point that it becomes routine.

And, most importantly, everything our staff person is doing is establishing the perception of legendary customer service that you not only expect from Sarah, but from everyone you will encounter in this business.

Any club owner or manager can teach customer service if he knows what he is trying to accomplish—something most owners really don't understand. Also, most owners are mired in routine training, covering nothing more than the basics of surviving the job at hand, and never train from the perspective that the key function with every job in this business is to deliver legendary customer service every day to every member.

Do These Things Now

- Be aware that the member always has a higher expectation in the relationship than you do. He always feels that what he pays is worth more than you give in exchange.

- Learn what the member's base expectations are in this relationship. There is no service until you meet, and then exceed, these expectations.

- Imagine perfect service in your club. If you can see it, you can break it down into parts and teach those parts to your staff.

Customer service is as simple as …
knowing the customer's name.

There is no greater insult than to take money from someone and then not remember that person's name.

We have used the excuse over the years that there are just too many of them and not enough of us, but we still get mad when someone who has paid for a year just disappears at the end of his membership and we never hear from him again.

Put yourself on the member's side for a moment. Can you imagine paying your membership for a year and then walking into the club for a workout and the "front counter person du jour" just stares vacantly at you as your scan your card and walk by the counter. How does it feel to that member who has invested a full year's worth of payments into that business, and no one even takes the time to learn who he is?

Not knowing a name is not business-threatening. Not trying to learn names, or to have the staff introduce themselves politely to someone they haven't yet met, or who they might have encountered but have forgotten the name, is totally unacceptable and a sure way to destroy a business over time.

Incentivize your staff to learn names. Make sure your computer system can accommodate pictures of the members and can flash the person's name in large print as he checks in each day. Reward your management team for seeking out members on the floor and making it a point to greet every member by their name as often as possible.

If you know the member's name, you have the start of a relationship between you and him, and he will be much more likely to stay longer and pay longer than someone who has been ignored for their entire membership.

6

Success in the Fitness Business Is Nothing but a Series of Basics

The longer you are in business, the further you move away from the foundational truth of that business.

The foundational truth is the short, preferably one- or two-sentence, definition of your business, which is a perfect exercise for owners just starting or old, jaded guys who have been out there for a while and who need to get the business back to being effective again.

In the world of small business, if you can't describe your business plan in just a couple of sentences, then you are probably building a business that is vague and that will be hard to market to the consumer or difficult to run on a day-to-day basis because you don't really know what you are trying to accomplish.

When most future owners start playing with this exercise in focus, they almost always begin with an emphasis on what they do and not on how they are going to do it. For example, a potential restaurant person might describe her new business as one that will create the best Italian food in town. This sentence describes the product, but does not take into account the delivery system, which is what you will really be selling to the consumer and is what keeps the customer returning to that business. Remember, there is a lot of good food out there, but there are a lot less truly great restaurant experiences to be found.

A tighter focus for our restaurant person might be: "We will create an Italian/Asian fusion experience designed and centered on the 30- to 45-year-old downtown trend set." In this example, she has declared a product and also a delivery system designed for one specific target market in her market area.

In the fitness business, we need to always start with this narrow focus. For example, a young owner might state: "We are going to build an upscale fitness center for the top 40 percent of the people in our area defined by the affluence demographic in the lower east valley." This statement clearly defines the target market as well as the needed delivery system (upscale is the definer), the potential owner can see this club in his head as it is described, and the statement also allows him to clearly visualize the members who would be using the facility.

In this example, the owner has clearly stated whom this business is for and whom he will target. Once you accomplish that goal, everything from that point forward has to match in the business. For instance, if you were going after upscale adults, the uniforms, staff choices, club colors, programming, marketing, branding, and even the music would all have to enhance your vision of the business. Start with your foundational truth and build from there.

Problems Arise When You Drift Away From the Foundational Truth

Owners who aren't making the money they want from their businesses often can't simply explain what they are trying to create through that business. Once you get past their initial response of frustration, "I am trying to make money here," you then discover that these owners have strayed from their focus. This drifting occurs more often the longer the owner is in business, since it becomes easier to dilute your direction over time due to staff changes, market pressures, or because you simply forgot what you built and have lost your way.

Let's look at the fitness owner described previously. He wants to open an upscale fitness business, catering to a very specific target market and located in an upscale part of town. He gets his club open and enjoys a decent level of success during the first few years he is in business. This type of club would have a strong training business, social events catering to the higher financial demographic, and would be a place for the wealthier folks in this community to meet and greet.

But this owner could also easily lose his focus in this market, therefore, starting his business down a path that won't be financially effective for him over time. For example, one of the regular members, whose son plays on the local football team and who has had private training at the club during the summer, brings the coach to the club. The coach was impressed by the fitness of the member's son and would like to arrange a deal where all the team members can train in the club during the summer.

The club owner likes the idea, likes taking care of good members, and especially likes the thought of a big check during the lean months from all these kids training in his club, and he makes the deal. Come June, the club now has 30 young males training there in groups for several hours every afternoon and in the early evening.

The owner is making money, the coach is thrilled, the players are getting advanced training, but the majority of the rest of the members really hate this situation because this formerly upscale adult haven is now overran daily by a bunch of loud, smelly (they are 15, and all young males that age smell), boisterous, high school football players. A few of the members complain, but most just quietly ignore the situation, although those in the silent majority are the members who will be the first to not renew or the first to leave for another club if given a chance.

The owner lost the focus of his business, but it may take him a long time to figure out where the money and good fortune of the club changed, if he really ever does. His foundational truth, based upon a focus on upscale adults, was watered down by the addition of the kids during the hours when the most conservative members train, which is always the early evening shift.

It was noted that once you establish your foundational truth, then everything after that has to match. In this case, the kids in the club broke the sequence because they are not part of the owner's long-term plan to build a club for upscale adults and then to make sure that everything in the business enhances that choice.

What does he do now with this mixed business? How does he market this eclectic business to an upscale crowd when any tours in the club will encounter packs of kids? Drift from your foundational truth, and you can lose the ability to go after a target-specific market in your area and you now become like every other generic fitness facility that claims to have something for everyone, but in reality has no meaning or identity for anyone seeking a fitness facility.

The Basics of the Business
Support the Foundational Truth

The fitness business is a simple business. Once you establish the foundational truth for your business, the application of just a few basic skills will put you on the correct path for success. These basics are:

- *Create* the concept.

- *Market* the concept.

- Learn to *sell* so you can develop a sales team that can convert 60 percent of your leads into sales.

- Create *service* that is legendary.

- *Train* your staff often to deliver this service and create the legendary experience.

- Everything you do has to lead to being able to *retain* as many members as you can over time.

These basics are sequential, meaning that one follows the other when you build a successful fitness business. For instance, you cannot market a new club if you're not sure of what you are marketing (failure to create first). You can't sell if you don't get enough leads into the business because the generic marketing failed. There is no service without the acquisition of new members, and there is no service without training the staff. If everything prior is done correctly, then the club will benefit from the highest level of retention possible. Break the chain, and you have a business that will be financially ineffective.

The Components Are Different for Every Foundational Truth

If you picked sports performance as your foundational truth, for example, then everything in the sequence would follow that choice. For example, the colors in the club would be much brighter and bolder than the upscale adult facility. The staff would also be younger, the music louder, the degree of finish leaning more toward an edgier look, and the marketing would be focused on an entirely different segment in the market. Once you pick a path, everything on the path then follows.

Customer service, which is a blend of the other basics, would be vastly different for the sports-performance center than it would be for the upscale adult club. The service training you would use for the adults would be laughed at by the kids in the sports programs, and the uniforms and dress in the sports-performance business would be considered underdressed and not appropriate for the upscale crowd. Most customer-service training is not one-size-fits-all as claimed in most customer-service books. Service for your business is a direct plan based upon the specific people who will be using your business.

The Customer-Service Model

Building a customer-service plan for your business has to be based on whom that business is targeting as a member. It is hard for any owner or manager to train a staff to deliver service if the training is generic rather than target-specific. For example, visit an expensive hotel, and the impeccable service is directly a byproduct of customer-service training devised for an upscale and wealthy traveler, or for a discerning and road-weary businessperson. Take that same service person out of that environment, and what he was trained to do might not work in other businesses based upon a different clientele.

Modeling customer service is as simple as choosing your target member and then listing a sequence of what you want to happen at every level of contact between that person and your business. There are no absolutes, and this is merely an exercise that helps owners and managers to begin to create an image of what good service should look like in their business.

The model we will build will be based on that upscale adult mentioned throughout this chapter. Keeping that foundational truth in mind, we will then narrow our focus down to a 45-year-old female member, Kathy Jones, who is a working real estate agent. She is in the top 40 percent of the demographics in this area, based upon affluence, and represents the population the club owner wants to attract and serve in this market.

What kind of customer service do we have to create to attract and keep Kathy as a member? This is the challenge every owner faces every day and goes way beyond just telling your staff to smile and be nice. Remember, if you use this exercise in your business, always start your service model outside the club since your marketing and other outside factors are nothing more than a projection of anticipated service.

Comstock

The Kathy Jones, Our Trial Member, and a Perfect-World Customer-Service Model

What kind of advertising would work for her, and why?

Every ad the club uses would feature testimonials of other adults near her age group rather than young hard-body models that women such as Kathy might find offensive or who might find that type of advertising sexist and chauvinistic. There should at least be one line in each of the testimonials that would rave about the club's service and how different that member was treated at your club compared to other facilities she might have belonged to in the past.

What would this club want in its Yellow Pages ad?

This person would not likely be interested in a list of equipment or services, especially since every ad in the yellow pages uses the same list of services, classes, and equipment, which does not help any of the businesses stand out from the others. She is a professional in her community and well known, so invite her down through a trial membership to experience the service she will receive. Lists and bullet points in advertising mean nothing to her. "To know you is to love you," which is the foundational truth of all good marketing, means everything when it comes to demonstrating true customer service.

How would you like her first experience with the club to go?

If you were chasing this type of member, then the outside of the club is very important. If she were representative of upscale folks in your community, then you would probably want the outside of your business to convey the image she is used to in the other businesses she uses. For example, she spends a lot of time in spas, banks, and other professional offices and maybe nice restaurants, so the image of your business starting with the outside should match that of other businesses she is used to in her daily life. In other words, she will not want to pull up to the front of your business and see wild discount specials painted on the windows or all your treadmills backed up to the front street with a lot of sweat-pant-covered rear ends facing the parking lot.

When the door opens, and she comes in to check out the trial membership, what do you want the experience to be?

Visualize a clutter-free front desk and a slightly older and more polished counter person who warmly greets your guest. The staff person is well dressed, well spoken, and very welcoming to the club. The staff person shakes hands with your guest, introduces herself, and asks a few simple questions as to how she can help her. Realizing that this person is in the club to inquire about a trial membership, your staff person, knowing that your salesperson is on a tour and won't be done for about 10 minutes, explains the situation to your guest, and then asks her if she would like a smoothie or bottle of water while she waits. When the salesperson arrives, the front counter person smoothly hands the guest over, using a practiced handoff routine the entire team has repeatedly learned in their customer-service training.

What kind of service image would you like your sales team to deliver?

Your salesperson invites the guest over to the information table, a high cafe-style table near the front with a great view of the club. Your club's sales team uses a table like this to explain the club and to do sales, since your target market, and almost every other human being on the planet, finds it offensive to be taken into an office and closed across a desk.

Your salesperson is professionally dressed in the club uniform, which might be a mock turtle and black pants for the sales team, well-groomed, and is approximately the same age as your target market, rather than the typical young, overdone male salesperson most clubs gravitate toward and who brings far too much testosterone to the sales situation. Before the tour of the club begins, the salesperson spends about five minutes at the information table getting to know the person and what she wants, her fitness experience, and what she is doing now for fitness.

The salesperson is not selling at this point, nor is he talking about all the classes, the training rates, or the hours. All he is simply doing is establishing a relationship with someone we hope will be part of the business, but through his training, he realizes that all sales are easier if the person experiences a touch of the club's customer service/caring attitude first. The salesperson gives the guest a tour, shows her the prices, and asks her to join. She likes the club, but would rather take the trial, which in this case is 30 days for $39.

What kind of training experience would you like to be known for in your business?

If service were perfect, your trial member would never be in the club during her first 30 days without a personal coach guiding her in some form. Group exercise, group personal training/coaching in groups of up to 10 people done with a challenging format and "badass" approach to getting fit, or semi-private training done in groups of two to four at a time, gives you an excellent foundation to engage your trial in a total support situation.

Roughly 80 percent of your trial members should be involved in guidance-based training during their extended visits. If you can get this percentage involved in these programs—meaning that during every visit the guest makes during their trial program they have someone leading them through their workouts—your conversion rates should be extremely high. The other 20 percent are those guests who "know how to workout" and will still be carrying Arnold's bodybuilding bible from the 1970s and are beyond help.

Most clubs, due to the nature of having every training session based upon one-on-one, can't afford to provide a true service experience to their guests, or even their members. Group formats are cost-effective, yet they deliver great service through the group dynamics.

What kind of experience would you like this trial member to receive from the club itself?

Your physical plant is, of course, part of the customer experience. If your trial guest Kathy were in your club for a full 30 days, what experience would she walk away with after spending that much time with your staff and hanging out in your business? The effect of a dirty club was discussed earlier, but that issue could be compounded if you add in a few pieces of broken equipment, training sessions that start late, no toilet paper in stall number two, and a few stained ceiling tiles and dead light bulbs. Taken separately, all of these are small things, but put together all of them add up to a negative experience and a lesser chance you will sign up this member anytime during her trial membership.

How would you stay connected to this person, even during her trial?

The goal of legendary customer service is to build a relationship with our members, and in this case, our trial members. The only cost-effective way to demonstrate service at this level is by going electronic. If service were perfect in your club, your trial guest would receive encouraging Twitter messages from your trainers and sales staff regularly, as well as a Facebook entry.

This is all subject to what is available in the electronic world at the time, but even if these two currently popular social networking formats go away, something else will be there that will allow you to touch your members cheaply and on an as-needed basis. You would also want to post workout tips on your YouTube account and have sample workouts done with bodyweight or readily available equipment that your members and guests can do at home if they can't make it to the club.

If the club service were on the legendary side, there would also be a social event each week and chances to get the members together in small groups, such as a kettlebell workshop on Saturday morning or a workout in the local park on a nice day. Most members and guests are thrown into the normal rhythm of the club and are forgotten except when we are ready to pound the person for a membership or referral.

Back to the Basics

Most club management evolves into nothing more than trying to maintain what you have and avoiding bad things happening in your business. For instance, if you have ever found yourself saying, "I need someone to cover that Saturday morning shift," you are already there mentally. Your goal is just to get someone to show up, open the club, and keep things going so none of the members get in your face about the club opening late and they had to wait 15 minutes in the parking lot.

The statement that should have been made by this owner is, "I need to get someone to work Saturday mornings who can set the club on fire service-wise and who can also tap the large money-making potential that exists in the club on a good Saturday traffic day." One statement is based upon avoidance of pain and the other is based upon trying to create incredible experiences in your business. But after a few years of getting your butt beat in an intense industry, all owners know that getting a warm body to cover a shift is easier than finding that person who can set the place on fire with great service. This is the challenge, but it is also what sets a great owner apart from an average owner: great owners are willing to learn to do the things average owners avoid.

If the service is right, then everything else usually happens in a good way for the business, too. Good service is a good source of referrals. Good service is the foundation of higher retention. Good service means a higher sales closing percentage. Everything good in your business begins with the plan to create legendary service, which can be taught and delivered if you return to the basics of the business and focus on modeling your perfect service world.

Do These Things Now

- Write out the foundational truth that describes your business.

- If you are not making the money you hoped for in your business, return to the basics that every owner needs to master, but that most stray from over time.

Customer service is as simple as …
sending birthday cards.

Sending the members birthday cards is retro, but the act of using this tool still has a customer-service impact on your members.

These cards should be addressed by hand and signed by the management team and assorted staff members. Sign a bunch of these all at once during a staff meeting so you can get a lot of names on each one and put them in the mail the day prior to the member's birthday. You should be able to print out the birthday list of the month with your club's financial software program. You can add value to these birthday greetings by including a $5 gift card for use in the club.

The largest group of members that get lost each year and fail to renew are the ones that feel the club is indifferent to them and their membership. Simple acts of kindness, such as sending a birthday card, individualize the membership process and lets the members know that they are thought of as individuals at your club.

You can take this a step further if you are in the right market. If you live in a smaller town, make sure that you send an acknowledgment concerning anything you might see about a member that appears in the local paper. For example, if a member is promoted at his job and it makes the paper, send him a small note mentioning the article and congratulating him on his success.

7

Complaining Customers
Are Good Customers

We all love the quiet members, you know, the ones who come in and pay each month, do their own thing somewhere out in the club, and barely flash a small, almost embarrassed smile as they pass the front counter.

These are also the same members who are silently plotting the end of your business by planning their escape and hoping they can quietly sneak away in the night. These members will not complain about the broken treadmill. They will not whimper about a cancelled class. They just sit and wait until the right moment when the accumulation of so many slights and inconveniences simply overwhelms them and then they flee from your business, and you will never even know what set them on the path or why they lost faith in your business.

This silent—but business-killing—exodus all stems from the perception that somewhere, and at sometime during their membership with your club, they were treated badly or that they noticed something in your business that offended them to the point that they don't want to be in your club any longer.

On the other hand, we hate the complaining members. Everyone has a small population of chronic whiners, complainers, and staff-hating and self-absorbed members who make it their life's work to constantly let you know how bad your business is and everything that is wrong with it. The bike is broken, the instructor was rude, the trainer smells bad, the beverages are cheaper at the gas station, you just fired my favorite instructor and I want my money back, and a litany of other complaints that come every single day in your business screamed by the same small group of members who must actually spend their time in the club just to find stuff to crush your spirit.

We hate these people because they never leave and can ruin any good day you might accidently be having by just approaching the front desk with that smirk on their face that means they have found yet another thing to bring to your attention. And every conversation with them starts with, "I hate to complain, but…"

The complaining member is actually what drives a lot of owners away from the business at some point because eventually most owners start taking the criticism personally. The personalization of all these complaints, even though many are justified, eventually takes the owner to the point of where he stops hearing suggestions and starts believing that the crazy bastard is out to get him. "Joe, Mr. Johnson is at the counter and wants to talk to you," the employee says almost apologetically. Inside Joe's head is the conversation everyone wants to have with their version of Mr. Johnson at some point: "You crazy old bastard. Don't you have anything else to do but hang around here all day, irritating my staff and pissing me off? Is there nothing that we do that makes you happy?"

Why Do These People Complain?

People who complain are taking ownership in your business, which is exactly what you want. It is painful, it is a nuisance, and it will wear you down, but it is good for your business. Most of customer service is being responsive, but we can't react if we don't know what is wrong.

What we forget is that when someone pays you for a service, they have basically entered into a contract with you that goes beyond the basic membership agreement you might be using. In essence, you are selling a membership to a private club that is only accessible by a monthly payment. In your world, you might have thousands of members, and this guy signing up today is nothing more but part of this month's membership count. But to him, it is a big commitment, even if it is only a few bucks, and it represents him becoming part of a club that separates him from others in the community that don't belong.

Strangely, you can compare his membership with going to church. The typical church might have hundreds, or even thousands, of members, but there is always that population within the membership that takes the responsibility for the leadership of the church. This group forms the board, volunteers for all the committees, helps with the fundraisers, and dutifully lets the minister know how things are going. The church becomes theirs, and their feeling of ownership is what makes the church successful and a vital part of the community.

It works the same way in a fitness facility, or at least it should. There will always be a core of the members who feel strongly that due to their support and investment in your business, even though it is only a membership payment each month, they are entitled to speak for the other members and to let the owner know that things in his business might not be up to the member's expectations and needs.

If you can create a business that is strong enough to develop a pride of ownership within your membership, then you have gone a long way in creating a business that will also be financially successful over time. Members who feel it is their club give it a base that allows you to grow your business over time with their support in the community.

What Do These Members Want?

Complaining is a form of showing pride and ownership. For example, how many wives feel the need to help their guy dress better, speak more clearly, lose weight, ask for that raise, or act more kindly toward the mother-in-law? If you are in a relationship, and care about someone deeply, then you will take pride in that relationship and pride in the person you are with, and all you might want is to help your significant other be better and grow. As a side note, most guys are virtually uncoachable after being potty trained, but it is good that the significant others don't give up on them and keep trying to seek change, although getting a guy over 30 to significantly change is like trying to teach a ferret to drive a motorcycle.

Members are exhibiting several needs when they complain:

- The need to show that they care and take pride in their membership.

- The need to help you run a better business, especially since it is "their" gym.

- The need to keep you keeping your promises, such as the ones that were probably given during the sales process. If you promised a clean club and working equipment, and sold that as part of the membership, then the members will call you out on that and keep you honest.

- The need for attention and recognition.

- The need to avoid inconvenience in their personal life, such as the irritating issue of an instructor who starts late or goes beyond the scheduled class time, making them late for picking up their kids.

Complaining means they want you to respond to these needs. The member states, "Your locker room is dirty." If you apply the list criteria, you can see that all of the basic member needs are met by this simple complaint dropped at the front counter as the member leaves for the day.

The member doesn't, however, know that your janitor just quit, your morning person called off, and that it is you and your out-of-work, drunken brother-in-law running a 30,000-square-foot club with 3,000 members; nor does the member care. She has pride in the place, which, in her mind, you obviously don't have because if you did she wouldn't have to point this out.

She also feels you are hurting yourself because she heard other members complain, and that you did promise to always have a clean club. Finally, she secretly likes being the person who told you, which gives her a little bit of personal satisfaction that she just won't live with "dirty" as the other members do, and that you did inconvenience her because it was distressing to shower in a dirty locker room.

This is the type of complaint that can crush your spirit as an owner. You are standing at the front counter, working yourself to death, and this crazy woman wants to point out that you are a lousy owner who doesn't care about the members, beat your children, and that your manhood is in question, too. She didn't really say this, but this is how you can turn a simple, "Hey, you might check your locker rooms" into a rave and soulless rant against your hard work. We hear what we want to hear, and the longer you are in the business, the more often these simple suggestions are turned into threats and accusations in your mind.

Digital Vision

Why Do They Stop Complaining, and What Does That Mean?

They stopped complaining because you stopped caring. Complaints are nothing more than customer-service complaints, and *all customer-service complaints are important*—whether you want to hear them or not.

The member stops complaining when the owner stops listening and responding. The member is usually telling you things that will help your business. When you stop responding to statements such as, "Hey, that class started late again," then you are failing to deliver customer service. *When you fail to listen and respond is the point when your business begins to fail.*

If a member voices the same complaint a few times but nothing happens, it will be the end of that member. The member, even though it isn't always phrased nicely or it sounds like whining, is giving you the secret to running a financially successful business.

It is not what you want that will make you money.
It is giving them what they want.

Dirty locker rooms are costing you retention numbers. Listen, and fix them because the complaining member just told you how to keep your members. Broken equipment is an inconvenience to the members. When someone complains, go fix it now, not later, because some member did just tell you how to improve your business. Member complaints are the key to customer service, but because of the adversarial relationship we develop with the members who do complain, we often stop listening, and that failure to respond can cost you your business.

Customer Service Ends Where Bad Business Begins

The classic theme in all of the old customer-service books is that the customer is always right. This adage has failed to keep its truth through recent years as a small percentage of customers have moved from being appreciative for good service to a level where their expectations and requests have become totally unrealistic. These new-age customers have acquired a sense of entitlement that initiates demands that can't be met accompanied by a total disrespect for you and your staff.

When customers become rude, nasty, mean, and their behavior is not appropriate for the situation, then they need to be removed, and more importantly, the owners and managers of the business need to often step into the situation and back up the staff. Complaining about a broken treadmill is one thing. Taking down a young staff person at the front counter over something minor in front of the other staff, members, and guests is not right and should not be tolerated.

The right solution is to remember that sometimes the only right way to handle certain customers is to remove them permanently from your business. Take them into the office away from everyone else, cancel their membership, give them a check, right at that moment, for any money you might still owe them, and walk them to the door. Getting rid of the members that go too far is good for the morale of the staff, and it's good for the other members as well.

There are also members that go too far in their supposedly helpful complaints, and they move from being a club asset to the club's pain-in-the-ass. These are the members that aren't necessarily rude or mean, but just can't help but endlessly pointing out every perceived flaw in your business.

Sadly, the line between helpful and disruptive is very thin, and those members who cross it usually do so knowingly for a variety of reasons that usually leads to the fabled owner/member conversation: "You have to go home now. We don't like you anymore."

This usually small percentage just has to tear you apart on everything. They make it their life's work to not only rip you, but to share their opinions with every other member who will listen. The skill is knowing which members are complaining because of the right reasons and those few who are complaining because they are just mean, unhappy people, and you are today's target.

The members doing the right thing are the ones who seek you out and thank your for taking care of their issue. The members on the wrong side of the customer-service line are the ones who ignore your actions and progress in the club and stay firmly planted in the negative each visit.

Customer service ends where bad business begins.

For example, let's say you fire an instructor. Your member, Allison, who loved this instructor, is now at the front desk, threatening to quit the club. You attempt to calm her down; she just gets madder and stalks away. She is now in the locker room and on the workout floor, sharing her anger and telling all the other members that they should quit, too, although Allison won't really leave because all she wants here is the attention.

Tomorrow, she is upset about you having to close the club locker rooms for a day while new water heaters are being installed and other plumbing issues are dealt with in the club. Allison is again at the desk, telling off your staff in front of your other members, even though you posted the close day for a month in advance, and she is again on the floor taking her case that you run a terrible club to the entire membership.

The only thing that will solve this issue is to ask her to leave: "Allison, would you please come into the office. I know you are very unhappy since Sean the instructor left, and I have also heard that you are very unhappy with the locker room being closed, even though we posted that closure a month in advance. Therefore, since I know you are so miserable about these issues, and you have expressed so much displeasure with us in the past, I have a check for the balance that I owe you back for this month, including a percentage of your membership fee. You're not happy here, and there is nothing that I can do to make you happy, so I think you will be much better off working out at another club."

Sometimes, you are better off to just fire your members. Give them what you owe them back, make sure it has a little extra so there are no disputes, and throw them out. Customer service ends where her impact on your business begins. It is also always important to keep your attorney in the loop. If you have a short list of people who need to go, chat with your legal person to make sure your back is covered, but do not hesitate to get rid of the person if the time is right.

Most of the time, people like Allison will just get quiet, apologize, and ask to stay. Most of the time, you are still better off with her gone, but that is a judgment call you will have to make in the office that day. The lesson to learn is do not be held hostage by your members. Her negativity drains you, drains the staff, and actually drains the members who are tired of listening to endless drama. It's just one membership, and you are better off without her.

But again, the skill is knowing when people are just complaining due to perceived ownership and pride in being a member and when they are just complaining to get attention, or because they are just mean and miserable and make everyone in their life unhappy. Very few people need to be tossed, but the ones that do need it earlier rather than later.

You Have to Learn How to Seek Complaints

You want complaints. Complaints are nothing more than loyal people who believe in your business plan hoping you will deal with issues that taint their experience.

Suggested methods range from the simple suggestion box to focus groups. Even though focus groups were discussed in an earlier book, these groups of your involved members are now no more effective than hanging a box on the wall and hoping someone drops a real thought in it. Focus groups, for example, turn out to usually be a meeting of personal agendas and seldom result in anything that helps grow your business.

The goal of a complaint, and don't even think about calling these problems "opportunities," is to gather information that will help you improve your customer service in your business as well as the member retention. This is important information, and there is only one way to get this that will help your business and that is to get in someone's face and ask.

Face-to-face interviews provide the best information because you not only get to hear about your business, but you can see the person's face as they tell you, which gives you the clues you need to understand how they really feel and how bad the problem really is.

If you are talking to someone in person, you can pursue random comments, react to facial nuances, and most likely the person will stray from the script and really tell you what you want to hear. For example, you might be using a simply survey with just five questions, which is the recommended format, but during the interview the person says, "These are good questions, but what I really want to tell you about is how lousy your trainers are and how good of a workout I had at your competitor's place."

Another example might be when you ask him a question, such as please list three things the club could do better. He starts, names three things, including a point about dirty locker rooms, and then just gets kind of quiet. You ask him about the locker rooms specifically, and he says they are fine and looks away. He is obviously not sharing his real thoughts, which you can now pursue, and you would never have gotten a sense of what he thinks by just using a simple form. You have to ask, and you have to see his face to learn the truth.

Comstock Images

In-your-face surveys usually are better if you follow these basic rules:

- Only use three to five questions.

- Offer the member a drink if that person will sit with you for just five minutes to share their thoughts.

- Try to do 10 to 25 per month, depending on the size of the club. Make it a habit, and look for new members each time.

- If you get something good, give something good. If the person gives you a great idea, or catches something you didn't know about that might have been costing you money, give him three months added to his membership. This guy is watching out for your business and needs to be rewarded.

- Only the owner or senior manager should do these surveys.

- If you have multiple units, travel and hit each one each month. It worked for Sam Walton, and it should work for you.

The following are some sample questions that will work for you:

- Name three things we can do better.

- Name the single-biggest thing you would change about our business.

- What is the one thing you like best about this club?

- Please tell me about my staff.

- On a scale of 1 to 5, how good is our customer service, and why?

- What three things could be most improved with our service?

- What equipment would you add to the club you might have seen lately?

- What classes or programming should we add?

- What is the weakest part of the club?

- Which club have you heard the most about of all the other clubs in town? What caught your attention?

- What would you change about our marketing?

You can post these questions online once in awhile, but it is still always better to ask in person. If you catch someone really full of good information, don't let him leave until he tells you everything. Anytime they have an issue is a way to improve your business, and that is what customer service is all about in a successful business.

When You Take It Personally Is When You Need to Go Home

It will be brutally hard not to internalize complaints after you have been in business for a long period of time. They will wear you down and eventually make you sometimes hate the business. Every owner who has been around for at least five years has said this at some point: "This would be a great business if it wasn't for those damn members."

It is easy to write that business is just business, and you shouldn't let a mean-spirited member ruin your day, but they will, as every owner has felt at some time. At some point, it feels personal, and it is hard to take it otherwise because it feels like they are coming after you personally.

Separating that anger is hard, but you have to learn to do it if you want to be successful over time. Remember, it's not like some drunk on the street walking up and commenting how weird your son looks. He indeed may be weird, but you don't need to hear it, and ugly is ugly and you can't fix that, either.

In the club, you need to hear it because bringing up the issues that might affect your profitability may save your business and are almost always things that can be changed. It is okay for your members to tell you your "child," meaning the business, is quite ugly, has funny ears, and needs its diaper changed. Listening and responding will build a better business, even if what you are hearing is painful.

Following are a few tips that might help you keep it under control:

- Always remember that you may not agree, but they may be right.

- Remember that they are paying you and have the right to complain in exchange for the support they provide your business.

- The few minutes of pain will most likely lead to more money in your pocket later if you just listen.

- Defending solves nothing. Take the beating, and move on. Understand that the member has to tell the story to purge their frustration and anger, and nothing you can say short of, "There will be 50 new treads here tomorrow" will solve their problem. Once it starts, it has to be finished.

- Take it to the office and away from the front desk.

- Reward complaints because it can lead to more money for you. If someone complains, give them $5 in club bucks (fake money) to spend in your business, but only hand it out to people who have caught something important.

Quiet members kill your business. They don't complain and simply take their business somewhere else, and you never had a chance to save them. These quiet members, however, are the ones we like most in the club because running a club business is very customer-service intensive and perhaps one of the hardest businesses in the world.

Complaints are good because people are vested enough in your business to take ownership. It's when they stop complaining that you should worry. Seek complaints, and build a better customer-service-driven business.

Do These Things Now

- Understand that complaining members are your best members, because they are emotionally connected to you and your business.

- Be afraid of the quiet members. These are the ones who will be the first to leave, and you will never know why.

- Realize that sometimes the member is wrong, and he needs to go home now.

- Learning to seek complaints will strengthen your business.

- Learn that one of the hardest things to do in this business is to learn to not take the constant member complaining as personal.

Customer service is as simple as ...
using the magic words.

There is customer-service magic in certain words that convey our intent and willingness to make the person's day better.

Many people use a defense mechanism (which is something someone does automatically without thinking about it), which gets in the way of their ability to deliver service. For example, a member approaches the front desk and asks a staff person if he has time to take a look at a treadmill that seems to be behaving erratically.

The staff person is a little stressed, glances up while trying to do three or four other things at once, and says, "Not right now, but I will get to it" and keeps doing what he was doing. The member turns away a little dejected because he knows that "I will get to it" really means, "I am busy here, buddy, and that just isn't important."

"Not right now" is just another form of "No," and "No" is not part of a customer-service culture. The staff person might have good intent, and may get to it, but he missed a chance to deliver good service in the name of the club.

His response should have included one or more of the magic service words:

- *Of course!*

- *Absolutely!*

- *I'd love to help you.*

- *Yes, I can do that.*

- *I'd be happy to help you.*

Using a combination of these words, the counter person could have responded, "Of course, I can help you with that, Mr. Johnson. Which treadmill is it? Give me just a few minutes to finish up here, and I will be right on it, sir."

Service is in the attitude, but it can also be the perception the customer gets through the use of a few simple words. These can be taught and should become part of your culture in the business.

8

Never Underestimate the Stink of a Dead Dog

Perhaps the best, or strangest, analogy every written about a bad employee is the one that compared the employee to a dead dog lying in the middle of the road. When it was a puppy, it was cute, and everyone loved to play with it. As it got older, it became a little obnoxious, and finally, the dog became more of a nuisance to the family instead of the once-loved family member it was as a puppy.

Over time, the family simply tolerated the dog, gave it space in the house, and apologized profusely when it snarled or intimidated guests. One day, the dog broke out of the fenced yard, wandered into the street, and was mangled by a delivery truck. At some point, someone cared deeply about the dog, but now that it is dead, no one was even interested in dragging it out of the street.

Many employees go through this same cycle in your business. We all love them when they are new and shiny, but some grow into obnoxious people who seriously affect your business in a negative way. The owners of these facilities often can't, or won't, deal with the obnoxious employee for a variety of reasons, but the end result is that the person stays too long in the business and puts a drain on the rest of the team and the members that cancels whatever good that person still might produce. When the person leaves, or is finally fired by an owner who just snaps, no one misses her, and the energy in the business quickly rises in relief that the wicked witch has left the house.

What Makes a Bad Employee?

The simple question of what makes a bad employee is more complicated than it appears. Everyone knows what a typical bad employee looks like and does on the surface. He dresses poorly, is often late, mumbles, is lazy, refuses to help out the other employees in your company, and is the first to leave you for a $.25 raise at another business. Everyone eventually hires this guy at least once, and he seems to be passed around from club-to-club all across America.

The more complicated bad employee is the one who produces a lot of revenue but is also disruptive to the business. This person is tolerated to a certain extent, because he does make some numbers, but this type of employee is also holding you hostage due to those numbers. Examples might be a good salesperson who is arrogant, refuses to help anywhere else in the club, and who won't train or help the other staff, or perhaps the group-exercise diva who fights every change you propose unless you do it her way, and if she gets upset, she always threatens to take her members and go to another club.

These employees represent the line that has been crossed where their contributions are now cancelled by their personal baggage that affects the owner, other staff, and, most importantly, the members in the club. These employees need to be sent home now (read: it is time to fire their lame butts), but most owners freeze and fail to address the situation for a number of reasons.

The bad employee has the edge in this situation by holding production numbers or vital information, such as how to teach classes, over your head as a threat of lost revenue or members. Once the owner backs away from these people, it only gets worse because the employee now knows that he holds the power over the owner. This results in territory expanding and more power plays later that will only make things worse. These situations never get better on their own, and the only way to either save the employee (which is rare) or to salvage the situation and return customer service and a positive energy in the club is for the club owner to intervene.

The hard issue is that you have to deal with these people immediately, not later, because bad employees kill your customer service, and therefore your retention. When an employee becomes more important in his mind than the business, meaning the other staff who work there and the customers who pay all the bills, then his world becomes very limited within your business.

For example, a trainer gets a full stable of clients, who are loyal to him and not the club, and he cultivates his personal image by telling these clients that the owner and the rest of the training staff are idiots, and that he is the only one in the entire club who knows how to train—the rest are just morons who don't know anything about training. He slowly builds his inner circle of clients, and then excludes everyone else in the business because that is how he builds and retains his status.

The rest of the staff suffers since they are constantly being put down to the members and their peers by this "superior" trainer; therefore, their ability to generate income suffers. The members in the club not training with this guy are ignored, or worse harassed, by this guy. Someone asks him a question, for example, so he quickly ascertains if they might have the potential to be a client or not, and if not, he refuses to help them and often won't even answer the basic question.

In essence, he has built a club within your club with members loyal to him, and in fact, he is actually in competition with you. The members, who are really your members, have been taught by him to be loyal to only him and his training system. The service in the club is lowered, because you are either one of his chosen few, or you are just another member in his way on the equipment, which he is quick to point out to those members that are slowing him down.

And don't forget the fact that he refuses to wear the club uniform since it doesn't show off his body well enough, he sells his own supplements through an online company he reps because he doesn't believe in the club brand, and that he is probably taking cash directly from the members since in his mind he is always underpaid for the work he does and the money he generates.

This is also the guy who fights all change because he realizes that if anyone gains more knowledge or information, his place in the club is devalued. For example, the owner brings in an outside trainer/educator, and the superstar trainer guy spends the entire meeting challenging everything he is hearing. He has to do this to protect his status as the club stud, but also he has to fight to protect what he believes is the one and only way and to keep anyone else from learning things that will enhance their status in the club.

This scenario can also play out with your group exercise diva or one-person sales machine. Each one stakes out their own territory in your business, builds their own circle, and then excludes everyone else. It is hard to run a customer-service-driven business when you have employees working against you in your own business.

But why do most owners fold so quickly and back down from dealing with this type of issue?

- You fear that you can't replace the numbers, so you tolerate the pain.

- You fear that you will lose members if the group diva or out-of-control trainer leaves and goes to another club.

- You fear that you can't replace the person, even if you tried.

- You fear that you don't have the information or skill set the employee has.

- You're too lazy to make him change, so you just ignore the situation and hope it corrects itself.

- You are somehow related to the person, as in your wife is the head trainer or sister is the group diva, and you know that dealing with the problem at the club will just mean you are really going to have to deal with it again at home.

The reality for any small business is that it is not how good you are, but it's how good your people are and how trained they are to deliver customer service. But when you have a staff divided by superstars, divas, and salespeople with bad attitudes, the rest of your staff can't ever amount to much as a team.

After all, why should the other staff be held to strict rules or bust their butts in the name of customer service when it is obvious that what you expect from them daily doesn't apply to all the staff evenly? The regular staff has no reason to perform since it is very clear that no one gets fired in the club for not following the rules, mistreating members, or ignoring club policies. Put a few numbers on the board, and the owner will pretty much let you do whatever you want, whenever you want.

Drag the Dead Dog off the Road, and Your Business Will Get Better

One of the most fascinating things you can read about people who fight addiction in their life is that they almost all claim that the drug became their personal reality. This means that for most of them, the reality of living in the real world is replaced by the perceived reality created through whatever drug they chose. Being trapped in the drug became their reality, and many said that they had forgotten the rules and the feelings it takes to live in the real world and were shocked when they returned from their lows to functioning at a higher level again with others not enslaved by the addiction.

This is the trap that most owners are buried under with these bad employees. You've lost control of your business and control of your staff, yet you've been functioning that way so long that you forget how good a business can operate without being held hostage by people who spend all their time in your business working against you. Yes, you might have some pain for a month or so as you make change and get this nasty drain out of your business, but somewhere down the road you have no idea how good you can really feel again when you gain control of your business and life.

Everyone can be replaced. You will find another salesperson, and someone new who has a caring attitude and is sincerely interested in people might actually end up selling more memberships than a too-slick, old sales dog who thinks he is irreplaceable. We are held hostage since we are locked into thinking that this person—and their method—is the only way, because he has told us that so long. But there are other methods, and other ways, to get sales done, or training, or even group exercise, and replacing the diva with a different model altogether will bring a lot of energy and new ideas to your business that might lead to growth instead of reduction.

Making change will also force you to become a better owner. Getting rid of that trainer might mean that you lose a few members initially, but now you are free to create systems that keep clients loyal to the club and not to individual trainers, and you might also now explore using non-solicitation agreements and other tools to protect your business the next time around.

Customer service is a team effort, and every employee must be committed to the member first. You and your staff exist for the sole purpose of creating a customer-service-driven environment that retains members through valuing them as part of the business. Anything, or anyone, that gets in the way has to go, which means that the super studs, the divas, and the old sales dogs either become part of a functioning team, or they are replaced by people who will, because there is never profit without keeping the customer first.

Do These Things Now

- Learn that some of your employees might have been there too long and are now part of the problem, not part of the solution.

- Realize that territorial employees might be hurting your ability to deliver customer service, and that these employees might also be affecting your retention.

Customer service is as simple as …
creating a waiting policy.

When you're busy, time flies by. When you're waiting for someone, it is like watching paint dry. You know it is going to happen, but you may spend the rest of your life simply staring at the wall, waiting.

We forget this in the club business. Someone comes in to get information, but has to wait until the club's salesperson is finished with his current guest. The front counter staff is busy, and time is flying. The salesperson is busy and thinks the 15 minutes it takes him to finish with his current guest is really only a few. The guest who is waiting, however, is bored out of his mind, and is now getting angry that he came in to potentially spend money and is getting ignored.

Part of a good service culture is to establish a waiting policy that automatically kicks in if someone has to wait five minutes or more for any staff person in the club.

This policy states that the person behind the counter has permission to tell the waiting guest, "I am sorry. The person you need to see will be at least five more minutes. May I buy you a smoothie or bottle of water while you wait?"

The waiting policy shows respect for the guest's time and also shows that the club understands the importance of customer service. Waiting five minutes staring at the workout floor goes a lot faster if you are engaged with a counter person who just bought you a smoothie.

The smoothie or water should be logged under the manager's account to keep the staff at the counter under control, but the important thing to understand is that this should be automatic and something the counter person can do without asking anyone.

This should also apply to all situations where a member or guest is waiting for a staff person and not just sales. If a trainer runs over for a paid appointment, the policy should kick in, and the training client should be given a bottle of water. Take care of the people who are trying to give you money.

9

Price Gets Your Club Considered, but Price Does Not Build a Relationship

The club price wars that have been raging since the end of the last century have changed how many owners thing about their businesses, and how they compete in their competitive market.

Early on in the industry, price wars were nothing more than skirmishes in the neighborhood, exemplified as one owner running an aggressive special to get people through the door, and by doing so forced his competitor down the street to react. For example, an owner might offer a two-for-one membership fee during the summer as a way to supposedly drive new traffic, but to also mess with his competitors, too.

The competitors in that market might respond with their own version of a membership discount, but most of the pricing parameters everyone in the market used as a base starting point were pretty much the same. These pricing guidelines all centered upon the member dues staying relatively the same, or at least within certain ranges that all the clubs knew about by calling and shopping each other.

For example, you might publish a price of $39 per-month/per-member, but when the member actually signed up, he might talk himself into anything from about a $30 per month membership to the full $39 retail price. Sign up with a buddy, though, and get a better deal. Sign up with your girlfriend, and get even a sweeter deal than you would have gotten on your own. Deals could be had, but most sales dogs stayed within certain pricing limits, and often clubs in the same market all stayed around the same price point.

The key point to remember is that there was far less competition in the 1980s and 1990s. Clubs could maintain a certain price line because there were so few choices for the potential members in a convenient drive time. Pitch a price to the guy sitting in front of you, and if he didn't like what you said, it was often hard for him to walk out the door and try another club since he might have to drive for 30 minutes or more to find one.

Maturing markets, where there is a higher concentration of clubs within your competitive ring, is a relatively recent development that began to change market characteristics in the fitness industry in the late 1990s. It is inevitable that when you have too many competitors in a market, someone will always try to turn the business into a commodity model, where the lowest price for a generic product wins.

Pricing as a competitive tool became more dominant at the turn of the 21st century. Clubs began appearing for the first time that based their entire business plan upon just the price as their primary attribute. This shift marked a change away from generic box clubs and generic pricing to clubs that gambled everything on only a single definer in the marketplace. For example, a new club might open with only a single differentiating factor, such as being open 24 hours a day, and that factor was the main focus in all of the club's marketing and sales.

The price clubs jumped in, touting $19 as their definer, and often built the price into their company name as their sole identifier and brand, such as Club 19. But it wasn't long before clubs that based their business plans on $10 per month quickly followed this move, and price became the central focus in the marketing. The better players in this game, such as Planet Fitness®, packaged the price well as part of a bigger picture, using advanced marketing techniques citing the "Judgement Free Zone®."

The price was still prominent in their marketing, although the first impression about these clubs gleaned through their advertising was that the price was wrapped up in copy that focused on what made those clubs different than others in the market. But it is still the low price that many people use to primarily identify the company and that brand.

The owners who use price as their sole definer in the market become that price, and what they charge becomes the only way they know how to compete. The weakness to this system is that price will get you considered, and even get you members, but it still doesn't build a relationship with your members, nor does it protect the business from competition.

For instance, what would stop a new club that has a decent rent factor from becoming the $5 choice in the market? If price is the only reason you are at a club, and a club opens in the market with virtually the same equipment, but a lower price, then logically every member that is with you for $10 is now a prime membership candidate for the new lower-priced business since price was the retainer, not service, and your price was just crushed by half if you were this $10 club.

When you're in the business of just renting equipment, then the lowest price will always win, and any price can be beat if the rent factor is right and the owner is crazy enough. Price gets you considered, but price is not always a sustainable business model since someone can always come in lower than you.

Price may have gotten you members in the beginning, but price won't keep those members in a competitive marketplace since there was never a relationship established beyond a little money exchanging hands between the client and the club.

It is interesting to note, however, that the people who seek out a low-price club are seldom the same people you would see in a higher-priced, full-service club down the street. There are actually two very different segments at play here, and if both owners identified and sought out their own segments, both of these clubs would survive in the marketplace.

A Relationship Is the Hardest Thing to Steal

Relationships are hard things to define, especially in business. If you want to understand the important relationship between a client and a business, you first have to ask yourself a few questions about relationships in the real world.

What, for instance, keeps someone from cheating on a spouse? Why do some employees work at a company for years, although they could make more money somewhere else? Why do people go to the same restaurant for years, although the food has declined a little and the place is getting worn out? What keeps people friends year after year, even though their lives have changed and they have lost many of the common interests they had when they were younger?

Relationships in our world of customer service can be defined as a *mutually caring and supportive bond between the client and the people who own or work in the business, based upon a foundation of trust.* While relationships are complicated to understand at the surface level most of the time, each individual relationship you explore that works always comes down to a feeling or commitment of trust between people involved. Without trust, there is no relationship.

In business, it is always good to start with the premise that people will stay longer and pay longer if they *believe in what you do and that what you are doing is in their best interest and won't hurt them.* For example, in the case of the employee staying year after year, he understands that the owner values him, pays him as well as the company can afford, and gives him other perks and considerations, such as time off or a company car. The owner, on the other hand, understands that he has a great employee on his team, values his hard work and does everything he can to demonstrate that he cares for and trusts the employee.

If both sides maintain their roles in this relationship, then it becomes very hard for anyone on the outside, such as a competitor, to interfere by stealing the employee for more money. It is only when the relationship is broken does the bond end. For example, the owner may sell his company, and the new owner has a different way of doing business that devalues the employee's previous role in the organization. When the value is diminished, and the bond of caring and mutual support is ended, then the employee is now free to move on without guilt or restrictions.

This type of relationship, where there is the bond of caring and mutual support, based upon this ongoing foundation of trust, should be the goal of every fitness business owner to achieve with his members, no matter how big or small his business. Relationships are what keep people staying longer and paying longer in your business.

The negative to this, however, is that for the last several decades in the fitness industry, we have done everything possible to eliminate relationships in the business and to change the club culture away from being member-centered. It is very important to consider this fundamental rule of small business:

> *Clients do not have relationships with a business or*
> *piece of equipment. Clients only have a relationship with the*
> *people who own or work in that business.*

While this rule should be the foundational truth for any type of fitness business, our ability to build and maintain relationships in this industry has been compromised because of the following reasons:

- We downgraded the role of group exercise in the clubs. It is unusual to find a club that isn't using some type of national group-exercise program to have a penetration rate in its membership of over 10 percent. Penetration rate means how far into your club's total membership does this program or service reach. For example, if you have 1,000 members and a group exercise penetration rate of only 10 percent, then you only have 100 members in the program. The flip side of that assumption is this also means you have 90 percent of your membership that doesn't support or care about this part of your business.

- Very few clubs have a decent weight-management program that penetrates beyond a few points in their membership base. Due to the intimacy of this type of program, weight-management clients tend to develop strong bonds with the club staff person that helps them change their weight.

- Almost all training and coaching in the typical fitness business is restricted to one-on-one training, which is priced too high for the bulk of the members, is too restrictive, and only appeals to about 3 to 6 percent of the club's entire membership.

- We have become machine convenient, meaning we buy acres of equipment to entertain the members with the mistaken belief that more equipment equals better service. People don't have relationships with equipment; they have relationships with people.

- We hire front counter people who are too young and too dumb to interact with the club's target membership.

- We have downplayed music and the experience in the club and replaced it with televisions on the equipment and mp3 players that isolate the members instead of encouraging them to interact with the other members and staff.

- We have stopped building sports bars/juice bars in the clubs where members can sit and socialize with staff and other members.

- Most clubs have eliminated open space in the club, which eliminates stretching areas and social nodes where members can informally chat and interact.

- The floor person has disappeared in most clubs. This was the person in a uniform whose sole responsibility was to help members during their visit. He would spot, pick up weights, answer questions, greet members, and do most anything else that was needed to be done in the main workout areas.

One of the strangest things about a modern fitness facility is that if you walk through one when it is fairly crowded, you will find that almost everything we have done during the recent years is meant to isolate the members from each other and the staff.

Check in at the counter on your own by running your card through the machine, get your old-style workout card, do the circle on the outdated fixed equipment, and go home. Feel like cardio? Get on a treadmill, walk for an hour watching television with your headset on, walk by the desk on the way out without getting thanked or acknowledged or even, "Have a nice day." Members can actually spend an hour or two in the club and never talk to a single person, which lessens the likelihood that this member will stay in the system long.

Most clubs don't have anywhere to sit and talk. It is amazing that someone can walk into a 30,000-square-foot club and not find anywhere to sit but on a machine. Even if the club has a few tables or a couch upfront, they were often never designed as part of the club's ambiance, but rather as something thrown in at the end to fill space, which again limits usage because everyone sitting there feels out of place.

People Who Have Relationships
Stay Longer and Pay Longer

Machine people leave early and they leave more often. Relationship people stay longer and pay longer. You can only build a relationship between people. Any type of people interaction in your business adds more to the relationship between the client and the club.

It takes the discipline of a born-again weight-loss person faced with a box of Girl Scout cookies to show up at a club every day and do fitness absolutely by himself. Show up, work hard, talk to no one, and go home, day after day for the rest of your life. This type of person should give up his job and become a monk, because the average human being can't sustain this long without losing faith. This is also the person who will be the most likely in the club to shop you for a lower price, since he has no relationship with anyone. It is all about him and the equipment, and the lowest bidder in the market will win.

Where we have made a big mistake in the industry is that we have forgotten what it was like to be a kid. Most everyone grows up doing stuff in groups of some kind. If you play sports as a kid, you belong to a team of some sort. Even the runners and golfers, where both sports are known as individual sports, belong to teams that practice and travel together.

Everyone else not in sports might have belonged to clubs, had a tight social network of friends, gone to church, or just hung out at the mall with a few buddies. Move on to college or work, and most everyone there had a group they hung out with, belonged to a business organization, or simply went for beers after work with coworkers. Somewhere, you received daily interaction as part of your life, and that community experience was a large part of everyone's early life.

Join a fitness facility, and all of that ends. Downgrade the social aspects, which either waste space or cost more to run in the owner's mind, and replace these things with dumb equipment, or even dumber staff, and then we all moan about how lousy our retention numbers are this year.

The rule is that a piece of equipment cannot deliver
customer service. Only your staff can deliver any real service,
and only staff can build relationships.

You Have to Put All Your Effort
Into the Touch Zones

Todd Levine, a talented owner in Rochester, New York, operates a couple of Gold's Gym® facilities. His flagship club is about 25,000 square feet and represents a lot of forward thinking compared to many other owners in the industry, and especially in that particular franchise, which had a history of building new clubs based upon the amount of equipment it could hold.

Todd's isn't a particularly beautiful club, but it is a very effective business, and visitors get a fresh perspective after spending a few days with Todd and his young business partner, George.

During a random visit to the club on a Wednesday evening in February, Todd and George had over a 100 members working with a team of five trainers doing a mass group functional workout. This workout was sold as a weight-loss challenge, but the reality was that it was nothing more than a large group functional training. The members were smiling, screaming, and having fun all over the club, and the energy was as good as it can get on a frigid February night in Rochester.

If you were watching this workout carefully, the interesting thing to note was that the trainers were seeking out the holes, or small open spaces, all around the club. They were using the walkways, the group room, a small, dedicated functional area, and just about any other space they could find that was open. The trainers and their groups bobbed, weaved, and leaped around the 60 pieces of traditional equipment that sat empty in the middle of the club and that was ignored by every trainer.

This started a discussion about what has come to be called money zones. Money zones are areas in the club that derive the most income over a year's period of time. Todd calls them touch zones in his club. He recently had a couple of owners from another club visit him on a Saturday, and he took them through his place at the peak Saturday morning traffic hours.

The group rooms were packed, the functional area, represented at this date by only a rack of old medicine balls and some old dumbbells, was also filled. The free-weight area was crammed to capacity, the cardio was going strong, and members and trainers were using all the rest of the space that was open.

He admitted that the functional area was weak in relationship to the rest of the club. Due to the popularity of this new program, and through the usage by the members and trainers, he completely expanded his functional offering, adding another 3,500 square feet that was available next door.

The epiphany moment for the guests was the fact that the fixed equipment was deserted. The club was running at a high capacity with over 400 members onsite at 10:00 on a cold Saturday morning, but everyone in the club was actually working around the fixed equipment, seeking other open spaces or workout options in the club.

The working areas that were filled with these trainers and members are called the touch zones. These are the areas of the club where members interact with each other and a staff person, rather than being on their own just using the equipment.

Group exercise is a touch zone because of the group dynamics and the relationship between the participants in the class and the instructor. Group personal training is a touch zone because of the relationship between the trainer and the group, and due to the relationship that evolves as the participants encourage each other through challenging tasks.

Even your front counter is a touch zone, because that is where you have a chance to demonstrate customer service to the largest number of your members on a daily basis as they enter and leave your business. It doesn't take much here to make a major difference in the overall effectiveness of your business, and just a simple "Thank you for coming in today" is a valuable touch that can affect how the client feels about that staff person and the business.

Perhaps a better term for these touch zones is "money zones" since touches equal member retention; therefore, the club makes more money over time if it puts more time, money, and training into developing these areas. Keep in mind in this story that Todd was one of the original Gold's Gym locations in the country, and his club was built when "he with the most amount of equipment" would always win.

During the visit by his guests, he clearly demonstrated that his single-joint fixed equipment had that lowest use of anything in his business, and that the members happily, and financially, responded to changes in the club's workout culture. The money zones made his business, and he credits his success on how well he and George get their members involved in anything besides just sitting on a piece of fixed stuff that is 30 years out of date.

As a result of this realization, Todd redesigned his club. He eliminated about 15 percent of his fixed stuff, opened up designated areas in the club for functional space, ordered about $4,000 worth of new functional tools, which represents a very large number of new toys for your trainers and members, and reset his membership structure to reflect group personal training. He also expanded his cardio area. Cardio is a touch zone, too, because without televisions on the machines, the members interact with each other and the staff as they complete their workouts.

The lesson to learn here is that during a flat year in the economy—this happened in 2009—this guy had a record year, and he did it using a simple approach. His focus was on working toward maximizing the strength of relationships within the business. Most owners will find that they have these money zones in their club, and most of your clubs will have almost the exact same areas that are full (as this owner found) and others that are getting little use.

An important thing to note is that most owners would simply complain that their members are still using the old equipment, and that any new training culture or approach wouldn't work in their businesses. In the example of Todd, his trainers and senior staff led the change by creating tools that introduced the largest number of members to the new ideas, and then put on a show during prime time, highlighting how much fun, and the results you can get, from doing something different. Left alone, members don't change. If you offer leadership and guidance, anyone can rebuild their culture and exploit the money zones in their business.

Customer service means exploiting these money zones and killing your black holes. If your members and trainers are working around your field of fixed equipment, get rid of some of it, and open up some training space. Add socialization areas, such as sports bars, stretching areas, and, most importantly, put all the effort in building the programs that touch the most people directly in your business, and make sure you obtain and develop the people who can build these relationships.

Your Staff Has to Match the Demographics of Your Club

The typical 19-year-old, gum-chewing, this-is-his-first-job, counter idiot will never be able to talk to a 45-year-old person who represents the target demographic of your business. It's been said other places in this book, but:

> *You cannot build relationships if the staff doesn't match the target demographics of the club.*

The term here is "disconnect." Potential members come to your club, for example, because they heard you specialized in a nicer club for adults. The person sees your advertising and drops by on a Monday night for a visit. The person behind the counter was hired because she will work cheaply and because you don't yet understand the power of the front counter.

The guest walks to the counter and is ignored because your staff person is on her cell phone with her back to the desk. She finishes, turns, and says, "How can I help you?" No warm greeting or welcome, just a harsh sentence because the guest is just another string of interruptions to her personal agenda.

This may sound harsh, but almost every fitness business, no matter who you are, has a version of this person. The disconnect between the guest and the staff person occurs because the guest expected adults and good service to match the image of an upscale adult business, but was greeted by someone who didn't fit the image and who did not show a warm and caring attitude of support.

You have already lost this person as a possible member no matter how good your sales staff is since the guest started the relationship being treated poorly. You have forgotten that at that moment the counter person was the single-most important staff person in the club, and she failed, due to poor training and the fact that this type of club should have never hired her at all.

In a perfect customer-service world, the person greeting the guest at the counter should have been somewhat close to his age, and been trained in giving a strong welcome statement, how to shake hands, and how to warmly help the person fit into the club while waiting for the sales team. Remember that this is also the person who greets every member, thanks every member as they leave, and who is in touch with most of the club's membership base on a daily basis. This person shouldn't be your cheapest hire; but during prime time should be the best person you can afford due to her effect on your business.

The rule here to learn is that your staff should be a direct reflection of the membership you are targeting. No matter what demographic you are seeking, the people who work in the club should be as close as possible to that target group in age and affluence if possible. Likes attract likes, and relationships are easier built between people who are somewhat the same. Diversity is a must for building a good club staff, but age and the ability to relate to the members is still an important driver for building customer service.

The key is the ability to communicate, which is perhaps the most important trait an employee brings to the job. Skills, such as how to sell, can be taught, but the ability to communicate is something the person has to take personal responsibility for and develop in himself.

The ability to communicate, and therefore relate, is the essence of building a relationship, and the relationship between your clients and the people who work in your business is the foundation for legendary customer service that goes way beyond the price of the membership.

Do These Things Now

- Understand that most any business concept you use can be copied or stolen. Relationships are the hardest thing to steal in the club business.

- Learn that your members don't build relationships with machines or your business. Clients will only build relationships with the people who work in your business and the other members.

- Understand that touch zones will have to be part of your business plan in the coming years in tough and competitive markets.

- Learn that your staff has to match the demographics of your club.

CREATING LEGENDARY CUSTOMER SERVICE IN YOUR BUSINESS

IT Stock

Section Two

Customer service is as simple as …
arriving early for class.

Owners lose control of their group programs and often end up being held hostage by the instructors. The class is at 6:00, and at one minute to 6:00 the door of the club busts open, and the instructor comes in doing the fast walk with her giant bag, microphone already on, and the proverbial big cup of Starbucks in her hand.

She teaches the class, which in her mind is nothing more than getting paid to work out, and then at one minute after 7:00, she is out the door, beating most of the class participants to their cars.

This person is not part of your customer-service culture. In fact, she is everything that is wrong with service in most clubs. She is late, has no interaction with the members, and is just there to pick up a check for an hour worked. She also has had no customer-service training, and very little staff training, because she has three other teaching jobs and a real job, and doesn't ever show up for team meetings.

She comes in, does her own thing, and leaves. It might be a decent class, but she is not part of what the club owner needs to do to keep members in the system staying longer and paying longer. There is function here in that the class was covered, but there was no service delivered.

This instructor should have arrived 15 minutes prior to her class (yes, you would pay her for this), walk the floor, inviting all the members to come try her class that night, taught the class, and then stood by the door, thanking every member as each one leaves for attending the class and inviting them to join her the next time she teaches. You can teach this and require it as part of the job.

Your group people have to become part of your team. Most never attend meetings and aren't really part of the club's service culture. The bad news is that for most clubs these instructors have the capacity to touch a lot of people during their classes, yet they get the least amount of service coaching of anyone on your team.

Make service training mandatory for these instructors. Teach them to be part of the service act, and make sure that what they are doing reflects on the total culture of the club and not just how the classes are taught.

10

Creating the Culture of Legendary Customer Service

Legendary service—every time,
every guest, and every member.

At first glance, this seems like such a simple sentence and one that might appear in any number of customer-service books. It is also a sentence that most business owners or managers would glance at once and then move on elsewhere in the book, looking for something more concrete to draw upon as they contemplate building a service-driven business. Look more closely, however, and there is magic in those simple words.

Creating service has to start with a few simple premises, or simple truths, that lay the foundation for all your future training and staff development. Without these simple truths, you will have a very difficult time building a service-driven program, since you really have no idea how you're going to get there, or you don't know where you're really going, Following are a few of the basic truths of customer service you need to understand before you can train others to deliver a higher level of service:

- Create the vision by using the "My house, my guests" analogy.

- Never lose sight of the foundational truth of your business, which is the club's mission statement.

- Start every new employee with three hours of staff training dedicated to covering *The 20 Laws of Customer Service in a Fitness Business*.

Customer service can be broken down into simple components and taught to your staff. All other staff training in the club, such as working with your salespeople or trainers, gets easier if you have a foundation of customer service embedded in the staff person's head first, because all procedures and sales techniques are usually nothing more than the direct application of your beliefs concerning how you want your members to be treated in your business.

Start All Training With the "My House, My Guests" Scenario

This analogy was briefly mentioned in the first chapter of this book, but we will discuss it in-depth in this chapter, including how to apply it in your staff training for service. Start all your training with every employee on the first day and the first hour by explaining the following statement and what it means to your business.

This is my house, and these are our guests.

You will always show the ultimate respect for the guests of our house.

You will always dress appropriately for our guests.

You will be courteous to our guests.

The guests of this house are the most important people in this business.

Disrespect the guests of our house, and you will be asked to leave our business.

Memorize these lines until you can mumble them in your sleep, and use them as guideposts to keep you on track as you create your customer-service plan. The following sections describe what each line means and how to apply it in your business.

This is my house, and these are our guests.

Most of the people who work in fitness centers would not be classified as real business people in the sense that they are not building careers that will take them into the mainstream business world. These same people may have a little customer-service experience, such as working at a retail store, but most don't have any advanced education as to what it takes to make a customer happy.

Because of the nature of the people we hire, managers and owners need to find different ways to get connected with the staff. Talking about numbers and accountability is good, and more owners should create systems that hold people accountable, but for most of our staff, their eyes just glaze over when you talk about creating service in your business. In other words, there is simply no connection between them and the business you own and how much you have put into it to get to this point.

The analogy that does work is the "My house, my guests" idea that helps the staff relate to something they can identify with, such as having people over to their house for some type of formal event.

"Customers" is a good word, but "guests" is much more powerful, and more importantly, more intimate. "Guests" connotes more of a friend relationship and much more of a caring attitude, while sometimes "customer" almost seems adversarial in nature. For example, we take care of the guests at our holiday party, but we service customers in the business. We need to get the staff thinking about developing the caring attitude of helping our guests, rather than thinking of our members as just people in line to pay for burgers at a fast-food place.

Try to get away from referring to your guests as members. Remember, customer service comes from the top of the organization and seeps downward. Your staff will directly reflect your attitude, and if you are disrespectful to your own members/guests, even in private with just staff people present, that will become the culture in the club, and that will be how your staff interacts with your guests.

The club business is one of the toughest of all small businesses because of the continual, in-your-face nature of the service demanded to take care of all the guests that flow through your business each day. You can never let down, and you can never be unprepared to deliver service if you are in your business.

Due to this intensity, many owners get defensive over time, especially the ones who have been in the business the longest. For example, many owners adopt nicknames for certain members that particularly irritate them. The member in the morning that always complains that the music is too loud becomes "old dude." The serious lifters become "muscle heads" or "plate faces." The older aerobic ladies, who predate the current term of "group exercise," are often the most hated people in the clubs, because they pay the least and demand the most. These women, usually the morning crowd, become "the crazy morning bitches."

No, these are not appropriate terms, but if you have spent any time in a fitness business, or any other business that demands constant service and attention to the customers, then the frustration for those clients who don't always appreciate what you are trying to accomplish becomes apparent. It's when you show this frustration to your staff, however, that the culture in your business becomes negative.

Using the phrase, "This is my house, and these are our guests" keeps the proper perspective, and helps you keep the culture of your business caring and supportive, rather than adversarial and negative. Simply put, we have a great business that our members often think of as their second home, and, therefore, we need to think of them as guests who are dropping by for an hour or two, and we need to show these guests the proper respect and courtesy we would for guests and family in our own homes.

You will always show the ultimate respect for the guests of our house.

Respect has to be taught, and it has to be explained. When you introduce this word to your staff, you can't just throw it out like a generic "Smile, and be nice to our guests." Respect has to be defined to be grasped by your staff, and exact examples and rules need to be added to make sure the respect translates for all guests. Following are a few hard examples you can use; but you need to create your own as well to match your business:

- We respect our guests by being on time for all appointments. We define "on time" as 15 minutes early so you are prepared and ready to go when the guest arrives.

- If a staff person is working out and the equipment is full, the staff will get off of their treadmill and give it up to a waiting guest.

- When you walk through the club, you will acknowledge all guests as you walk within three feet of that guest. You will stop, face the guest, shake hands, thank the guest for stopping by today, turn, and pat the guest on the shoulder and say, "Hope you have a great workout."

You will always dress appropriately for our guests.

We will dress for our guests (uniforms will be discussed later in the book). Dressing appropriately is showing respect for the guests, who are the ones who pay to be here each month, and who pay for the right to be treated with respect for their support of what we do here. We will dress as to not offend or intimidate any of our guests.

You will be courteous to our guests.

All staff has to be taught common courtesy as well. This used to be taught in school, or by caring parents, but common courtesy is a lost art that is very much still needed when you have a fitness business full of guests, and a young staff that has never had any training at all in even the most basics of being courteous to other people. Following are a few rules to begin to build with in your business:

- We address all members appropriately. This is regional and situational, but teach the staff to err on the side of respect. For example, in Southern states, most young people are taught to still refer to older adults as "Sir" and "Ma'am." This works there, but might not work in New York, although respect for the older businesspeople who are your members works there as well. What is not appropriate almost anywhere is a younger staff person calling an older female by her first name without being invited to do so. No matter where you live, establish rules that demonstrate respect for your guests, teach those rules early, and then enforce as needed.

- All staff will say "Please" and "Thank you." It is not appropriate, for example, to ring up a bottle of water, and then slide the change back with a "There you go." Every time you interact with a guest, you have a chance to demonstrate that their business is appreciated, and the simple rules of common courtesy help us make that point.

- You will say "Thank you" as the guests leave the house. Every guest is thanked every time as they leave and for every transaction.

The guests of this house are the most important people in this business.

You have to teach the staff who really pays the bills in the house. Most staff thinks most owners are wildly rich, and it is to your benefit to change their thinking by directing the money aspect toward the members.

It does not hurt, for example, for most owners to share what it really costs to run a business. Most young staff has no idea that you pay $3,000, or even $12,000, for just utilities, let alone the rest of your expenses. By relating your expenses to member payments, and the fact that you can't pay your bills if the members don't pay theirs, keeps the perspective of why the business was created and why we have to be nice to the people who are really paying all the bills around here.

Disrespect the guests of our house, and you will asked to leave our business.

Staff will make mistakes, and sometimes these mistakes damage a guest. But the intent of that staff person, and the ultimate damage he caused, can result in the staff person being let go.

Let's look at two examples. In the first one, the staff person made a mistake, but there was no intent to harm. In the second example, the staff person made a mistake, but it was harmful to the member.

- *Case 1*: The club's trainer was walking the floor and noticed a guest struggling with a new exercise. The trainer stopped, showed the member how to do it correctly, but as he turned to go, he stepped on the guest's cell phone and smashed it.

- *Case 2:* The club's counter person was stressed and took an inquiry call at the front counter. The person had a lot of questions, but the club's salesperson was on another call and wasn't yet available. The staff person was in a hurry to get off the phone and go home, so she was impatient with the call and mad because she couldn't get the salesperson to take it off her hands. As the salesperson hung up his call, the counter person put the person on hold and yelled to the salesperson in the office behind the counter, "There is some stupid bitch on the phone that has a thousand questions. You can deal with her." That comment was rude enough, but it got worse. The counter person had hit the wrong button and the guest/inquiry on the phone had heard everything, which she strongly noted when the salesperson picked up the phone to talk to the salesperson.

Intent is everything. In Case 1, the trainer apologized, and the club bought the person a new phone. The trainer was trying to do the right thing, but it was a simple accident, and the trainer should not be reprimanded, nor should he have to pay for the phone. In fact, what he did (helping the member) was behavior we want from our employees, and the club can pay for a new phone for the guest.

In Case 2, the intent was harmful, and the staff person was fired immediately. Hurt a guest and you go home, because the guests are more important than you are. In this case, the owner heard of the call and personally called the inquiry and apologized. She also let the person know that the club's staff person who insulted the caller was fired immediately. The owner further gave the caller a free six-month membership to the club; because your reputation is everything, and you don't want negative word-of-mouth spreading in your market, especially over something so harmful to a potential member.

Never Lose Sight of the Foundational Truth of Your Business, Which Is the Club's Mission Statement

When you spend your life fixing all kinds of businesses, you come to realize that there are really just a few fundamental laws that govern whether a business owner will succeed or not. Even if you read endless business books, and limit yourself to just the literally thousands released during the last few years, you will find that most of these books can be boiled down to the same key points buried in a lot of fluff and filler that make that book unique. One of the basic elements recurring in all the good books is that you must seek the foundational truth of your business.

The foundational truth is usually a single sentence that defines the business and why it exists. Stray from your foundational truth, and you will usually fail at some point. Drifting from the foundational truth affects all businesses, no matter how big or small. If you can't define your business and the purpose of that business in one sentence, then you can't make the decisions you need to make, train your staff, or even market your business, because you don't know what the hell you are trying to accomplish.

When you explore your own foundational truth, start with the question: "Why do we exist?" Then ask, "What are we trying to accomplish with this business?" Avoid the trite "making money" statement. Making money is what happens if the foundational truth is correct for your business.

If your business isn't performing the way you expect, then always return to the foundational truth first. If you can't define your business simply, and what you are trying to accomplish with that business, then how do you train staff, market, and even paint the place; because you are making random decisions based upon the situation at hand, rather than informed choices based upon fulfilling your truth.

Walmart, the retail giant known throughout the world, may have the best example of a foundational truth you could find. Walmart's foundational truth can be defined as: "To lower the world's cost of living."

If you understand your foundational truth, then every decision you make in your company either matches that truth, or works against that truth, which makes that decision something to be avoided. For example, Walmart is known for getting the best deals from its suppliers. If the company is living by its foundational truth, which is to lower the world's cost of living, then it has no choice but to aggressively seek better deals, since saving money through its vendors results in more of a savings for the people who shop there.

Mission statements are as old as the business itself, and are usually worthless, because most are too self-serving or too generic to be effective. But mission statements done correctly are really nothing more than simply stating the club's foundational truth, which is why are we here and what are we trying to accomplish?

No matter what your current mission statement says, consider dropping yours and using this one instead. This mission statement exists for one purpose, which is to help the staff focus on delivering legendary customer service. It is simple, and it is clean, and probably more effective than the one you are using now that only appears on your website or in your brochures.

When you train your staff, start with this simple question: Why are we here? The answer is your foundational truth and also your mission statement:

We are the best part of our guest's day, every day.

Your training then involves making this statement come true. If we really are the best part of the guest's day every day, then what do we have to change to make that true? Do we greet people properly? Are we clean enough for our guests? Are we happy, upbeat people, who act truly glad to see them each day? All these are questions that validate your foundational truth.

This foundational truth also allows you to test what you are currently doing in your business. For example, if your group classes start traditionally five minutes late in the evening, due to the previous instructor always running over, then you have failed the test of the foundational truth, because how can you be the best part of someone's day if you make them wait due to the rudeness and lack of respect the instructor is showing the guests waiting for the next class.

This instructor may think she is providing great service by giving her class a few extra minutes every day, but she is really irritating the guests who have to pick up their kids on time or have other obligations that are time sensitive. Her perceived extra service is really a lack of respect for someone's time.

More importantly, you have to do what you say you will do. The schedule states clearly that the class starts at 6:00 p.m. and ends at 7:00 p.m. Customer service, and living up to this particular foundational truth, is always doing what you tell the guest/client you are going to do. If you state the class is one hour, then make it an hour, since your guests plan their day and schedules accordingly.

Build This Statement Into the Culture of Your Club

This statement, "We are the best part of the guest's day, every day," should be the first and the last thing the members see as they enter and leave your business. Ideally, this should be made into a very large display that hangs behind the front counter or somewhere else in your entry area that is very noticeable. Think big here, maybe in the 3x5 foot range, or even bigger if space in your lobby permits, and be sure that someone professional does the art, including embedding your logo as a light background screen.

Any employee who has been with you more than 90 days should get up on a ladder and sign the board as a rite of passage into the business. By signing the board, you are acknowledging that you not only understand the power of this statement, but you are always willing to accept that responsibility as an employee in this company.

New hires should wait until they complete their initial 90 days before they are offered the privilege of signing the board. Putting your name on this board should not be taken lightly. By signing, you are guaranteeing that you will make this happen for all guests/members who are part of the business.

Smaller versions of the board should be displayed in both locker rooms and in other key areas around your business. Smaller clubs should have at least one strong version tied to the entry area. This statement should also be part of any marketing materials or handouts the members receive from the business as well.

As a side note, don't forget to create a hierarchy of employees by seniority. Employees that have been with you at least a year should receive a small, but very nice, pin to wear on the collars of their uniforms. For example, if you were the Workout Company, then each employee could receive a silver "W" at the end of one year of service. Being a senior employee is a status for the other employees to achieve, but more importantly, it gives the members a sense of stability in the business and that there are senior people in the organization that have the skills and knowledge to help them solve problems in the club.

Start Every Employee With Three Hours of Staff Training Dedicated to Covering *The 20 Laws of Customer Service in a Fitness Business*

It is much easier to create customer service if you have a basic tool that covers the fundamentals you are trying to accomplish in your business. Employees need a go-to tool that keeps them focused and that states your entire belief system concerning customer service in one short document.

The 20 Laws of Customer Service in a Fitness Business is a good starting point for your business, but you may need to change a few of the rules to match your personal beliefs and your type of business.

The 20 Laws of Customer Service in a Fitness Business

1. Always remember that those who are paying to belong to this club are people who we consider guests and are not account numbers or just another member.

2. Do exactly what you promise, when you promise.

3. Always show the proper respect for our guests by being on time, prepared, properly dressed, and ready to take care of their needs.

4. Answer the phone within three rings, using a positive welcoming statement.

5. Greet our members at the door as if they are coming home.

6. Know everything about what we offer, and always be prepared to answer questions and help our guests get what they are looking for in our club.

7. Thank every single member every single time they leave the business and whenever they make any additional transaction with our business.

8. All managers will be available at any time while on duty to help solve a guest's problem.

9. Keep the guests informed about every change or issue in the club immediately if it affects the quality of their visit.

10. We promise to be the best part of the guest's day, every day. Always remember that we work so our guests can enjoy their time with us.

11. We are here to make things easier for our guests.

12. Always be courteous, always be smiling.

13. Never complain about any club problem to our guests.

14. Use the guest's name every chance you get.

15. Any questions from our guests? You find the answers.

16. If you can, handle it yourself instead of passing it along to someone else.

17. Strive for profitability. The profitability of our company creates opportunity for everyone who works here and a better experience for our guests.

18. Do everything in your power to make this the cleanest facility in town.

19. The safety of our guests is the most important thing in this business.

20. Take this job seriously, but not yourself. Remember, we are the best part of their day, every day, so make it fun.

Any owner or manager should be able to take these rules and turn them into at least three hours of staff training if not more. When you introduce customer-service training, one of the keys is to always have an example of what you want done and how the staff should behave and respond in certain instances.

For example, if you're discussing Rule 3, which states the need to be on time and prepared, you might reference trainers and the need to be there 15 minutes early so they can have the equipment ready if needed, the trainer is fed and has hit the restroom, and that he has the workout of the day ready to go. Arriving at 2:00, when the appointment actually was scheduled to begin, doesn't enhance the service, since the trainer is on time but not prepared for the training session.

You can also use actual examples from your business or create ones that make the point. For instance, if you see a staff person doing something that is valued as great customer service, write it down on an index card and work the actual example in later during the training. Real examples have more power and help the staff person "see" the desired action being carried out.

When you first start your training, put all your effort into the things that make the most difference in the shortest period of time, such as answering the phone more professionally, greeting members as they arrive, and thanking everyone as they leave. Remember that customer service is nothing more than hundreds of little things done well that all add up to a legendary experience with your business. Start small, but go for the impact items that the members/guests will notice quickly.

Customer-service staff training also is more effective if it is personal. By personal, we mean it is something you do side-by-side with your staff standing at the front desk or walking the floor.

Your staff learns by seeing it done correctly and not in a room, sitting at a desk taking notes. The classroom format of teaching is where you tell your people what is going to happen, but the floor is where you show them how it is actually done.

For example, if you are standing at the front counter at 5:00 p.m. with your new counter person, he will learn more by watching you go first. When a member/guest walks by on the way out, and you say, "Thank you for coming in today, John. We appreciate your business," your staff person gets an immediate idea of what service looks and sounds like when done correctly. Let the staff person then try it, and correct as needed. Remember again:

> *The classroom format of teaching is where you tell your people what is going to happen, but the floor is where you show them how it is actually done.*

The members also appreciate seeing senior staff working the club no matter how big the club is. The guests love to see the managers and owners involved in the process. This demonstrates the caring attitude, and it also lets the guests know that you are keeping yourself aware of what is happening in the business, which gives the guests a sense that you really do give a damn about more than just taking their money.

Do These Things Now

- Create the vision of service in your club by introducing the "My house, my guests" analogy.

- Use the mission statement to create the foundational truth for your business.

- Start every employee with three hours of staff training dedicated to customer service.

- Introduce *The 20 Laws of Customer Service in a Fitness Business* to your staff during the first three hours of training.

Customer service is as simple as …
dress codes for the members.

Most of your members have a little common sense. Many don't and are as dumb as a kettlebell.

This lack of common sense is often reflected in how members choose to dress in the club. There are the guys with the 14-inch arms who feel the need to wear the string tops. There are the women who are overweight, but insist on wearing the little bikini workout bottom in class. And then there are the old guys who like to wear the running shorts split high up the side but insist on not wearing any underwear.

Every club has these members, and for everyone that you have running loose in your club, you have dozens of regular members that are horrified by that member's lack of decency. In other words, that member's bad taste is costing you other members, who slip away at the end of the membership because they are offended.

The members need a dress code. It should be part of their membership agreement, and it should be hanging on the member boards in each locker room. If the members understand it when they sign up and it is displayed in the club, you can enforce it.

The key words in the code is "deemed appropriate," which leaves it up to the owner and managers to decide if something is not appropriate for the club. You need a generic phrase in your code because the members are just too creative for you to anticipate everything they could possibly show up wearing.

There are, however, a few things that we know don't work in the club that you should automatically list:

- *Appropriate athletic shoes only. No street shoes, boots, or sandals allowed in the workout areas.*

- *Only shorts, sweat pants, tee shirts, tank tops, and spandex accessories deemed appropriate by management may be worn.*

- *Clean workout clothing is required. Management will address any unsatisfactory hygiene condition immediately, and corrective action may be required.*

- *Please avoid the use of heavy perfume or cologne.*

- *No belt buckles, blue jeans, or loose jewelry items may be worn in the club's workout areas.*

Respond quickly to things that bother you or the staff, because if it bothers you, then it is probably bothering many of your members, and failing to take action may cost you renewals later.

11

Start With a Culture of Success That Can Be Applied to All Members

The group class was full on a Monday night at prime time. The instructor, who was in the club 15 minutes before her class began, walked through the club, inviting all the members to take part and join her in the group room.

Class began exactly on time, and the instructor did a masterful job of handling the full room. During the class, she noticed a woman who was new to the club struggling with the moves. The new member also seemed to be somewhat new to fitness and was obviously deconditioned. The new member tried to keep up, but she was clearly getting frustrated with the changing moves and class basics everyone else but her seemed to understand.

After the class, as the instructor stood again at the door thanking each member for attending that night, the new member wandered out slowly, thanked the instructor for the class, and headed toward the locker room. She was moving slowly, her head was down, and the instructor knew that she might never see this woman again in class if she left the situation as it was.

The instructor thanked the last student and then caught up with the woman. The woman expressed her frustration that it had been a long time since she had worked out, and that group exercise had seemed to change in the years she had been away from fitness. She admitted that she just didn't know if she could do it anymore, and that maybe it had been too long since she had been in a club.

The instructor surprised the member by asking if she might have another 15 minutes left in her. The woman moaned softly, but smiled and nodded yes. The instructor led her back to the group room that was now empty until the following hour. The instructor put some music on and then took the member slowly and patiently through all the basics that she had struggled with during the class, giving the woman a chance to feel that she could do it. The instructor set a very easy pace, checking for understanding rather than moving at workout speed. The member responded quickly to the moves and was immediately smiling at her success.

After the brief remedial session, the instructor walked the guest to the locker room, chatting about the club and kids. Several days later, the guest was back in the club and participating in another class with her new friend, the instructor. Instead of a lost member, the instructor's extra effort had resulted in a loyal member that had already mentioned the club to her sister, who was also in the class that night.

The instructor had never mentioned the incident to the owner, who had found out by a small note the member had left at the counter, recounting what she considered as the extraordinary service she received from the instructor. The owner took the instructor aside later, thanked her for being part of the team, and gave her a $10 gift card to her favorite coffee shop.

What separates this instructor from so many others is her attitude. What separates this club from so many others is the culture of success and of customer service that led to the instructor making the decision to help so easily. Proper attitude can be taught, and a culture of customer service and success can be created in your business.

We Do Everything We Can to Create a Culture of Failure in the Clubs

In most fitness businesses, the member never had a chance. The current culture in the club business, which is the culture of failure, has been slowly building for decades. Everything we do in this business is designed to lead to short-term success for the club and failure for the member. For example, look at these common practices and the effect each one has upon a typical member, or potential member.

We run advertising with offers or specials based upon a percentage off of some type of membership.

For instance, the club might run a membership fee special that is half off if you come in now. Percentage-off special offers are the most mistrusted of all sales techniques, and we are already creating a culture of predatory sales practices before the potential member even appears. Sadly, many of our club owners are young and inexperienced, or are not very sophisticated in marketing and business, so they are easily led astray by an ad consultant who talks them into these discount offers, which is the same offer he just talked the furniture guy down the street into and the clothing store he worked with earlier.

The entire sales experience, and first impression of the business, is based upon a single, 20-minute hammer session in an office.

As it has been said in other parts of this book, fitness has too many moving parts and is too complicated for a single-visit close. This means that we often let a member try the club once and then expect him to sign a membership agreement in the office at what is probably the worst single moment to ask for the sale. The guy is beaten, tired, and frustrated, and now we want him to be happy about signing up for a membership?

Even worse, the guy doesn't even get a chance to work out first, and he is simply taken into the office after a brief tour and then hammered hard by a young salesperson using out-of-date hardcore sales techniques originally designed to move cars, but not to help someone get started in a service business. The relationship begins with pressure, and the potential member now understands that this company is just a sales machine, and really is not interested in his long-term success in fitness, which again demonstrates the culture of failure rather than success.

If the person does sign up, he is handed off to a bored trainer, who is just looking for qualified clients.

The new member is supposed to get three workouts according to club policy, but the trainer prequalifies the person as not interested, or not financially able to sign up for personal training during the first visit; therefore, he puts the guy on a simple circuit with a workout card and blows him off.

The new member, who is somewhat new to fitness, has maybe one or two assists from the staff and then is on his own. He follows the circuit for a few weeks, getting a little success from doing a new workout, but the success quickly plateaus, and he gets frustrated. But unless he is willing to sign up for one-on-one training, which he can't afford, he is really left to figure out fitness for himself, relying on fitness magazines or help from other members.

This club is good at getting new members, and at having a lot of equipment, but the new member is quickly discarded to find his own way. Eventually, he will just give up, probably pay to the end of his agreement, honoring his commitments as he always does, and then quietly go away. Failure was built into the equation from the first encounter with the trainer. The club's entire training system is based upon help for a small percentage of the club's financially elite, and all the other members are left to either figure it out on their own, or to just quietly fail and leave.

What we used to think was good business not too many years ago is actually the basis of the culture of failure in today's market. The members are now more educated in fitness and want more than help and support than most clubs are designed to provide. Even the non-profits in the fitness world still can't break out of the model that is still based upon just a small number of members really getting help.

Building the Culture of Success in Your Business

If you are seeking the culture of success, which is the foundation of legendary customer service, then you need to question all of the typical business practices a club currently uses. Most of what we do is left over from an era when the member was expendable and easily replaced if he left. In today's more mature markets, where club owners have more competition than they ever dreamed of in past years, we need to question every business practice we use and start going down a different path. This new direction should lead to the creation of a fitness business that supports and cares for its membership, knowing that replacing that member is harder than it has ever been in the industry.

You have to start with your business's perception in the marketplace.

Price-driven ads send a distinct message to the consumer: this business is sales-driven, and it is all about the price. You cannot hold two opposing thoughts in your head at the same time, but this is what we try to get the potential member to do when we advertise a price special and talk about service in the same ad.

You simply can't be a great service club when you advertise price-driven specials that lead to a single, high-pressure sales encounter. When the consumer sees these ads, he automatically catches the disconnect, which is the claim to have great service at this club, but wait, the club also offers outrageous price specials, such as no membership fee this month, that the consumer knows can only lead to getting pounded during his first visit to the club.

Again, this has been said in every book in this series: the member is not as stupid as you think he is or hope he is. The potential members look at these ads and know you can't be both a great service club, and a club that tries to attract members with wild discounts and sales practices. Service and deep discounts are opposing thoughts, and these ads are worthless over time in the market as tools to attract new members.

Trial memberships, on the other hand, are tools that do convey customer service, starting with the first encounter between a potential member and your business, which is often done through the person looking at a piece of your advertising he just received. Trial memberships are simple tools based upon the concept of exposure marketing. This type of marketing is based upon the premise discussed previously, which is "to know me is to love me."

There are three types of trial memberships a club owner might use:

- *The paid trial*: An example of a paid trial might be 30 days for $19. The risk is low, and the potential member gets enough time to really get involved in the club.

- *The risk-free trial*: This trial is based upon a fixed length of time a potential member can try the club at no cost. Risk is the biggest barrier to inquiry, and this trial works well to introduce your business to a large number of people who wouldn't normally respond to a price-driven advertisement. Risk is nothing more than fear of loss: "What if I try this and don't like it? Now I am stuck with a payment and will just lose money." An example of this type of trial might be "The 21-day risk-free trial."

- *The fixed-time trial*: This trial works well in smaller markets where you might have a large population of people who have never even been into a commercial fitness facility. For example, you might base this trial period upon the premise that your mission is to let everyone in your community try fitness for the first time with no risk and no obligation.

You can also talk about the need for fitness and cite all the numbers that support the fact that we are getting fatter and more out of shape as a country. The trial itself is based upon opening the club up to the entire town during a slower month, which might be May, for example. During this month, everyone in town can try fitness free and experience it first-hand. You would also do special clinics and have a lot of information handy that talks about the need to move and eat better.

All of these trials are based upon the following verbiage (risk-free trial):

> *We are so proud of our club that we would like you to come try us absolutely free for 21 days with no risk to you nor with any obligation. We understand that many of you are nervous about getting started with a fitness program, and we would like you to experience our club and our service before you make up your mind.*

> *We're proud of our club and feel it is the best in town, but talk is cheap. We would like you to come meet our staff, and meet the other members in our club, and try us with a full club membership for 21 days. We will give you all the help, coaching, and support you need to get started before you even consider becoming a member.*

> *At the end of this trial membership, if we haven't earned your business, then we don't deserve to have you as a member, and you are under no further obligation. Please give us a chance to prove to you that you can be successful*

with a fitness program and that we're the club that can give
you the service and support you need and expect.

Trial memberships help move your business's perception in the marketplace toward a customer-service driven model and away from a perceived sales machine. Trial marketing is also more effective if you couple the trial with a testimonial format.

We often forget that fitness is an emotional event for most people, especially when they first consider getting fit, or when they get started doing something new that involves movement and fitness activity, but few ads or promotional tools used by most club owners really tap this emotion.

Fitness is scary to new people. Fitness is difficult if you haven't done it in a while. Fitness is frustrating to many people, since exercise requires doing movements the body may not have done since they were five years old, or just isn't used to yet, because of the years of rust and inactivity.

Most importantly, fitness can be embarrassing, because it requires going into a business filled with a usually young, fit staff and a lot of fit members and admitting you are fat and don't feel good about your body. Admitting that you are far from perfect has to be one of the most difficult things you can do in the world, especially when you have to admit it to people you know will make a judgment about your fitness level and how out of shape you really are.

Telling your mother you are out of shape and getting back, "No honey, you look good with a little extra weight" is far different from walking into a club and having a trainer look at you and then just sadly shake his head and mumble to himself something that sounded like, "They don't pay me enough to fix guys like this." Fitness is emotional, and being out of shape and being judged for that is perhaps one of the greatest barriers to even getting people through the front door of most fitness businesses.

Testimonial ads are the only tool that can tap this emotion. Pictures of real people who have been successful pursuing fitness lets other people know that they can do it, too, and they can do it at this club where there are so many other success stories that are inspiring.

The combination of testimonials and trial memberships is the perfect solution to start creating a culture of success before the potential member even walks through the door. Testimonials help the future member feel that if this guy can do it, so can I, and trial memberships back up this belief by completely killing the risk factor. Trial memberships also demonstrate that the club is willing to prove that it has the information you need, accompanied by great service, before you spend money or commit to a membership.

There are a few rules that you should apply to using testimonials:

- Use normal members in your club's target market who have had reasonable, not excessive, success. Everyone can identify with someone who has lost 20 pounds and kept it off, but most people have trouble identifying with someone who has lost 100 pounds, or the equivalent of another entire small person. You might have changed a life with the 100-pound weight-loss person, but there just aren't a whole lot of people out there in that condition who will respond to that type of person in that type of ad. Stick to real people in your community who have had realistic success stories and are walking billboards of what your club and team can accomplish.

- Use videos whenever possible. Videos are the most important club tool of the future. You should have a video-driven website, feature videos on the social network sites that change daily, and use a flat screen in the sales areas that features at least 10 members who have been successful in the club. Remember, it is one thing to read about someone changing their life through fitness, but it is much more powerful, and much more believable, to see someone actually work out and hear their story.

- Don't forget to have the person always emphasize the service he received at your business and the help and support he had from your staff. Service sells, and it sells even better if one of your customers is telling the story.

- Use professional photographers whenever you can. These images are part of your brand and you don't want to run high quality ads with lousy pictures. Also get releases from your member, because once you get a collection of testimonials you will be using them for years.

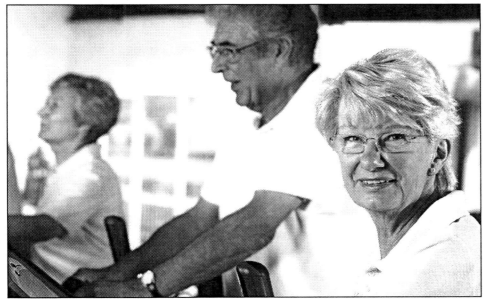

Hemera/Thinkstock

Create a membership system that has many layers and options where everyone who wants help can get it at a price they can afford.

We exist to change lives and any fitness business should be nothing more than a delivery system designed to change as many lives as possible.

Change lives, and people stay longer and pay longer, which results in more income for the business, usually more profitability, and a chance to change more lives in the future.

The tool that enhances this mission to change as many lives as possible is customer service. Every member who pays us each month to belong to the club in essence trusts us to facilitate this change, and every member who pays deserves some respect from the club and its team. This glowing and somewhat simplistic business idea breaks down, however, when it comes to the direct application in most fitness businesses.

In most clubs, there are usually two distinct classes of members. There are the ones who have the money to purchase one-on-one help, and therefore get the best results from their membership, and then there is everyone else going through the motions practicing self-inflicted fitness.

Everyone else is defined as all the other members still doing their original circuit workout from the day they started, the members carrying sweat-stained copies of *Men's Health*, and the wannabe bodybuilders still carrying around Arnold's 1977 hardcover edition of *The Education of a Bodybuilder*. All of these people are seekers of a more fit life, but almost all will be failures since the club simply doesn't have a system to help them that isn't restrictive and expensive.

If we want to keep more members staying longer and paying longer, then we have to design a membership system that allows everyone to get help at a rate they can afford.

Doing this requires that you stop copying the traditional one-on-one business model and move to a system that is more inclusive for more members, yet more financially successful for the club due to a much higher percentage of your members paying a monthly fee that is higher than your rate for just a simple access membership.

The current system only serves one type of client.

The traditional training model only serves one type of client. If you are on the average a middle-aged, fat, white guy and have money, you get a trainer. If you're not, then you are much less likely to seek out the services of the club's training department.

The club loses money, and fails to deliver great service, by limiting its business plan to only a single user group. If you want to generate the highest revenue possible from the most members, and deliver service to the widest range of clients, then you need to expand your model to seek out the other types of clientele who are waiting for you, but are untapped because your model fails to serve them.

Following are all of the categories you could be serving in your business by expanding your current training model and by making it more inclusive.

The deconditioned people

This group, defined by the statistic that about 63 percent of the people in this country are either overweight or obese, really doesn't do well in a mainstream fitness facility. Unless the deconditioned person can come up with money for one-on-one training, he is pretty much underserved by most clubs. These people simply need much more help during their first 30 days than most clubs can afford to give using the one-on-one format.

It is interesting to note that most clubs fail these clients, due to the limits and restrictions of their business model, and not because of the owner's or manager's lack of awareness that these folks need more help or because the club's management doesn't care. The model itself is wrong, and is where the barrier exists, because most owners just can't afford to throw that much one-on-one help at people who need constant attention during their first 30-days.

The traditional one-on-one clients

This is the standard client serviced by the standard model. This is a failing model in most clubs, however, if you look at the numbers. One-on-one training usually only has a penetration rate of about 3 to 6 percent of the club's membership. Penetration rate is again defined as how many people in the club's total membership are involved in a given program. In this example, a club with 1,000 members, and a penetration rate of 5 percent with one-on-one training, would only have 50 consistent training clients.

Some clubs try to compensate for this by showing a higher rate of training, using $75 per session for example, and then discounting for anyone who buys more sessions, or packages. In this instance, the club might offer five sessions at $250 (now $50 each) or 10 sessions at $400 (now dropped to only $40 each). Besides killing the credibility of your trainers, who started out as $75-per-hour trainers, but are now worth only $40 per hour, you are still limiting your program to only a single type of client.

Most one-on-one training clients like the pampering and the status that comes with having a personal trainer. These people seek this out because of the results they get, the guidance they receive, but as equally important to many of them is that fact that they can afford it and the other members can't. It is elitist, it has status for some, and this type of training was always designed to be that way. The trainers themselves perpetuate this by fighting for bragging rights on who can get the most per hour, therefore, continually seeking to drive up the training rates in the market.

These elite clients have a place in the club, and if a member drives up in a Bentley and wants to train, take a lot of his money and give him the training. But there are other types of clients, in much larger numbers, who are not being serviced by this model you need to chase as well.

The social dynamic/group dynamic category

These are the clients that prefer to do things in groups and who seek the energy and fun from doing things they like with a lot of other people pursuing the same activity and goals.

The business concept behind attracting these people is that they can share the cost of the trainer. People need access to more information to make change in fitness, because most people just can't figure it out by themselves. Training in a group allows a wider range of people, who understand they need help, to get this information at a reduced rate by going through the process with others and sharing the cost of that education.

People grow up doing things in groups. If you were an athlete, you grew up on a team. Even if you were an individual-pursuit athlete, such as a track person or played golf, you were still part of a team and trained and travelled together. If you weren't into sports, you might have been a Boy Scout, Girl Scout, in the chess club, or somehow involved in doing something with a group of people. Even the guys in the computer clubs still get together to exchange tips and combine expertise.

We have killed the group dynamic in most clubs. Training is done one-on-one, the cardio equipment has personal televisions, and we encourage members to bring their mp3 players. We not only limit the personal connection, we strongly discourage it in most clubs. Except for clubs who have vital group-exercise programs, there is nowhere in most facilities to meet and interact with other members, especially since many clubs don't have stretching areas or any type of socialization node, such as a sports bar.

Training in a group is more fun, you will get better results because of the peer pressure, and you can save money if you share the cost of the trainer. The club also benefits more by being able to generate a higher return-per-session. For example, if your best trainer can get $75 per hour, then that is your ceiling for her for every hour she works. You simply can't get more than the proven maximum of $75. But if you think about creating the group dynamic experience, you can now raise your return-per-hour. For example, you might charge $75 for one person, but you can charge $40 per workout for four different people in a semi-private environment; therefore, generating $160 for the same length of time.

It is important to understand that you can add this layer without cannibalizing your one-on-one business. The people who do one-on-one are not the same people who seek the group experience, and the majority of your existing one-on-one clients will prefer to just keep doing what they are doing if you do add the semi-private option to your training business. Most semi-private training would be done in groups of two to four people, but experienced trainers can sometimes manage groups as big as six people.

One of the false assumptions that prevent many club owners from trying this model is that they believe—usually through the influence of the trainers— that everyone has to have their own individualized workout. Unless the person is injured, or needs sports-specific training, such as someone getting ready to do a marathon, then the rest of the members can do things in groups, sharing a common workout. For example, the head trainer might post the workout of the day for the semi-private clients listing kettlebell swings, clean and presses, squats, pull-ups, and dead lifts. An experienced trainer might have a member who has been training for a while do two minutes of swings with a 53-pound bell and the new guy might do 30 seconds with a 35-pounder. Everyone can get individual help and guidance that suits that member within the confines of the group, but everyone still does the same basic workout.

The challenge seekers (those who simply can't find a hard enough challenge in most mainstream fitness businesses)

This is the group most clubs never see and wouldn't know how to service if they did appear. These people are in the 25- to 45-year-old age group and are the ones who are doing radical training in their garages, doing the cult workout of the year. These are also the same people who would be bored to tears working with a traditional trainer by themselves. This group wants a challenge, wants to do the training that their favorite athletes are doing, and are concerned not only with looking good, but with functioning well as a skier, bike rider, hiker, kayaker, or any other weekend lifestyle sport. These people almost always train in groups, because the peer pressure drives the results and helps take every workout to the next higher level.

These are also the people who usually know a lot about training since they read all the hot fitness publications, explore fitness online, and read the training books. We usually call this group the "badass" fitness group, because they are seeking the badass, make-it-hard, challenge-me-as-much-as-you-can workout, and have no interest in traditional fixed-equipment circuits or body-split bodybuilding workouts done 1972-style.

This group thrives in group personal training/coaching with groups of a trainer and up to 10 members. The group training sessions should be very aggressive and would be structured consisting of a program that is usually done for a full month before being changed. This should not be called a class, because that term forces a comparison between the club's group personal training and its group exercise program.

Group exercise is generally included as part of a simple access membership to the club, but you want to charge for group personal training. There is a sample pricing structure later in this chapter.

The key point is that there are really four types of clients that need, or who are seeking, help beyond the most basic information that most clubs offer, but most clubs merely offer help to the traditional one-on-one client. By limiting your help to just the 3 to 6 percent of the people who can afford training, or like that type of training relationship, you are in effect neglecting the other 94 to 97 percent of the members who can't afford, or who simply don't like, that type of working out.

The interesting thing to note is that when asked directly, most owners cite that almost everybody coming through the door, which stated statistically might be as high as 95 percent in most clubs, needs help of some type and can't get started on their own. Even the folks from other gyms and who have been working out are often doing homemade or dated workouts that are ineffective or dangerous.

Yet knowing this hasn't led to any changes in the training model for most clubs. The clubs simply don't change, or can't afford to change, the current model that limits help and service to the majority of their members.

Building a price model that can service a deeper penetration rate in your membership

Following is a sample model that is designed to touch the largest number of members in any given club. *When you add layers, you are really adding a variety of different price points that will appeal to a wider range of clients.* This model is also based upon the assumption that the one-on-one training model is not effective in most clubs. The traditional model only generates restricted income from the entire membership base and also restricts the return-per-hour the club can obtain.

Done correctly, most clubs should only have about 10 percent of its training revenue come from the traditional model. Most clubs could in fact benefit from charging more for one-on-one training and making it more elite for its membership and for its image in the marketplace. Setting a higher standard with your one-on-one price would also guide more members toward the semi-private and group models where the club can reap a higher profit margin and serve more members.

Important note: Do not panic by trying to force your existing members into a new system. If you use this model, you would do it for new members forward. Most owners balk at using a newer model, because they always relate change back to the members they already have in the program: "I know Joe, and Joe won't do any of this new stuff, and he sure won't pay more." Leave Joe alone. Don't mess with your current members in the model you are using. If they want to keep buying sessions, then sell them the sessions, but stop failing to grow your business because you are afraid of a bunch of members holding you hostage. Honor the deals you have made, but move forward from there.

This model is also based upon the assumption that you will at some point stop selling sessions and packages and move to an EFT model (members are drafted monthly for their training directly from a credit-card or bank account). Sessions and packages are weak tools, because the cash flow is so inconsistent. You sell a package, get the cash today, which is nice, but then you have to service the person for several more months without any matching influx of money.

Your goal in this more advanced business model is to:

• Offer a system that allows a wider range of members, as defined by workout type and price sensitivity, to become active in your business.

• Stabilize your cash flow by switching away from short-term packages and sessions to 12-month training programs based upon a monthly EFT.

The training clubs have long suffered from having all of their membership based upon short-term tools, such as packages, and the mainstream fitness clubs have based their memberships upon longer tools, such as a 12-month term.

Both businesses could benefit from combining these memberships into one model. The training clubs could develop a large receivable base, which is the combined total of all their members paying monthly for their training. This eliminates the inconsistent cash flow that is so detrimental to these small businesses.

The mainstream people should strive to get the highest number of members possible into a larger monthly payment and include the membership to the club as part of the training membership.

One of the biggest changes in the industry during the first decade of the new century, and maybe one of the biggest changes in the last 30 years or so in the business, was the necessity to show the lowest entry point/membership price possible in order to get as many members as possible into the club, and then work hard to drive up the average EFT sale.

In the past, clubs have been able to hold the line and not drop their single-person rate, but the combination of the economy, the maturing of the marketplace with more competitors than ever before, the advent of the lower-priced club model, and a more astute clientele looking for more options is forcing everyone else to change. This change will drastically affect all mainstream fitness clubs for the next decade, and all owners and managers need to tweak their current price models before falling sales and declining revenues force you to change what you are currently doing.

The Customer-Service-Driven Price Model

Illustrated in this section is a service-driven pricing model that would be typical for most clubs. You may have to change the numbers up or down to fit your market. You can also consider changing the following:

- Change the price as needed for your market. Remember that it is easier to raise your price than it is to lower the price. Start lower than you think and raise the price at set levels as you gain confidence. For example, you may start group personal training at $89 x 12 months and raise that price by $10 after you sell your first 20 memberships.

- You may also alter the length if you are a little nervous and need to get some experience first. You may, for example, start at only three months rather than 12, keeping in mind that the three months is still better than packages and sessions.

- The higher price pampering membership is for a club that has members who want everything, but don't want to feel that they are getting hit for small change every time they come through the door. This membership should be all-inclusive and can, depending on what you have to sell, include sending full supplements to the person's house each month, perhaps a massage or two a month if you offer them, a recovery shake during each visit, and bottled water as needed. Add value to this membership, and target about one out of 15 as a reasonable sales number for your club. The range in prices reflects different services you might be able to include.

- One-on-one training should be priced to be only about 10 percent of your total training. Your future is in groups, where you can service many more members at a higher return. Price your one-on-one memberships higher than your competitors so you obviously can claim of having the best trainers in the market. "Yes, our training is the highest priced in the market. We have the best trainers and charge accordingly." Money people want and expect the best from you, and your trainers can't be the best if the guy down the street charges more for his people.

The Foundational Pricing Model

Simple access to the club

This membership is for anyone who has fitness experience and just wants to work out on his own, or for someone who is just wants to take part in the club's group-exercise program.

- $49 one-time membership fee and $49 a month for 12 months

- $49 one-time membership fee and $39 a month for 18 months (This is a value membership designed to offer the potential member a lower entry point into the club.)

Personal coaching options

This membership is for anyone who feels they get results faster when they work under the direction of a certified personal coach and who wants to know that he will always have someone there to help and guide him during each workout.

$49 one-time fee, and $699 to $1,299 a month x 12 months/unlimited personal training

This membership includes:

- Unlimited personal coaching/training for the month

- Unlimited group personal training classes

- Unlimited use of the club

- The membership to the club is included in the price for no separate charge.

- Extras the club offers, such as spa services, supplements, or shakes that raise the perceived value of this membership.

    (This is the pampering membership. The price range is dependent on what you have to include and the value you can add to increase the perceived worth. The person is guaranteed a trainer if he calls at least 24 hours in advance, or he can have the first available trainer if he calls with less than 24 hours notice.)

$49 one-time fee, and $360 a month x 12 months/one-on-one personal training

This membership includes:

- Personal coaching four times a month

- Unlimited group personal training classes

- Unlimited use of the club

- The membership to the club is included in the price for no separate charge.

(You may buy additional sessions per month at four for $360, or you may buy eight workouts a month for $720 a month x 12 months.)

$49 one-time fee, and $200 a month x 12 months/semi-private groups of two to four people

This membership includes:

- Unlimited small group coaching

- All semi-private coaching is offered at times set by the club.

- Unlimited group personal training classes

- Unlimited use of the club

- The membership to the club is included in the price for no separate charge.

$49 one-time fee, and $129 a month x 12 months/group personal coaching/training in groups with a maximum of 10 people and one trainer

This membership includes:

- Unlimited group personal training/coaching

- Unlimited group personal training/coaching is offered at times set by the club.

- Unlimited use of the club

- The membership to the club is included in the price for no separate charge.

(You may buy punch cards priced at 10@$180 for members who want to attend on a random basis.)

The fundamentals

This is an orientation class offered approximately four to six times per week as needed for your business. This group caters to guests and new members who are deconditioned and who may need to start with basic movements before they could even attend a semi-private workout.

Guests and new members may attend this fundamental group free during their entire trial, or the entire first month as a new member. The goal of this group is to get people grounded in the basic workout moves they might encounter elsewhere in the club, such as their first visit to a semi-private workout. Do not forget that the goal is to teach the guests how to work out, not to give them a fixed workout, which will come later.

Don't make these groups too complicated, which is the direction too many trainers take. This group should be designed to build a feeling of success since many of the participants will be guests and not yet members, so you want people to start slowly and gain confidence before venturing elsewhere in the club.

Start with the simple basics. For example, you might introduce a kettlebell swing, a light pressing movement, a bodyweight squat, some type of pulling movement, and maybe a light deadlifting movement. Keep them off the machines if you can. Contrary to popular myth, machines are far more intimidating to the beginners than just working with a trainer using bodyweight or a very light medicine ball.

Don't forget to coach cardio in these fundamental groups. Many of our new guests and members still believe that the secret to weight loss is staying on a tread for an hour or two. Coach controlled cardio and how to get the most out of the shortest sessions you can, basing the workout upon some type of interval training.

iStockphoto/Thinkstock

Group Training of All Kinds Is the Answer to Building Great Customer-Service Experience in Your Club

Club owners and managers discovered years ago that it is just not profitable to try to get a lot of new members and potential members started with one-on-one training. There are simply too many new people who needed help, and it just costs too much to get so many new people moving in the right direction.

Where we made a huge mistake in the industry was when we realized this situation was affecting the business, but we then made a bad choice when it came to fixing it. Instead of finding a method that would allow us to get every new person in the system, as well as giving our guests a great service experience, we just stopped helping people and left them to pursue fitness on their own.

This was the juncture where we picked "We will help you with one or two workouts, and then you are on your own" as our business plan. We couldn't afford to help, so we didn't, and only the wealthier members ever got the help they needed to reach their goals. Every other member was left to fail on his own with a minimum of help and support, usually involving simple circuit equipment and big workout cards with all the circuit machines and seat settings listed on the front.

The question we really should ask ourselves in this industry is: "Did we embrace the traditional 12-piece circuit because it worked so effectively for our members, or did we go that way because it reduced our cost, and we used this equipment as a substitute for member service?"

The alternative to no service, or to being machine-convenient, is to get everyone involved in some sort of group training. Group training is cost-efficient, and the members enjoy it more than the more boring one-on-one ordeal, or worse, just going around in a circle by yourself. Group training also, as noted previously, gives us a chance to introduce a much wider range of price points for clients who seek training, which is something not possible with a traditional one-on-one model.

Trial memberships and the group experience

First perception is everything, whether you choose to believe it or not. We often judge people and businesses based upon a very limited amount of time spent with either.

There is almost always truth in the old adages, and the one your mom probably used on you as you first learned to dress yourself, "You never get a second chance to make a good first impression" is still maybe one of the most powerful rules that can be applied to any type of small business. This is especially true when it comes to servicing the potential members who inquire about your services and offerings.

Because most clubs are nothing more than sales beasts that need to constantly be fed, all the emphasis on potential members visiting the club is based upon systems and procedures designed to get him to buy during the first visit.

In the hardcore sales world, there are no "be backs," and there are no second chances. If you really are power selling, as demonstrated by the quote attributed to the sales manual of a national club chain: "No potential member leaves the office unless they are crying." It's harsh, but this quote also reflects the culture of our business and also represents the foundation of a culture of failure.

The dilemma is that we want potential members to have a good experience, but we also don't want to spend any money to enhance that experience. The solution that too many clubs choose, therefore, is to put extreme limits on the first few workouts and then add a heavy sales pitch.

The following is what is wrong with this solution and why it simply doesn't work anymore:

- The clients are too sophisticated to believe the drop-close and high-pressure applied by dated salespeople.

- Fitness is too complicated, especially if you have shifted to a functional training base, to demonstrate in only a few workouts.

- The trainers who do the training with the guests simply go through the motions since most of the potential members don't represent future business for them. This attitude results in a weak workout or two and the potential member ending up with a poorly designed circuit and a giant workout card. This, by the way, is now the person's image of service he will receive in the future from this club.

- The cost of the membership for most clubs is high enough that most potential members really do need a night to think it over before they can commit to a membership that might represent $400 or more. People rarely drop $400 on impulse because that amount of money is large enough to put it in the realm of a family decision, or at least in the, "That's a lot, so let me think about it tonight, and I will get back to you" category.

- Even if a club wanted to help the person really experience fitness and what it can do for him, it is still too costly because of the traditional one-on-one model.

By adopting the model that was discussed previously, if you channel all potential members into group situations, you then have the ability to demonstrate how you can change their lives because the group experience is so cost-effective in comparison. In a perfect-world scenario, the potential members would follow this track in a fitness business dedicated to selling memberships and to delivering great customer service.

The guest/potential member has the option to try the club with a risk-free trial membership.

Risk is the biggest barrier to inquiry. Trials kill all risk and get you the maximum leads possible for your market. You will still sign up about 30 percent of all sales the first visit, but those who don't sign during their first visit are now given an option to truly experience fitness, and most importantly, the level of service you can offer in comparison to your competitors.

The guest/potential member, if deconditioned, starts in the fundamentals for as long as needed.

The fundamentals group should be fun, restricted to a few exercises so the person can gain confidence, and done in groups so the guest will meet new people and become grounded in the club. If you use a 30-day trial, the member might spend the entire 30-day period just repeating fundamentals a few times a week until a minimum of conditioning is obtained.

Remember, most clubs will give this same potential member only one or two workouts with a very bored trainer, and then the guest has to go solo in the club. You, on the other hand, are willing to let this person truly get some training and feel some success, because you have the advantage of the cost-effective group-training model, which the other clubs don't have and can't match.

If the guest progresses quickly, or if he was in decent shape, he would be sent to the semi-private groups where he would get more coaching and learn more exercises.

Again, your goal is to achieve a business built upon the culture of success and service. In this example, your potential member is never in the club for the duration of the trial without a personal coach, either in the training department or through the group-exercise program.

If the guest was in good shape, he might be given permission to enter a group personal training session, which should be known as the club's most challenging workout option.

This type of program should be one of the many different reflections of your training philosophy that separates you from the others in your market. This type

of training should be one of your strongest differentiators, because of the challenge it offers, but more importantly, you can now offer training to a much wider range of people than any other competitor due to the shift toward the group experience. The more people you touch with correct training, the more people will stay longer and pay longer. This type of training demonstrates service during the trial, but also drives results once the person is a member.

Guests who prefer group exercise are channeled there for the duration of their trial membership.

There is a key number to remember in this process. If you have 100 guests during a typical month using this system, about 20 percent will just want to be left alone and do their own thing, even if we know that it is wrong and ugly. The other 80 percent, however, will get channeled into your programs that involve a guide or coach, such as group exercise and the personal training department.

Remember that if a member has a relationship with the club, through his coaches, then he will stay in the system longer than people who just go around in circles on the machines. This rule also applies to our potential members. You are far more likely to convert a guest into a real member if their only experience in your business for a full 30 days was under the direction of a fitness expert of some type.

Any guest who becomes a member during his first visit would be given a 30-day Full-Access Coaching Pass.

These types of members should represent about 30 percent of your new sales and are usually direct referrals or "buddy sales." These new folks are presold into your business due to a relationship with a member, or because of your reputation in the market. Keep these new members from getting lost by giving them a Full-Access Coaching Pass that gives them entry into the semi-privates and group personal training for a 30-day period after enrollment as a member. Make this pass special, and oversize it at 4x5 inches. This pass allows your new members who haven't joined through the trial program to still experience the same help and support that is the basis for your service, as well as giving the club's sales team a chance to upsell the new member into a higher-priced coaching program.

Changing From the Culture of Failure to the Culture of Success

Don't forget that in most fitness businesses, the member never had a chance. If we admitted that is the way of life in most fitness businesses, the owners and managers who run these facilities might seek change that would lead to switching from a total culture of failure to one of success. If our goal is to change lives, then everything we do in the business has to be designed to help our members be successful in chasing their fitness goals.

The culture of failure, however, is so embedded in the present fitness environment that most of the owners and operators just take what they are doing as commonly accepted business practices. Actually, we are in the business of selling memberships, not in the business of support and service.

We run price-driven advertising that puts the emphasis on a one-visit sales encounter. We pressure during the first visit, even though the guest might not have been in a fitness business during the last 10 years, because the goal is the membership, not service or to gently get someone into the club so we can help him be successful.

If some brave soul does sign up, we restrict the real information he needs, only available through trainers, to an elite few. The member becomes a sales statistic for the month, and the club's team moves on to hunt for other prospects to feed the sales machine.

Our members are on their own and often ignored by the counter staff and the trainers. If someone accidently loses weight and gets in shape at most gyms, it is probably due more to a random act of divine intervention than it is due to the club's efforts on behalf of the member.

Do These Things Now

- Build your future business around creating a culture of success.

- Examine everything you do to see if you are inadvertently creating a system of failure in your club that could be hurting your sales and retention.

- Trial memberships are a base tool you can use to start changing the perception of failure into success with your potential members in the market.

- Create a membership system that has many layers and options where everyone who wants help can get it at some price level.

- Learn that the traditional one-on-one system limits any help you can give your members and guests.

- Build your new system around a much wider range of potential business that exists in the market.

Customer service is as simple as ...

eliminating clutter.

Clutter is just another form of being dirty in the member's mind.

To you, it is a broken piece of equipment in the corner that was forgotten for a few months. In the member's mind, it is junk and sends the message that this club is really kind of dirty and full of stuff that doesn't work anymore.

Everyone that works in a club becomes club blind. This means that because you spend so many hours in the club, you stop seeing it as it really is. Clutter piles up, but we fail to notice because it just didn't appear magically all at once; the stuff just insidiously grows and grows over time, one layer at a time, until you have major piles of crap that no one on the staff even notices.

The worst offending areas in the club are all the group rooms, the edges of the workout areas (such as under the dumbbell racks), and the front counters. These are the areas that either get high traffic, such as the counter, or are forgotten because no one on the management team has looked in these spaces in months.

The rule is simple: Clutter offends your members because they associate the clutter with being disgustingly dirty. You have to thoroughly clean your club quarterly with the single-most thought in your mind of throwing everything out that is not being currently used.

Quarterly is a good practice to get into because if you haven't used it since the last cleaning, or if the piece of whatever is still sitting in the same spot as it was last quarter, toss it. Don't worry about going too far, and if you are going to err then do it on the too-clean side.

Customer service is clean, but no matter how clean your club really is, if it is cluttered, then it is dirty in the member's mind.

12

The Fortress of Customer Service

Every guest, every member, every transaction, and every daily visit all revolve around the front counter. Yet, almost every front counter kid in the world is too young, too undertrained, and often too dumb (proven by the fact that he was hired simply because he was available and could do that shift, and not because of his overwhelming skill set) to create any type of positive service experience that helps build the club's brand.

Even the typical front counter design itself works against your business. Most are cheaply made, too narrow, too high, and a cluttered mess that looks like your grandmother is having a yard sale of mostly leftover junk that the staff keeps moving around to find room to add more junk. No one ever throws anything away at the front desk, because no one ever uses the unidentifiable garbage that is lying there. Since no one is really sure if you can live without these piles of unidentifiable crap, every year more clutter accumulates, giving the counter a worse look.

Your front counter is your fortress of customer service. The counter is where you touch the most souls on a daily basis. The counter is also where most membership sales are really made—not in the sales offices as you are led to believe by the sales teams.

Good service at the front desk keeps your retention numbers higher and your sales closing percentage stronger because your members are paying for the personal, caring touch that can only be consistently delivered by the counter people, who are the ones who come into contact with the largest number of members per day.

Start Your Quest for Better Service at the Front Counter

Believing in something and then carrying it out are two different things. For example, most owners believe in doing the right things for the members, but those beliefs are never translated into reality, because there is a breakdown between the top of the organization and workers who have to carry out the mission.

The pyramid model is a perfect example of why the industry has such a terrible customer-service reputation. Think of a typical drawing of a pyramid. It has a wide base and tapers toward a point at the top.

If you place the owners and managers at the top, and the club's workers at the bottom, the problem of delivering customer service in a busy fitness center becomes more obvious. If you want to hammer the point home even more, take your pyramid and sit it upon an even wider base of the members.

Management
The workers in the club
The members in the club

This pyramid represents the makeup of a typical fitness organization. There are a lot of members, a lesser number of workers to take care of them, and at the top, a few managers who are supposed to provide leadership for the workers, which are really the only club staff who are actually in daily contact with the largest number of members.

If you step back and take a hard look at this pyramid model, you will also notice that the slightly narrower band of workers separates the members from the owners and managers. This is important to note since that barrier actually operates as a filtering system. Members interact with the workers, and the workers decide what to pass up to the management team.

It also works the other way, too. The management team states loudly, "We believe in customer service," but it is really up to the workers, who are the only ones who are in daily contact with the bulk of the members, to carry out that edict.

What does this mean to your business? It means that no matter what you believe as an owner, it is the knucklehead at the front counter—who you desperately hired to fill a hole left by an employee who simply disappeared, and who has about two hours of training—who is now the face of customer service for your $2,000,000 investment in this club.

No matter how you feel the customer should be treated, the new guy who just turned his back on a customer to answer his personal cell phone is the guy destroying your brand, member by member. You filled the job and got the coverage, but you're also killing your business slowly through one poor interaction at a time.

The counter people are the most important people in the club. They are your brand. They determine how hard the sale will be for the sales team, because they were the first to meet and greet and were the ones who formed the first impression of the guest.

They also determine your retention rate due to the level of service they provide, which can go up and down throughout the year, depending on the quality and training of that counter staff.

This group of staff also strongly affects your daily cash flow because it is up to them to get the members interested in what the club has to sell, and even a simple, "Hey, did you notice that your favorite bar is on sale by the box today?" can add to your bottom line significantly throughout a full year of business.

Who Is the Perfect Counter Person?

Sit in a chair, and close your eyes. Now purge every worthless counter person you have ever had from your mind. If you were hiring today, who would be the model staff person you are looking for in your business that in reality is the single-most-important cog in your customer-service machine?

Most owners that play this game seldom come up with a model that matches the people they actually have working in their business. This is a lot like some woman sitting on the beach in the sun, dreaming of some movie-star hunk and then opening her eyes to find her 30 pounds overweight and slightly drunk husband sitting in a Speedo® next to her. There is fantasy, and then there is the harsh reality of what you really own. For some reason, we dream of getting the talented staff we need to deliver great service, but we still keep hiring the same old bunch of dummies over and over again.

But if we can imagine the perfect model, then we can find and train the perfect model. These points are at least a starting point in our quest for counter perfection:

- Confident with great communication skills

- Can multitask

- Dependable

- Professional presentation and dress

- Interested in fitness and working out

- Has a prior work history that includes customer-service experience

- No fear of asking for money

You Have to Have Adults to
Deliver Real Customer Service

Most of the owners who look at this list would say, "Yeah, that would be nice to hire someone with all these traits, but in my market you just can't find those people..."

The unspoken finish to that sentence should read "...can't find those people for what I pay." This person is out there, but they won't work for what you are willing to pay. You pay peanuts, you get monkeys, and monkeys can be trained to do tricks, but monkeys can't be trained to solve the level of problems you would encounter in a typical fitness business.

McDonald's has mastered the *art of perceived customer service*. This company has, through the development of tight and extremely structured systems, managed to take an endless variety of employees and turn them all into a unit that gives the impression you as the customer are receiving customer service.

The kid stands behind the register dressed in his uniform, where he is told to stand for his first four hours of his shift. The uniform might be so last century, but there is power in your team dressing as a unit, and these uniforms also take the decision-making issue of "What should I wear to work today?" out of the equation, which is good for young males who have trouble dressing themselves. Everyone looks the same, and everyone looks professional in a uniform.

This young guy working the register says hello and welcomes you to McDonald's and then asks: "May I take your order?" You choose, he says "Thank you," the order is electronically placed, and a few minutes later your food pops up on a tray. You are thanked again, and as you walk to your table, you mumble to yourself, "That was quick and easy." We now equate quick and painless with customer service.

The kid was nice, because he was taught exactly what to say and how to say it (anybody see the monkey and the trick analogy?). The service was quick because the technology behind that simple burger, despised as the enemy of health and fitness by everyone who has ever worked in the fitness industry, allows a quick delivery system. You ordered questionable food from a trained kid, and it appeared moments later, forcing us to now equate speed and a simple thank you with customer service.

On the other hand, hotels—such as the Arizona Biltmore—have mastered the *art of true customer service*. The hotel does have great systems, but the people who work at the hotel understand their roles in the company, and more importantly, how to deliver true service. For example, this particular hotel is somewhat sprawling with a number of buildings surrounding a very large central courtyard. The hotel was a Frank Lloyd Wright project, and in many ways might be one of the most beautiful hotel properties in the country.

Because the guests are housed in different buildings all around the property, there is a certain amount of walking that has to happen to get to any meetings, which are held in the hotel's main building, or in the small convention center on the outer edge of everything else.

A female in her 50s was struggling with an armload of brochures, a giant purse, and a briefcase down a walkway, heading to a morning meeting. Seconds before she dropped everything and probably ruined her day, a groundskeeper who barely spoke English dropped his gardening gear and ran over to help her. He smiled big, gave her a slight bow of his head, and then gently took all the brochures from her. She tried to get reorganized and take them back, but he kept saying, "Please, please, no" and nodded with his head for her to keep going.

He followed her to her meeting, refused a tip, and hustled all the way back to the job he was working on. It turned out that he was also a supervisor in the grounds department at the hotel. He returned to the job he was working on, picked up his tools, and continued as if that extraordinary service he just delivered was something he did every day, which he probably did and considered that help a routine part of his job.

Who trained this guy? Who had the sophistication in service training to spend time with a gardener supervisor and teach him that helping a guest was part of his job, even though he probably only knew basic English? This situation was not part of his normal day and was something that would be very hard to systemize in his training. In essence, he had to solve the problem and weigh what he was doing at the moment as his real job in contrast with helping a guest who was having difficulties. How did he know that the guest was the most important thing at the moment and the guest's experience was the choice he had to make?

The difference between the kid at McDonald's and the worker in Arizona is that one company builds systems that give a perception of service, while the other company creates employees that understand the true purpose of customer service, which is to ensure that everyone who works there will do everything possible to make sure the guest has a legendary experience during their stay.

The other big difference is that the fast-food kid is taught to fill a role, but he isn't really taught to solve problems. Solving problems is the role of the manager, and they do it well at McDonald's, which is probably why they are the kings of the fast-food nation. The front-line kids that make everything happen are really interchangeable, which is the strength of their system, but also creates kind of a mind-numbing service experience. Walk into any of their restaurants, get in line, and the procedures are always the same, and in this case, the sameness is what sells and builds the brand.

Where we go wrong in this industry is that we don't understand that we need both of these service systems to be legendary, because the dollar amount of the transaction in our industry is simply so much higher. We will tolerate quick and impersonal for a $3 meal, but the expectation of what constitutes good service changes when the cost increases.

In this industry, we need to develop systems, such as thanking every person every time he leaves the club after a workout, but we also need to hire people and teach them problem-solving skills that can be handled at the front-line level and not always by a manager.

Our failing is that we hire kids, undertrain them in the mastery of even the most basic systems, and then also expect them to handle the literally dozens of problems a typical front counter person might be overrun with during a shift.

For example, members on any given shift might lock their keys in their car, have a payment problem on their membership, hurt themselves on the floor, need to sign up for training, and want to renew their membership. Some of these require simple systems that can be duplicated each time, but others on the list require the person to solve a problem and to help the member in front of them now.

This is why we only seek adults to represent our businesses.

The false assumption involved with hiring front counter people is that cheaper pay is better for the business. But what if the front counter person really is one of the most important people in the club due to the sheer number of people he touches throughout a typical day?

In most markets, the difference between a kid at the counter and a reasonable adult with some common sense and basic customer-service skills is only about two dollars an hour. Two dollars an hour over a month's period of time works out to be about $336 difference in pay (40 hours x $2 x 4.2 weeks in a typical month), or the price of a cheap membership.

The accountant model of running a business suggests that front counter people are just simple fillers that keep the place open, do basic grunt work, and are totally interchangeable. The people beyond the counter, such as the managers, salespeople, and trainers, do the real work in this model. You have to have counter people, but they are merely mindless idiots that come and go throughout the year.

On the other hand is the customer-service model. This model is based upon the belief that the people who have the largest amount of contact with your clients are the ones that are the most important in the organization.

For example, a membership sale is much easier if your front counter staff was warm and friendly and created a powerful first impression for your guest, as opposed to a salesperson who has to overcome a rude counter person who ignored the guest or who simply grunted and just sat the guest in a chair in the corner until the sales guy arrived. In this example, the trained and courteous counter person might have actually made the sale for the club, and the rude, poorly trained counter person might have cost the club the sale.

The simple rule is to buy adults and recognize that every single person who enters your club as a member or guest has to run the front counter gauntlet. Keeping that in mind, who do you want representing your business and affecting the retention of every member you own, as well as having a direct effect on the sales effort of your team?

Stop thinking of counter people as fillers, and start thinking of them as the most important people you have representing your company. Another scary way to think about it is that your brand is only as good as the dumbest person on your staff because he pulls everyone down to his level instead of everyone else on the team pulling his image up to theirs.

The Basics Behind Developing an Effective Service Counter

You don't make money in offices; you make money at the front counter and on the floor. Even the salespeople perform better if you take the offices away and give them tall cafe tables near the front counter, or on the edge of the workout floor. Keeping potential members in the environment that excites and inspires them is more effective than taking them to an office and out of the action.

You have to change your thoughts about what the front counter is and how it operates. The old thought process was that the counter was a throwaway that could be done cheaply and all the real money had to be saved for the equipment in the back of the club.

When the new generation of club architects and theorists, such as Rudy Fabiano, began to explore the possibilities of fusing fitness with entertainment, and with a touch of upscale service, the old model was replaced with that of a more modern upscale hotel presence. In nice hotels, the front counter is really their centerpiece of customer service. These counters are staffed with the best and brightest they have because the bulk of the customer-service experience for the guest is going to be determined by how well these people do their jobs.

But the counter itself has to be a tool that supports customer service. Most fitness centers in the past have built counters that are totally contradictory to the customer-service experience. These counters were too cheaply made, giving a bad first impression, often too high, and many times resembled a highly protective walled environment meant to protect the club from armed invaders instead of a tool to aid in the delivery of customer service.

There are a few basics you might consider when it comes to building a service-centered counter. When you rebuild your counter area in your mind, and then in reality, hold the thought that the only purpose for this counter to exist is to aid in the creation of legendary customer service.

The First Impression Is Everything

Once that door opens, the counter should beckon the guest or member as an island of warmth and service. Most clubs almost bury the counter, and often it is somewhat hard to see exactly where you need to go when you first walk into the door. Following are a few points that might help you build a functional service counter:

- Keep the pathways to the counter clear and open. The counter should be an obvious first destination as soon as someone walks through your door.

- Kill clutter. Members think clutter is just another form of dirt. There should be *nothing* on the top of the service counter. This means you have to get rid of all your boxes of credit-card applications, candy for sale for charity, open boxes of munchie bars (they should have their own rack), sales information, sign-up sheets, and anything else that gives the impression that is this is a tired and dirty club.

- Check the height of your counter. Ideal height for a counter is 42 inches, but you also want a lower section on the end where two people can sit in chairs on the member side, and a staff person can sit in a chair on the other. Sometimes, simple customer-service issues can be handled outside an office; but you don't want people to just stand there while you are taking care of their problems.

- Lower the ceiling over the front counter when you can. This doesn't always work, but sometimes it does help to lower the huge expanse most clubs have over their entry areas and compress that space into something more intimate and warm. If you do this, use incandescent lighting (warm bulb lighting of some type) to give the area a more inviting appeal.

- If you are doing a sports bar/juice bar area, always combine it into your front counter. Sports bars work when they become people-watching spots. Keep the check-in on one side and put the people on the other side or end. It is fun for the members to sit and drink a recovery shake while seeing who is working out that day. Add a number of televisions, which are a cheap visual, to the bar as well. A key note here is that the televisions should be set with the bottom edge at seven feet off the floor. Most people put the televisions too high, which makes watching them difficult. You want people to sit and spend money at your bar, and the longer they sit, the more they will spend.

- Get a large check-in screen, and tilt it so both the member and the staff can see the check-in. Most good check-in systems flash the name as the member runs his card through, allowing the staff to see the name and use it as he greets the member.

Teach Two Key Techniques to Your Counter Staff to Help Them Be a Positive Part of the Sales Effort

There is a lot that can be taught to the counter people to help the sales people get better numbers. Out of all the things they can learn, however, are two key items that should be taught early in the development of anyone who is working the front counter on a regular basis. These two techniques are:

- You have to develop a waiting policy.

- You have to script out and practice a handoff strategy for the counter people to use when they transfer a potential member to a salesperson.

The Waiting Policy

If a potential member, or a regular member that is waiting for someone on the management team to help him with a service issue, has to wait for five minutes or longer, then an automatic waiting policy should kick in.

> *Thank you for waiting, David, but the person you need to see to show you the club will be tied up for about five more minutes. While you wait, may I buy you a bottle of water, or would you like to try one of our smoothies?*

Don't overthink this policy. It exists as a simple way to show respect for the person's time, and the policy itself should be something that can be taught to the staff in a brief, one-hour-or-less staff training. Following are the basics you would want to include:

- If the person has to wait for more than five minutes, the staff person at the front counter has permission to buy the guest or member a drink.

- Create a special account the staff can use to track these in the club's point-of-sale system designated as the special manager's account.

- Always be courteous, and apologize for the wait.

- Make sure the person is not left standing at the counter. Move him to a seat at the smoothie bar or at a table where he will be comfortable during his wait.

The Handoff From the Counter to Sales

The handoff is another scripted tool designed to highlight the club's customer service. You want to show off a little, and you want to give a completely different first impression and service experience than your competitors. We actually hope that a potential member visited a competitor first so you have a chance to contrast just how good your people are and how different the person will be treated as a member with your club.

Customer service is a powerful tool once you understand how it affects your business. You can have a mediocre club in programming and equipment and still survive if you put more training into your people. Service training is the hardest thing for a competitor to take away from you in your market. If you have good people who are well-trained, you can take on almost anyone, but most owners simply won't do the work it takes to build a legendary staff.

The handoff is just a tool that shows we are polite and that the experience in our club is different. If your salesperson is busy and the guest has to wait, then the handoff script would be used when the salesperson does arrive to meet his guest. Again, this technique can be scripted and should be memorized by your entire counter staff, then practiced with your sales team.

In this scenario, Sylvie is the front counter person and Matt is the club's salesperson. John, the potential member, has been waiting for a few minutes for Matt to finish something in his office and to get to the front counter. As Matt approaches, Sylvie executes the handoff:

> *Hi Matt. I would like to introduce John to you. He is here to get some information about the club. John, this is Matt. He is the best person in the club to help you with getting some membership information. By the way, John, it was a pleasure to meet you.*

> *Again, my name is Sylvie, and if you need any help in the club please come find me. I am usually here during the evenings, and you can almost always find me here at the front counter. Thank you for coming in, and we look forward to having you as a member.*

This would be one of those core fundamentals anyone working at the counter needs to know. Practice this at least weekly with anyone who might have to do it in the club as part of their normal routine.

If You Do Nothing Else, Put More Time and Effort Into Your Front Counter

If you do nothing else in this book, put whatever effort you can into creating a better front counter experience. Design and build a service-friendly front counter, staff it with adults who have great communication skills, and then train your staff with at least these five things that are mentioned several other places in the book:

- Greet the person warmly with a strong opening statement, such as "Welcome, we're having a great day at the Workout Company."

- Use the person's name whenever possible. Cheat if you have to by getting a software system that displays the name as they check in each day.

- Thank every member every time that person leaves the club.

- Develop a waiting policy that demonstrates respect for a person's time.

- Practice the handoff so you can set the salesperson up for a more successful sales encounter.

- These five things are more than most clubs in the country do, and just these alone will set you apart from your competitors.

Do These Things Now

- Start your quest for customer service by putting your first effort into your front counter team.

- Stop hiring cheap kids for the counter, and replace them with adults who can deliver service and help your business grow.

- Take a fresh look at the structure of your counter. First impressions are everything. How does your counter hold up under a severe look?

- Teach your team a waiting policy and a handoff strategy for guests.

Customer service is as simple as …

giving back.

There is an old saying that your parents have probably used on you at least a few times in your life: "The world does not owe you a living."

This line was probably paraded out when you were complaining and moaning about how unfair it was that you had to cut lawns for spending money or had to put on a silly fast-food uniform and head off to work when you were 15.

The lesson, of course, is that you get out of life what you put into it, and the sense of entitlement many people occasionally feel doesn't really match how it works in the real world.

Sadly, many club owners feel this way. They borrow money from their parents, put years of dreams into building their first club, and actually get mad when the community doesn't respond by showing up by the thousands to become members.

These same owners become even angrier when competitors open near them and start to take away what business they have. Most of these owners are lousy owners and never do figure out the business. They simply won't do the work necessary to grow the business. Many fail because they just can't believe that others can't see their dream as they do. Being in business gives you the right to compete, not the right to be successful.

One lesson to learn is that you have to have the support of the community you live in to be successful. You want, you want, but what do you give back to the people in the market who you depend on to survive?

Become involved in a charity. Work with kids who can't afford fitness. Send trainers to the local old-folks home to help get fitness programs going. Do something besides being just a taker. Give back to your community, and they will give back to you.

13

Ring, Ring, Ring—You're Already Too Late for Customer Service

Nothing upsets people more than bad service on the phone.

Adults smash their cell phones on the floor. People put on perpetual hold, waiting for the next available agent, scream at people who aren't even there. Otherwise rational adults spray spit in anger when they talk because they are trapped in voice-mail hell. Nothing represents poor service more strongly, or can give a business the golden perception of legendary service, as how that business handles the telephone calls it receives.

Customer Service on the Phone Is Not a Random Occurrence Left to the Discretion of Your Staff

The business telephone is still the initial contact and first impression for so many of your potential clients who have yet to set foot in your business. Someone interested in fitness might get online and look up clubs in their area, or the person might receive your advertisement with your phone number and call.

For the duration of that brief interaction between a caller seeking information and a member of your staff, that phone call is the sole representation of your customer service and brand. The caller has nothing else to judge you on except the quality of that call and how he is treated. He also will decide from the outcome of that call if he wants to take the next step and come and see the club in person. If you get a lot of calls, but few actual leads in the club, then the quality of your phone technique and service is very poor.

But this service also extends to your existing membership, as well. Once someone becomes a member, he now has a relationship with your business and his expectation of service is now elevated. This increased level of anticipated service, as noted previously, is not always perceived as equal with higher expectations on the side of the member.

The club management often loses sight of the individual member, while this same member, who just sent his payment in for $49, feels he is paying a lot of money, and, therefore, deserves a lot of respect and service when he calls. If this same member calls in for information about a class or program, how that call is handled is often a major factor in whether that member might renew in the future. If you don't appreciate my business now, then I will take it somewhere else to people who do when I am done with my membership here.

Keep this member on hold, or act like you are angry because you are busy and feel put out by having to provide information by phone that the guy could have easily gotten on the website, and the member will remember this when it is time to renew or pay his next membership payment.

On the other hand, a courteous call that is respectful of the member, who, if you remember, is the one that helps pay all the club's bills each month, could just as easily lead to a happy member who will renew or even bring a referral in the future. Good service is contagious in a positive way, but lousy service is a life-threatening disease that is often fatal to the business over time.

Clubs have to also look at phone training as an investment. Typical fitness businesses might spend $3000 to $7000 per month in marketing dollars to get the phone to ring with inquiring members and then waste every dollar of that amount because the club owner and managers failed to train the front counter people in the proper etiquette of phone service and in how to properly hand off the phone inquiries to the club's sales team. Money spent in training your counter staff is really money invested in your sales-acquisition efforts and member retention and might be the most important training you can do with your staff each month.

Start Your Phone Training With the Rules of Phone Etiquette

There are probably only about 12 people left on the planet under the age of 30 who haven't grown up with cell phones and advanced computing skills. These 12 are monks locked in a cave and are waiting for the end of the world, still linked to the outside world through old-fashioned landline phones, fax machines, and answering machines. The world has passed them by while everyone else has gone totally electronic.

The downside of this is that most of our employees in this industry are under 30. They spend their days text messaging or by sending out brief, coded messages through the social networks. Everything is brief, shortened to key code words, and a entire conversation between two 20-something people might consist of five real words, seven grunts, a couple of "LOLs," and a :) at the end. These might be short, effective calls, but they are hardly the kind of tool that is transferrable to the real business world, especially when these people are now in charge of answering your business phone.

When you hire anyone, no matter what their age, always assume that they have never seen a phone before in their life, and start with the absolute basics of telephone etiquette. Remember:

Good service is nothing more than a series of basics mastered by your staff to a point that the customer never recognizes the techniques.

Following are the easily taught rules of mastering the business phone. You have to role-play these obsessively to get your staff to come across as natural. If you can't find the time and energy to train your people, simply remember that every time a staff person messes up an inquiry phone call, it probably costs you about $500.

If that isn't motivation enough to spend about two hours a week, which is what you should dedicate to phone training with your entire staff, but especially with your front counter team, then try flushing a $100 bill down the toilet, and remember that bad phone service to your existing members by that undertrained staff of yours is flushing these like you were making them on your color copier.

Phone Etiquette Made Simple

- You always have to answer the phone by the third ring. That is money calling on the other end. Respect that money by answering quickly.

- Answer live. Do not ever, and it means never, let something electronic replace real customer service. Answer live and within three rings. The people on the other end of that phone are trying to give you money, or are people who have already spent money with you, and will continue to do so in the future, if you treat them with courtesy and respect. Voice-mail hell is not customer service; it is something to be endured because you have no choice, such as a root canal or colonoscopy.

- Always use a strong opening statement: "Hello, we're having a great day at the Workout Company." Make it quick, a little loud, and with a lot of energy. Skip the traditional "Hello, thank you for calling the Workout Company. This is Sarah, how may I help you today?" By the time the counter person has gotten all of that out of her mouth, the caller has fallen asleep, face down on his desk.

- Thank every inquiry when he first calls and again at the end of the call. The person had a choice and could have called any of your competitors, but he decided to call you. Be grateful for the call, thank him for checking out your business, and maybe your club will be the last one he calls that day.

- Develop a professional screening system for your team. The worst insult for a caller is when you ask, "Who is this? Okay, let me see if he is in." What this really means, and everyone in the world knows it, is "Let me see if he wants to talk to you." Teach everyone the same simple screen that gets the job done as well as sets a minimum expectation of customer service: "He is with a member at the moment. May I take a message, please?"

- Get in the habit of returning all calls at a set time each day. This is professional, and gives the caller an idea of when they might expect to hear from you. For example, "Matt is not available at the moment. He is with a member. May I take a message, please? Matt usually returns all phone calls between 1:00 and 2:00 each afternoon, so what is the best number for Matt to reach you at that time?"

- Call everyone back, even if the answer is a definite "No." It is a professional habit to develop early in your career that will serve you well through the years. Even if the call is from a salesperson, call and just say, "No, thank you, for now, but I appreciate your interest, and if I ever need your service in the future, I will certainly call you." Quick and polite, and then get off the phone, but you did handle it professionally, which is what you want from the people that you have to call during your workday. Treat other people as you would want to be treated.

- Absolutely no gum is ever allowed in the gym for any member of the staff. Smacking, chomping, rolling it around in your mouth, and chewing with your mouth half open is disgusting in a business environment. You are not a cow; you are a human being. Get some strong mints, and get over it.

- If you have to put someone on hold, and you will in the course of a busy day, always ask permission, and then wait for the person to respond before clicking him off.

- Develop a short, key-person list that is kept displayed behind the counter for the staff to use. Sometimes, there are people you need to talk to when they call, such as your accountant and banker, or perhaps you're in the middle of a construction project, and you just need to be available to certain people involved in the project. Keep a list in writing by the main business phones, and teach your staff how to handle those calls as well. For example, "Matt is with a member right at the moment. May I take a message? Oh, hello, Mr. Parker. Matt said he would like to talk to you when you called. May I put you on hold and see if I can interrupt him? Thank you, I will be back with you shortly." These are simple statements that any staff person can learn if you practice and role-play enough. Your brand image is on the line here; what kind of impression do you really want to leave with the caller?

Phone etiquette is nothing more than common courtesy with the intent of showing a little respect for your caller. But no one understands how to do this anymore because no one teaches this anymore except the really good hotel chains and some retail stores.

Courtesy is a lost art that has to be taught to everyone on your staff. The good news is that most of your staff people really want to do the right thing if given a chance, but most of them simply don't have the tools and never had anyone in their life show them the basics of being nice and respectful to the paying guest. If someone is paying you to be a member, or is trying to give you money as a potential member, be nice and courteous, or he will simply give his money to someone else.

IT Stock

Don't Forget the Power of
the Phone to Help Drive Sales

We have been taught in this industry for years that it is the salespeople who can make or break a fitness business. Most of the major chains, and many of the independents ran by the old sales dogs or chain guys, stack the club staff according to that belief with a load of talent at the top and nothing but warm bodies at the bottom.

The salespeople on these teams get the most training, get the most promotions, and are the stars of the club. The counter people, on the other hand, are usually the youngest and cheapest that can be hired, and as mentioned in Chapter 12, are just young faces that are expendable in most clubs with no real bearing on the club's business.

In today's market, with a much more sophisticated buyer and member, the opposite of this is probably closer to the real truth these days. Sales is a team effort where everything counts, and the salesperson is just one of many who work together to create new business for the club.

In an unscientific survey, but worth noting due to the fact that it included over 100 different members from five different clubs, over 50 percent of those members surveyed, when asked what the single biggest factor in their decision to join this club was, stated: "I really like the people here."

It is documented that the first thing people look for in a club is convenience to their home. But members do make calls to a few target clubs first and might visit several before deciding which one is best for them. It almost always starts with a call, and whoever takes that initial call, even if he passes it on to the club's salesperson, is part of the sales team whether you recognize it or not.

Keeping the fact in mind that someone is out there trying to spend money, what kind of first impression do you want to make in person when someone visits your club, or on the phone during an inquiry? Do you really want to just leave it all up to your salesperson and hope he is having a good day and can overcome the bad first impression made by your undertrained counter person who handled the initial inquiry so poorly before she even passed it off to the salesperson?

Imagine calling for membership information, or walking into a competitor's club and hearing or seeing any of these things, which are all actual incidents from someone trying to get membership information from clubs around the country during a three-month period:

- A counter person talking on his cell phone as he checked people in and then waved the guest toward a clipboard and guest inquiry sheet. He never said a word to the guest; he just waved and pointed with his free hand.

- During the inquiry call, a somewhat stressed counter person put the phone down on the counter, but didn't put it on hold and then yelled, "Hey, Billy, there is some dumb-ass on the phone that wants membership information. Doesn't this guy know we close in five minutes?"

- A counter person at a $16-million non-profit said that she would be happy to show the guest around, handed over a brochure, and then gave a room-by-room tour. If you called this club to get information, you weren't invited in to see it initially, but instead the counter person asked for your address and then sent you a three-fold brochure you could have first before you made up your mind if you even wanted to see the club.

- Two counter people were at the end of the check-in counter, talking to a small group of members. As the guest stood waiting, one of them broke free from the group and wandered over, stating, "Yeah, what can I do for you? Oh, a membership? Wait here, and let me see if I can find Danny. He was eating lunch in the back. Hang on for a moment, and I'll check." He left the guest just standing at the counter while he searched the club for the missing Danny.

- A counter person dressed in almost Friday-night party clothes because the owner never told her that bare midriff and tight jeans aren't business attire.

- Trainers standing behind the counter eating out of Tupperware® while supposedly covering for the counter person, who was on break. The phone rings, and the trainer takes the call while still shoveling in rice and chicken at the same time.

- No one at all behind the counter, and after 10 minutes a person walked through the door, carrying a sandwich bag, and said, "Hey, you been waiting long?"

- Wrinkled, scruffy people in tee shirts and jeans working the counter of a $4-million national franchise gym and answering the phone with less than an hour of actual service training.

This list could go on and on, but the point is that all of this negative-image behavior works against your business. These people don't help your sales team; your sales team has to overcome the negative first impression the potential member has from trying to get through this madness.

If you think about it, how desperate is that potential member who gets abused on the phone first and still shows up at the club. This could only happen in a market where there is only one club, since no one given choices would choose a business that starts the relationship by treating the potential client so badly.

Based upon what not to do, when you build a service club, remember:

Everything counts when you try to build
a brand in a competitive market.

The counter people, the counter area, and especially the phones, are part of your sales effort. When a potential member arrives at the club to inquire about a membership, you have to control every aspect of the sales experience.

How to Practice Delivering Good Customer Service Over the Phone

The phone rings every day, so you practice every day. You never know when the next call might be a potential member, or a regular member who is upset and who you need to save with a little customer service.

The phone is the first line of first impressions, and you have to make phone training first and foremost in your thought process. Following are a few training tips you can apply immediately to your business. Don't wait; train now, and if you don't know how to do it, then do it anyway, and you will get better with time:

- Train for at least two four-hour blocks spread over two weeks when you first introduce phone training. Wear your staff out when you first introduce the concept of phone service with the intent of erring on the overkill side. There isn't much else in your business more important than mastering the phone with the plan that all training leads to increasing sales and retention.

- Once you lay the foundation during the first two weeks, then train for one to two hours per week forever. There is no such thing as overtrained on the phone.

- When you practice phone techniques, get some old phones to use as props, and make sure the staff sits back-to-back during their training. If you can see each other's face, you can pick up cues that would not be available in a real calling situation.

- Script out everything, and put it into the staff's training manuals. Write down exactly what you want them to say, and practice the scripts. Do not let the staff do their own version of the scripts, which many try to do if you don't enforce what they are learning: "That doesn't sound right to me, so I'll just do it this way." Throw this person out of your club. She is poison and it isn't far from doing her own thing to going all the way back to just making up whatever sounds good at the time. Service is not random; service is systems based upon a series of basics that can be taught.

- Consider taping calls. The technology is getting so much easier to do this today, but you do have to state on the phone in a prerecorded message that this call might be taped for training purposes. There is nothing more powerful as a learning tool than to think you are the master of what you do and then have to listen to a recording that shows you are the phone fool.

Phone training should be one of the first things we teach the staff, not one of the last. Because the phone is taken for granted as just a part of our daily existence, coupled with the fact that most people live with a phone stuck to the side of their head every day, we don't really think we need to train people on something most of our staff is doing on their own four or five a hours a day.

Everything counts in building a legendary business, and the phone is often the first think a potential member encounters when considering your business.

Do These Things Now

- Start combat phone training for your entire staff immediately.

- Start your training with the rules of phone etiquette.

- Always answer the phone within three rings.

- Always answer the phone live.

- Train for at least two four-hour sessions when you first start your training, erring on the "too much is a good thing" concept.

- Practice the phone with the counter people at least one hour per week for the rest of your life.

- Script out everything you want said, and practice from the scripts.

Customer service is as simple as ...
                    the perfect training session.

Trainers lose track of who is paying whom to work out.

Most schedule back-to-back sessions, but don't manage their time in these sessions very well. They start a session late and then run over on the next one. The paying training client shows up on time for his service, but ends up warming himself up on a treadmill, waiting for his turn with the trainer. All of this is terrible service and directly reflects on your image in the market.

There are several key things you must change if you want to deliver the maximum service possible in your training department. Listed are a few important ones you can start with:

- *The maximum length of any session is 50 minutes. If the trainer can't get it done in 50 minutes, get new trainers. Don't sell sessions as an hour; sell them as sessions up to 50 minutes maximum, depending on the shape and condition of the client.*

- *Eliminate 30-minute sessions. You can't provide service in a 30-minute session that really takes the trainer 40 to do anyway, which is one reason they all run over so often.*

- *You cannot warm someone up on a treadmill. You are getting the person warm, but you aren't getting the muscles he will use loose. The treadmill warm-up isn't effective, and isn't service. Everyone should do some form of trainer-led dynamic warm-up. You sell leadership, and treadmills don't provide leadership.*

- *Start every training client at the sports bar. Tell him what you are going to do to him today.*

- *Do it to him. Take him through his workout.*

- *Take him back to the sports bar at the end of the session, and tell him what you did to him. Most importantly, tell him what he will be doing next session based upon the results of this one. Build continuity into all of your sessions.*

- *People are paying extra for these services in your club. Appreciate the business, and treat the paying member with respect. Put the show on, and make the trainers do the work they are paid for instead of relying on a treadmill to provide the service.*

14

Greet Every Member With a Strong Welcome Statement

Everyone has a place in his life that is his home-away-from-home. It might be the neighborhood coffee shop, where they shout out your drink before you even get to the counter, your favorite restaurant with your table, or a quiet bar you hit on the way home just to sit and wind down before hitting the rituals of home that you know await.

These places all have one thing in common: each one gives us the feeling that we belong and that we are surrounded by people who recognize us and who appreciate us for being part of their business. These places add value to our lives and are often cherished as something very important to us because these places become sanctuaries where we can retreat for a while and get away from all that is demanding and stressful in our lives.

People want to feel this way about their club, but often the owners and staff deny this to the members by the way they choose to operate and train their staff. The people who join a club are seekers, not only looking for a place to pursue their fitness journey, but also a place where they can belong and be part of a larger community searching for the same goals in their lives.

This sense of belonging needs to be cultivated in your club. As noted a number of other places in this book, people who have a relationship with your business will stay longer and pay longer. Part of that relationship is the sense of belonging to a business that becomes more of a retreat and less than a business one just happens to spend money at occasionally.

It All Starts When the Door Opens

Golden retrievers might be the goofiest dogs in the world. People who own them and love them refer to their pets as hairy four-year-old children. These dogs spend their lives endlessly playing, seeking attention, and being happy, just like most four-year-old kids, once fed and then left to play on their own without adult restrictions.

Golden retrievers and four-year-old kids might also be the perfect role models as to how your front counter staff should act every time the front door of the club opens and a member, or potential member, walks through ready to work out or find out what you do and how you can help him reach his goals. Everyone coming through that door has high expectations of help, support, and guidance, and if we replaced our typical front counter hires with kids and dogs, we might actually be better able to meet these lofty needs our guests are seeking to be fulfilled.

If you have a golden retriever and leave the house for even a minute to get the mail, he is at the door when you get back, wagging his tail, smiling, and waiting to get petted: "Hey, where you been? Just got the mail, huh? Seems like you were gone for a long time. Glad you're back. I missed you. I love you, dog dad, and am I ever glad to see you."

The kid would be the same. You go to work and come home, feeling bad after the business beating of the day, but when that door opens and the kid is there, everything changes: "Daddy! Daddy! Daddy! Mommy, Daddy is home. What did you bring me? Can we play now? Guess what I did today? Can I follow you into the bathroom? Please? *Please*?"

The dog and the kid are the same. Both love you unconditionally, and both are very happy to see you walk through that door, which is the way we should be, too, when a paying member, or someone who is trying to give us money, walks through ready for us to be excited to see them.

If you remember from Chapter 10, we want to be the best part of the member's day, every day. If that is our goal, then it starts when the member arrives to his special place, his sanctuary away from home, his one place that is all his without business, family, or other distractions. Just for a little while, it is all about him and about his time and his space.

The Welcoming Statement Is How You Set the Tone That This Is All About Them

Many people arrive at your door, beaten and tired. Most really don't want to stop in the club that day and would probably prefer a strong drink to an intense training session. It is either early in the morning and they aren't even awake yet, or at the end of the workday, where the life has been drained out of them. It is up to you to change the energy.

Hello, we're having a great day at the Workout Company.

This simple welcome statement should be energetically shouted to every person who comes through your door. We are in the energy business, and energy is transferrable. This is our house, and we should always show that we are excited to see the guests of the house.

The "great day" line is perfect for use in a high-volume club. Yes, it could be repetitious to the staff, but most owners never really get tired of counting money generated through more sales and higher retention, so it is probably worth teaching your staff to use this strong greeting.

If you have a lower volume membership club, then add this:

> *Hello, we're having a great day at the Workout Company. Thank you for stopping by. It's good to see you.*

The idea is to set the tone for the person coming through the door. Assume that they had a rough day, or stopped by and took a sales beating from your competitor, and raise the standard by demonstrating that we are happy to see you, appreciate you coming in, and that no matter how your day has gone, it is going to get better now.

If you have staff who can't do this, then get new staff. This is your house, and these are your guests. All staff have to respect the guests of this house. One of the ways we demonstrate that is by showing our appreciation for their visit that day. If you can't respect the guests of this house, then you need to go home now, and the club will find people who do care and respect the people who pay the bills in this business.

The Potential Members Bring an Energy All Their Own

Walking into someplace you have never been before is much harder than most people realize. The regular members and the staff have gotten over that stressful feeling after their initial visit, and the club really has become that sanctuary or familiar place to work.

Being out of shape also adds another layer of stress for the potential member. Most owners and senior staff people in the club are long removed from being out of shape and fearful of fitness. But to the newbies, who have little experience with fitness and only know it as something that they need and that it will be somehow painful, walking through that door can be excruciatingly stressful.

Being out of shape is also embarrassing. You have to get off your couch, admit you look like the out-of-shape, fat uncle you used to laugh at as a kid, and then walk into a club where you just know that everyone will be in shape but you.

The strong welcoming statement at the door, which encompasses everyone that walks through sweeping the potential members up in the energy, helps deflate the stress and eliminate the feeling that you won't fit into this enclave for the tight butted and ripped. The potential member expected the worst, but was surprised by an energetic person at the counter who went out of her way to make the guest feel like they are welcome in the business.

Implementing the Welcome Statement

At first glance, using this statement is deceptively easy. How hard can it be to just tell your staff to shout out a simple phrase every time the door opens? It is much harder than it looks, but still very important.

The team gets busy and forgets a few times. One member, who comes in after a fight with his wife and is in a foul mood, asks why you do such stupid nonsense every time he walks through the damn door. The staff then equates a complaining member with everyone who walks through the door, so now they want to back off.

The fitness business is a game of numbers. You have to get members, collect money from members, and then you have to figure out a way to keep the ones you do get. Just a few members a year can often be the difference between a good year and a flat year in this business.

Customer service is the one common denominator that separates you from your competitors and is also the one base tool that will keep members staying longer and paying longer. The extra members you need to make a difference might be the ones you get and keep because your service was just a little better than anyone else's in the market.

It is said that anything done consistently for 21 days becomes a habit. When you introduce the welcome statement, pound it hard for the first 30 days. Stand up there and do it yourself until it feels natural. No, you don't have to scream at the top of your lungs every time the door opens, but you do have to convey a sense of energy and enthusiasm that we are glad to see our guests in the house that day.

Lead by example, and then hold the rest of the team accountable after you master the greeting. Customer service is about money and someone's willingness to pay you for your product. Create the environment that makes people feel good about being part of your club and your business.

Do These Things Now

- Greet every member with a strong welcome statement.

- Remember that a welcome statement eases the fear of a guest who has never before been into your club.

- It will take about a full month to get everyone on the staff using the welcome statement. Be relentless, and keep it going until it becomes a habit.

Customer service is as simple as ...
something small, something free.

Member appreciation has to happen more than just one or two days a year.

Your good members pop into the club a couple of times a week, and after a while it becomes a routine for them. This is good for getting in shape, but like all routines, this one can often become boring, which spells the beginning of the end of that relationship.

Surprise your members weekly with small things that cost you little to provide. Breaking their routines by doing something that puts a smile on their face, and shows a little appreciation for them being there that day, is not only good service, it's good retention as well.

Following are a few inexpensive things that you can do that the members appreciate:

- *Put out a bowl of fruit on the counter on a busy Monday.*

- *Give away bottles of water on a busy day.*

- *If it fits you and your market, buy a keg of beer and have an informal party on Thursday night.*

- *Get a special order of tee shirts with something fun on the front, and hand them out personally to each member on a Saturday morning.*

- *Organize a bike ride on Saturday that leaves from the club or local park, and ride to a destination where you have water and snacks waiting for everyone.*

- *Free recovery shake on Monday for every training client.*

- *Dedicate an entire month to get everyone in the club involved in group training of some sort (and then try to convert them with an upgrade at the end).*

Do something weekly, and remember you don't always have to spend a lot to put a smile on someone's face. Customer service is a perception of caring that the member creates in his mind. Sometimes, just a free apple can create a powerful feeling of a business that cares.

15

There Is Nothing Sweeter Than the Sound of Your Own Name

The fitness business in the coming decade will be about individualizing the membership process. The larger chain clubs that treat members as if they are just a sales number to be counted or replaced will start to fade. The players who are left in the field will have to embark on the process of making their members feel unique and special in their businesses if they want to survive into the future.

When you experience legendary customer service in your own life, it always seems like it was aimed directly at you. For that brief moment, the business singled you out and made you feel special and appreciated. This ability to take the systems of good customer service and apply them so each person feels it is all about them is what turns a good club into a legendary business with raving fans that are proud to be your members.

Your Name Is the Most Individual Thing You Own

Even if your name is Bob, Mohammed, or Jesus (known collectively as three of the most common names on the entire planet), your name is your name, and when it is spoken directly to you, it conveys a sense of personal intimacy not achieved when you are referred to as "Dude," "Buddy," or "Girl."

The breakdown we have in most fitness businesses is that the volume of members works against the individualization process. There are simply too many of them and not enough of you to get everything down to a personal level. You do, however, for the sake of member retention, need to find a way to make a thousand members or more feel like you know them personally.

Perhaps the simplest tool you can use is to create systems that allow your staff to learn and remember the highest percentage of member's names possible. Your name is personal and is the one place to begin when you want to individualize the customer-service process for your members.

As Always, Start at the Front Counter

Always start where you can get the highest amount of success in the shortest amount of time. The front counter, our fortress of customer service, is where every member is touched at least once while that person is in the club, which is why you need to start your emphasis on learning names with the counter people.

Once a staff person begins to use names, it becomes a habit, but most staff people just don't try to gather and use names as part of their daily routine. It is easier to just smile and wave than it is to start the process of trying to learn the names of a large membership. But like everything else in customer service, using names can be taught and built into the daily life of your staff in your business.

You can tell a staff person what to do in an office, but you can only show him how to do it on the floor. Effective customer-service training can only be done by direct application done in conjunction with immediate correction and feedback.

This means that if you want to be effective with training of any type, you need to stand there and do it with them. Effective training for the teams in the clubs always has these parts:

- Tell them *what* you want done and how to do it (this is done in the office).

- Tell them *why* it is important (you are more likely to get buy-in from your staff if they know why the task is important and that almost everything they need to learn can be directly related to enhancing the guest experience and member retention).

- *Show* them what the new skill looks like when it is done correctly (this is the *how to do it* part of learning a new skill).

- Let the person *practice* while you watch.

- Provide immediate *feedback* and *correction*.

- Let the person *practice again*, using the corrected skills.

- Do it until it is done the way you want it, and *then do it some more.*

These steps apply to any type of training. Most club owners and managers usually shorten this process by only doing the first step, which is to simply tell the person what to do. If you only do the first step, then you are automatically assuming that the person knows why it is important to the company and how to actually get it done.

Most owners that only tell someone what to do are also assuming that the person has all the same information in his head as they do in theirs, which is seldom the case. If you want an effective staff, you have to do all the steps whenever you teach a new skill to any staff person. Never assume the person knows what you are talking about, even if the task is considered too simple to mess up, because we all know that a typical staff person left to his own devices can pretty much destroy any simple job.

Jupiterimages

The Name Game

The simplest way to get the staff interested in learning names is to compensate them. Direct compensation demonstrates the emphasis you place on the task, and small rewards are kind of like dog treats. The dog sits; he gets a cookie. He sits again; he gets another cookie. The staff learns some names; they get a $5 coupon for lunch. They learn more names; they get another coupon for lunch. Positive reinforcement is the same whether it is a dog or staff, and both of them can learn new tricks if the reward is worth the effort.

The name game is very simple. Stand with your front counter person, and tell her if she can name the next five people through the door by first name before they get to the computer, then you will buy lunch today (the $5 sandwich-shop coupon).

Do it randomly throughout the day. Change the reward, but keep it small because the game itself is the important thing, and the fact that it is important enough to you to test and reward. If the staff person hits five in a row several times, up the ante to something worth $10, and go for 10 people.

If she doesn't know the person, then teach her to shake hands and introduce herself. For example:

> *Hello, I am sorry, but I don't know your name yet. My name is Sarah, and you are?* (Paul.) **Paul!** *It's nice to meet you,* **Paul.** *How long have you been a member? Thank you for coming in today,* **Paul,** *and it was nice to meet you.*

It seems a waste of time to have to script out a brief conversation such as this, but by teaching your staff person to use this type of tool, you are helping to ensure that she will be more likely to remember the name, since she was forced to use it three times in the conversation. She hears the name in response to her question, repeats the name, works it into her first statement that it is nice to meet him, and then uses the name one more time as she thanks him for coming in today.

When you use the name game for managers, the stakes have to be higher and the game tougher. Managers should be able to randomly name the next 25 people through the door. That seems like a lot of names, and it is, but no one said developing a legendary customer-service business would be an easy thing.

The managers should have a little risk to themselves built into the game as well. If the manager can't name the next 25 people, then he should be forced to do a nasty job in the club or kick in a small fine in a penalty pot used for a group meal.

Most staff people get pretty good at this name game in just a few weeks, and once you start it, do it at least several times a week forever. You might actually put it on your calendar and plan in advance when you are going to hit them at the counter. If they know they are going to get tested at certain points, they might also be more enticed to start learning more names on their own.

Cheating With the Computer

Modern computerized check-in systems give you an easy way to cheat with the names. Most of the better systems flash the member's name in large print on the screen as the member runs his card through the scanner. Situate the screen so the staff can easily see it along with the members. Get an oversized screen to make it easier to see the name from a distance.

Many of these check-in systems also have pictures of the members stored as well. If it is slow at the front counter, pull up the last 10 members who have checked in, and send the staff out to introduce themselves to anyone they don't know. It is good service, and the members feel a little special if you run them down in the club to make sure the staff knows whom they are.

We forget the power of using someone's name, but the simple act of just greeting a member with a "Hello, Johnny. Thank you for stopping by today" is the easiest and probably most sincere form of customer service you can provide.

Do These Things Now

- Start teaching your staff to use the member's names every chance they have during their day.

- Start using the name game to train the counter staff first.

- Teach the staff simple techniques that will allow them to introduce themselves to all members if they are not sure about the member's name.

Customer service is as simple as ...

the 13/1 rule.

There is a small percentage of your members who never have a problem opening their mouths and sharing with you every opinion they might have ever had about your business and how you run it.

But this is a small percentage compared to the large majority that quietly go about their business and never say a word to anyone. These are the ones that you need to give special consideration to since they just fade away without a whisper if they are upset or frustrated in the club.

The 13/1 rule states that if one person complains (the small percentage), then there are probably 13 other members who feel the same way about the situation, but are too shy or polite to say anything (the ones who just leave if there is a problem and never utter a word).

For example, if a member complains about the proverbial stinky member, you have to weigh the issues within the realm of only a single complaint. This means that maybe the stinky guy just had a bad day, used a dirty tee shirt because he had forgotten to bring a clean one, or came directly from his construction job that day and just didn't smell very good.

On the other hand, if three or four members tell you the same thing, then the 13/1 rule kicks in. If you get four complaints, multiply that by 13 (representing the quiet members who feel the same way but won't complain), and you probably have a trend that demands you take action now to deal with the issue.

Ignoring bad situations in the club is never good customer service. Something that irritates a member enough to complain is usually just the tip of something bigger that is working its way through your business. The 13/1 rule is a tool that gives you a better perspective as to how bad a situation could be in your business.

16

The Lost Art of Saying "Thank You"

The relationship between the paying client and the club owner has become decidedly one-sided in recent years with the perceived overload shifting toward the club.

We have, in truth, become an industry of takers, and the culture we have developed in most of the country's fitness businesses is designed to take as much as possible, and, therefore, giving very little back to the people who support the clubs and pay the bills. There are a number of supposedly valid reasons we use to justify the fact that the members are now little more than just a membership agreement and a sales number.

This idea is easy to prove. Just look at a typical club's sales department compared to what it puts into member retention. Most clubs have dedicated salespeople and a dedicated sales manager and not a single person whose job description is solely based on keeping the members already in the system. We are an industry of front loading, meaning the next prospect through the door is worth much more than the members in the back who already signed up.

In order to justify the fact that we don't really care much about the actual members, we tell everyone that the line of new equipment was purchased for the members and that big-dollar remodel in the locker room was another gift from the attentive owner to his membership that they just didn't understand or appreciate. Fitness businesses are very capital intensive, and we often use that factor to justify the lack of any type of customer service.

The reality is that replacing equipment and keeping up with the worn-out parts of your physical plant isn't about member service at all; it's about your need to keep your business open and presentable for the new sales you are chasing.

Equipment is not service. Equipment is part of your investment to keep your business functional so you can stay in business. A restaurant guy who buys a new pizza oven to replace the one that finally worn out isn't buying the oven and then claiming he did it for customer service. He bought the oven so he can keep the doors of his business open and stay in business.

If you remodel your locker room, it isn't an exciting gift to your members and something special; it's just part of what you have to do to stay in business. The sad thing is that a lot of owners who dump money into a new locker room get upset when the members fail to drop to their knees and bow in thanks for the upgrade.

The members are paying you each month to be a member, and keeping the physical plant working and decent isn't customer service to them; it is just a base expectation they view as normal in exchange for the money they spend with you each month. "Hey, cool, the cheapskate owner finally fixed up the locker rooms before someone got killed tripping on the nasty carpet" is the more common response you would get from most members about that remodel if you weren't afraid to ask.

If you want to build a customer-service business with a high retention rate, then you have to learn the difference between the current industry perception of what service is to our members, and what the members actually value in their relationship with you. The difference is that the current industry perception is all about the club, while you really should be working on what you can do to make each paying person feel like an individual.

Customer Service Is a Series of Small Things Done Correctly That Touches the Individual

You have to feel good about the money you spend. Someone who works his butt off, putting in 50 hours or more a week, and then spends $49 per month with you wants to feel good about the money he has gifted you with each month. The important thing we forget is that:

The money was spent by an individual,
and he has to be recognized as an individual.

Customer service has to be individualized to work. You can't build a customer-service business, with the goal of maximizing your retention, by attempting to service the entire group all at once. Customer service only works if you bring it down to a level that each member feels something was done for him personally.

For example, an owner in a club with about 1,500 members tried running a member-appreciation week in his club. The goal was to do something every day to thank the members that were coming through the door. He gave out tee shirts on a Monday, free munchie bars on a Tuesday, and he put out a big bowl of fruit on Wednesday.

One of his regular members, a lady in her 50s who was known to the staff as a little bit of a pain in the butt, stopped and picked an apple out of the bowl, walked up to the owner, and gave him a kiss on the cheek. "Thank you. The fruit is such a nice touch. It is nice to know that you really appreciate your members," and she turned and left.

This was the same lady that chewed on him for replacing some of the equipment she liked, and was used to, with a new line. He received more attention and recognition from the members, which is what he was seeking from the equipment investment, with an apple.

The difference is that the equipment was an investment he had to make to keep his gym competitive in the market, and that purchase was perceived by the members as just another routine change the owner had to make in his business since the old equipment was kind of beat up anyway.

The fruit, on the other hand, was something the members perceived as going beyond the normal operational procedure for the club. The perception of the apple to the usually grumpy member was a positive gesture that was perceived at an individual level rather than a large investment in equipment that was merely seen as the owner taking care of business.

The Power of "Thank You"

One of the strongest customer-service gestures you can learn that individualizes the service process for the members is to learn to say "Thank you," not only for each new sale, but also for all of the major and minor milestones the member passes through with your business.

The rule to learn is that you need to always continue to *validate the sale*. Validating the sale means that the member knows that you, as the business owner, recognize that his money was spent to enhance your business and that you are appreciative of that transaction. Listed are most of the occurrences that happen in your business over time between the member and the club that deserve special recognition.

Every single member is thanked every single time they leave the club.

"Goodbye, Mark. Thank you for stopping by today." It is that simple, but again, this is something that has to be taught and practiced for a few weeks so it becomes part of every counter person's daily routine. You also need to recognize anything else the member might have done for you that day. For example, "Thank you, Mark, for stopping by today, and we especially appreciate the extra business. Thank you for buying that training package." Learn to say "Thank you," and thank every single member every time that person leaves the club.

Every potential member is thanked at the end of a trial membership, even if the person doesn't become a member.

Send out a small, standardized letter that says thank you for considering your business. Following is some sample copy that would work well as a handwritten thank-you card. Yes, handwritten and hand-addressed is old-fashioned, but that is what makes it effective and also generates a much higher chance that a hand-addressed card will get opened:

> *Thank you, Justin, for trying our club as a trial member. I am sorry we didn't get you as a member this time, but we do greatly appreciate you giving us a chance to meet you. If at any time in the future you are looking for a place to work out, I hope you will think about us and give us another chance to earn your business.*

Every person is thanked once they do become a real member.

Anyone joining the club should receive a small gift at the end of their first 30 days as a member. This gift is another way to validate the sale, arriving just when most members think that you have forgotten about them and that they are now just another member in the pile. It is suggested that you send something practical that will be used, keeping the cost under $5. Water bottles with screw caps or stainless coffee mugs work well here. Send a personalized letter, using the member's name, addressed to the member, but using a standardized form letter, along with a five single-guest passes with expiration dates valid for 12 months.

Every member is thanked at the end of the member's first year.

The end of the first year is a critical time for the member. He is either on a month-to-month membership, which is easy to cancel and walk, or you are trying to get him to sign for another year at a time (the recommended way to chase renewals). Either way, the person has spent money with you for an entire year and needs to be recognized for that effort.

If you are using open-ended memberships, meaning the person goes from a contractual obligation to month-to-month, at least send a thank-you letter for reaching their first anniversary date and with the invitation to stop by the desk during the next visit to pick up this year's gift package.

This package should be simple and based upon usage in the club, such as a spa package or training, and should include a tee shirt as well. Keep the tee shirts rotating in your system using fun sayings on the front, such as "Sweat: The perfume of the skinny" with your logo on the sleeve or on the top of the neck in the back. No one is wearing the giant logos on the front of the shirt anymore, and members don't really want to be walking billboards for your business.

iStockphoto/Thinkstock

Keep in mind that the person can come get the package and then cancel the next month, which likely won't happen often, but is a factor when you consider the gifts. Offer a training upgrade for the month or something dependent on using a service in the club and keep the hard cost of the items you give down to the cost of a tee shirt.

If you are using a closed-ended membership, meaning the member finished one year and then resigns for another year at the same rate, then you can up the ante a little. For example, you might send a letter at the end of the member's year thanking him for his business and pointing out that he just reached his first anniversary date with you. In celebration of this date, if he will stop by the club, he can pick up his special thank-you gift.

The gifts in this case should be a little nicer since you are trading another full year's membership in contract form for a small gift of appreciation. This gift should be a hard goods gift, such as a messenger bag or nice workout bag that changes yearly. The rule of thumb for spending would be to keep the cost to less than one month's dues.

Before you fall to the floor, screaming at that perceived cost, keep in mind that you are already willing to spend money each month to chase new leads with no guarantee that you are going to get anything back in exchange. For example, you might spend $4,000 for marketing and get 80 leads through the door, which is a cost of $50 per lead. This is just the cost per lead, and you still haven't made a sale yet.

In this same club, which has a monthly membership of $49 per member, you could give a renewal prospect a very top-end messenger bag, which you might get at wholesale for $30, and know that the result will be a 12-month membership with payments of $49 per month. The most important thing to remember is that you incur no cost until you receive a $588 signed membership agreement ($49 x 12). In other words, you are buying a full membership for less than you would have spent just to chase a lead and made a paying member very happy through your demonstration at a personal level of your appreciation for his business.

This should be done every year. If someone pays you for a full year and doesn't miss a payment, say "Thank you," and give them a reasonable gift in appreciation for the loyalty and continued support. Remember from earlier that we are a front-loaded business designed to chase new members, and most club owners have nothing in place to keep the members already in the system staying longer and paying longer.

Birthdays

Get the member's birthday, and send the person a hand-signed card every year. Have your staff sign a pile of the cards during a staff meeting so each one sent is a reflection of your entire staff. If you can personalize the card by noting something personal, such as "Congratulations on that new job," then you are even further ahead.

Any large purchases deserve recognition.

Some of the smaller clubs have gone to rewarding any major purchase as part of their routine business. For example, one club owner who was training-centric in his business would send a bottle of wine whenever a member made a large purchase in the training department. He kept an account on Wine.com and just spent a minute or two sending a gift valued at about $25 to each member who spent a decent amount of money. The wine appeared the next day on the member's doorstep with a thank-you card attached. This is very cheap for the impact, and it definitely individualized the service aspect.

VIPs

This is an old idea that seems to get better every year. Members who stay with you over time should be recognized for that achievement. Technology makes it so much easier now to recognize these people with special privileges and services in the club that this is a low-cost way to give some special "love" to those who support you over the years.

The VIP program is based upon years accumulated as a member. Once the members go through these milestones, they should be recognized with extras unique to their time spent with you.

The three-year member

Every member who passes this level should receive a special membership card with extra benefits that are extended to him as a member. The card at this level should be gold, following the standard credit card configuration, with a big VIP on the front. Most of the better third-party financial-service companies can easily do this mimicking the card stock mailer you receive with your credit cards when they are issued.

The benefits might include 5 percent off of any product or service in the club, as well as the chance to bring any friend or relative to the club who can sign up for no membership fee (waive the fee and get the first month dues up front). This is a status play for the member who can now claim that he can get his friend a deal at the club, which he can, and you just got a new member for less than the cost of your typical marketing.

The five-year member

The member would be issued another card but this time it would be silver, similar to a platinum credit card. The benefits would be increased to 10 percent off anything purchased with the right to sign up a guest for no membership fee and the member would now be given an extra benefit where he could gift once a year a three-month membership to a friend or relative.

Again, get off the floor and think about this. You as an owner will spend big marketing money to get someone in the door as a lead, yet here is a proven member, who has paid you for five straight years, referring a guest for three months (just another form of a lead). Leads come in all forms and shapes, and you have to think creatively to be competitive in your market.

The 10-year member

This is the black card member. Increase the benefits to 15 percent off everything the club offers, unlimited guests, and two three-month memberships that can be gifted each year. Make the card solid black with a silver VIP on the front.

Member Referrals Are Something We Want But Don't Get Enough of in the Club

You want the members to refer their friends, but when they do, you hand the person a ball cap, a cheap tee shirt, or a free month added to their membership. You get what you pay for in referrals, and if you don't value the referral, then the members will stop giving them to you.

The members who refer guests to you obviously know what the memberships cost each year. If someone just hand delivers you a prepackaged membership, it has to be worth more to you as an owner than a month added to the member's time.

For example, the following is the cost of what it might take a typical club to buy a new member:

- $4,000 in marketing/80 leads through the door: The cost is $50 per lead.

- $20 in commissions for the sale.

- $5 in basic startup costs, such as marketing materials, handouts, the membership agreement, and maybe a very cheap tee shirt.

You are already at about $75 to get a new member in this example without considering any labor costs to service the person for the first 30 days. Trying to buy new members is expensive with no guarantees of success.

Referrals are passive business, which means that you had to spend little of your time, money, or energy to make them happen. Even if you run an aggressive member-referral program, you are really not incurring much expense unless you get direct members, which makes traditional marketing look like an even worse deal.

The rule of thumb is to be aggressive. It is worth your time and money to spend the equivalent of the membership fee and first month's dues to acquire a member. For example, the club has a membership fee of $49 with monthly dues of $49. Would it be worth it to you as an owner or manager to spend $98 to buy a deal? The answer should be a big yes.

Let's say that you divert some of your marketing dollars to a small campaign where you mail all the members a special letter stating that for the month of November you are going to give every member a new mp3 player (valued at about $100) if they bring a guest in that becomes a new member.

Remember that you are not incurring any cost unless you get a sale. The promotion is passive in that the members have to do all the hunting for leads for you. You sit back and just hand out mp3 players in trade for signed membership agreements.

Most importantly, you just said "Thank you" in a big way to an existing member who thought enough about your business, and who really, really wants a new iPod, to bring in his brother to get signed up. The gift, which is substantial, validated the effort and the value of the referral the member happily gave you.

Saying "Thank you" and showing appreciation is a lost art in this business. Due to competitive markets and increasing costs over the years, we stopped trying to individualize the service process, replacing it in our minds with the cost of new equipment and physical-plant renovations. We had to spend the money anyway, and it is a lot easier to justify that what you did was service when you just spent $75,000 on treadmills.

Service should be an individual process where the person who is spending money with you receives something that is directed at him as a person. Service does not have to be huge to work, but it does have to directly thank the person who is doing business with you.

Do These Things Now

- Recognize that money was spent by an individual, and he has to be recognized as an individual.

- Validate every sale every time.

- Every member is thanked every time he leaves the club.

Customer service is as simple as ...
hand towels and spray.

You cannot escape the "nasty factor" when it comes to running a club.

The nasty factor is the inevitable situation where a sweaty body is going to come into contact with a piece of equipment, or that same sweat-soaked individual is going to drip on something. Try as you might, if you run a good gym and are an advocate of real fitness, then you have to end up with sweaty people, or you aren't doing your job correctly. Anytime a member leaves dry, you probably failed, and he did nothing to get in shape that day.

Get hand towels, and force the members to carry and use them in the club. You should also have bottles of spray disinfectant easily accessible as well.

There are two sides to this discussion. Some club owners don't feel that providing towels and spray is good service and actually setting those things out gives the perception that the club is dirty and that the staff isn't doing their job.

The other side is that if I am going to put my back on that bench, I am going to wipe it down myself first. Yes, you might have cleaned it, but how many people have been on that bench in the last hour since your crew came through and wiped it down.

Try telling your female clients that the bench they want to use was thoroughly cleaned last night by the cleaning crew, and hey, it is only 6:00 in the evening the following day, so there could have been no more than 40 to 50 people parked on that bench since then.

The proper decision is to err on the side of the prissy members who never trust anyone. In today's world, where there is 24/7 news coverage about forms of flu and other strange diseases that we may, or may not, ever face in this country, the members want a sense of controlling their own environment. Give them the spray, give them the towels, and also make sure there are dispensers of hand sanitizers as well.

Just as a side note, do not buy white towels. They slowly turn gray, and white towels are stolen more often from the clubs. Get bright colored towels, similar to shop towels, that come in funky orange or some other ucky color.

17

Service Beyond the Front Counter

If you master service at the front counter, you can now venture out onto the floor and start to gain control of the rest of your club.

Even weak club owners put a lot more emphasis into the front areas of their business than they do the back. These clubs aren't necessarily customer-service driven, but they do have most of the action in the business taking place somewhere near the front door. For instance, these clubs do have a check-in area, offices near the counter, and usually the salespeople are located near the front door as well, all putting the emphasis on the front of the house.

Locating everything near the front door is efficient in many ways, especially in sales, but the logistics of this arrangement forces a business to have all the action happening at the front with the back of the house being often neglected. In many cases, the only time anyone on the staff really ventures to the back areas is for a sales tour or if the team is looking for another missing staff person.

This neglect of your workout floors and group rooms often reflects in the perceived customer service in the business. If the front area of the club is busy and well-kept, but the back is neglected and somewhat dirty, then the owner is sending a clear message that it is important to put money into signing someone up, but it isn't really important to do much for the membership after the fact.

Following is a list of 12 easy things you can do to add some depth to your back shop with out spending a lot of money.

The three-foot rule

This rule states that if you as a team member are walking anywhere in the club, you have to stop and acknowledge the person. Many staff people, especially the managers, walk through the club focused on paper in their hands or are walking fast so the members don't grab them with a petty complaint. It is the member's club and their time, and you are fair game if you are on the floor, but should also take responsibility and teach the team fixed customer-service practices they have to use any time they pass within three feet of a member. Following are the exact steps your staff should memorize and practice to demonstrate good service on a club walk-through:

- Stop as you pass the member.

- Face the member, and make eye contact.

- Shake hands.

- Acknowledge the member with a "Thank you for coming in today. It is good to see you."

- Give a friendly pat. This means for you to give the member a little encouraging pat on the back of the shoulder, or upper arm, as you walk away after your encounter. Add the words "I hope you have a great workout" as you leave.

The locker rooms

Someone on the staff should walk through their respective locker rooms every 30 minutes the club is open. Check for toilet paper, close the lockers, pick up any debris on the floor, flush the toilets as needed, wipe the sink if applicable, and in general make sure the locker room is ready for the members and sales tours.

Unless you are really broke, or just starting out, the staff should not be expected to double as a cleaning crew. It is hard to develop a professional staff when part of their job is to stay after work and vacuum the floor. The team is responsible, however, for doing whatever it takes to keep the club in service-ready shape during normal operational hours.

The locker rooms are a strong first-impression area, and a member that is having a bad day due to something else outside the club will often punish the club because of a dirty locker room. He walks in after a tough day of work, opens his favorite locker, and finds an old cup of coffee left over from the last user sitting in the bottom and a pair of slimy workout briefs hanging on the hook. Don't give the member a reason to quit over something as routine as a 30-minute locker-room sweep, which should catch all the problems the members create as they enter and leave each day.

The club sweep

The staff also should be trained to do a planned walk-through every hour to make sure the club is ready for business. Planning the walk means that you list certain key areas on a sheet on a clipboard, such as the stretching area, so all of the traditional trouble spots are checked at least once every hour you are open. All you are looking for is bad news.

The members often surprise us by spilling a drink in a corner and just leaving it, getting sick and covering it with a newspaper but not telling anyone on the staff, dropping a pair of underwear on the floor as they exit the locker room, or leaving strange surprises in the tanning rooms—which you should be eliminating from your club due to all the bad press and increasing liability the tanning industry is generating. We are in the health business, and more and more research demonstrates that there is nothing healthy about indoor tanning. Walk with a purpose to keep the house clean for the guests, but plan this walk to cover all the key problem areas, and make sure the staff does it regularly on the hour.

Consider getting service specialists back on the floor.

Years ago, most clubs had floor workers whose only task was to help the members any way they could while on duty. These people spotted the members on lifts, answered questions, helped to adjust seats or settings, explained the treadmills, and helped with just about anything else the member might need during a typical workout. These employees faded in popularity over the years, but the idea of a service specialist is making a strong comeback. In fact, even ACE (American Council on Exercise), the premier certification and education company in the world, has launched a service specialist mini-certification that is very economical for the club owner but covers everything a new employee would need to know to be effective on the floor short of becoming a real trainer. These service specialists are valuable and give the illusion that service is everywhere in the club.

The owners and managers need to be visible.

The club's owners and managers have to have a presence in the club. One of the key findings in IHRSA's *Guide to Retention*, mentioned earlier in this book, was that members perceived the service in the club to be better if they could find a manager or the owner on the floor or behind the counter during prime hours. It seems that just the presence of a senior person gives the impression that the management team is really involved in the club and cares enough to be part of the club's culture.

The owners and managers should also make it part of their daily routine to occasionally walk through the club, greeting all the members they can touch and thanking them for coming in that day. It may seem like somewhat of a waste of time in your busy day, but in fact it is much like being in a restaurant and the chef pops out of the kitchen to personally go table to table, inquiring about the food and your evening. It is a personal touch that demonstrates that those in charge care about the business and what you think, too.

Nothing is ever left broken on the floor.

If you can't fix it now, move it off the floor now. This applies to all equipment. You do not ever want a piece of broken equipment to be sitting on the floor for days. This is extreme, but use some common sense. If a cable breaks on a piece of fixed equipment, and the company tells you that it can't get the cable to you for a week, do you really want that piece of equipment as part of every sales tour for the next seven days?

The broken piece of equipment also sends out a strong message to the members as well. The first day it is broken, they grumble, but after the first day it becomes a personal issue between you and them. By the end of the week, it is common knowledge in the club, due to all the members sharing their complaints with each other, that you must be broke and going out of business if you can't even fix a stupid little cable. If you can't fix it today, or know the cable is coming tomorrow guaranteed, then get it off the floor before it becomes a liability.

This obviously applies to cardio as well. The rule here is to always buy the same matching pieces. For example, not too many years ago, it was in style to have different brands in the club of the same type of equipment. For instance, a club guy might buy 16 treadmills, but he would get four each from four different manufacturers.

This was supposed to give the illusion that the club owner was really getting everything available in the industry and had the best equipped club in the market since he at least had something from every company in the industry. This proved to be a false assumption that actually did a lot of harm to a lot of owners because they couldn't get decent pricing by only buying four of something, and it made it very hard to keep all those different brands running at the same time since all were differently built and all took different skills to service and fix.

What the members really want is 16 pieces that actually work and that are spaced at least eight inches apart so you don't have to smell the person next to you. Buy 16 of the exact same treadmills so you can buy replacement parts for just one brand instead of four, which no one ever did. It is more important to keep things running, which is why you buy top-end equipment, versus variety and going for the cheap brands in the industry.

Try to lay out the club to help sort the members.

Little people seldom want to work out with big people. Women seldom want to lift weights with monster guys who spit, fart, and drop stuff. Some people love televisions and want a lot of visuals while they work out on the cardio, and others would rather work out with just music in a different part of the club. When you do the club layout, remember that everyone has different expectations for the business and that you should try to address a few of these when you decide where to put things. Following are a few hints that helps give the perception of more service:

- Keep the childcare in the front near the front door so the mothers don't have to drag the kids throughout the entire club, risking death if the little four-year-old wanders off and is smashed by a huge dumbbell, who dropped a huge dumbbell.

- Split the cardio into two distinct groupings once you get past 40 pieces. For example, if you have 60 pieces of cardio, consider putting 20 pieces into a quiet area with no televisions and the other 40 into television heaven. Also, consider not putting televisions on the cardio. You are better off just using that money and buying even more pieces of equipment from the same company.

- Do two different dumbbell/free-weight areas. Have one area for the bigger people with the traditional weights and another area with the dumbbells going up to 50 pounds or so. The smaller people will gravitate toward the lighter area, and your bigger people will stay in the other spot. It is interesting to note that most clubs are restricting the size of their dumbbells to 80s and less. They just don't want the very few people who use the larger weights and scare the other members. Unless you are a sports-specific business and need anything bigger, you might consider restricting or removing some of your bigger bells.

- You do not need a women-only area in your coed club. This is a myth started by men who own clubs and who know nothing about women and want they want from a club. The women still have to come through the front door, which negates the escape to the women-only area. Coming through the front door kind of kills the no-men, no-mirrors, and no-makeup idea that makes a women-only club more successful. This is why every club owner who tries an area such as this ends up with just a few points of penetration in his membership and eventually wastes the space. You would be better off with a soft area that women and men who want, or need, a softer space with its own cardio and functional equipment can work out. The false assumption is that it is just women who want a softer space, but in reality many of your members of both sexes would love a space that is less intimidating, more user-friendly, and that is away from the members who are already really in shape.

- Don't forget the changing areas in the women's locker rooms. This is regional in nature, but these are coming back in many more clubs around the country. Many women don't like to change clothes in front of the other female members. Plan your locker rooms to include special changing booths that are private or do extra space in front of each shower stall that is an enclosed changing area where a woman can step in, disrobe, shower, and then put fresh clothes on before she reappears in the locker room.

Stifle your need to fill every inch of space.

Far too many club owners must have been horribly bitten by the empty-space monster when they were children because it is a universal rule that empty space in any club will be stuffed with equipment and eliminated at first chance.

How we work out has changed; therefore, how you lay out the club also has to reflect what is happening in the market. Pick up any fitness magazine, and even *Muscle and Fitness*, once the bible of bodybuilding, has added articles about various aspects of functional training that involves an upright adult using tools such as med balls, ropes, and kettlebells in open spaces. Weirdly, you can visit clubs that are 30,000 square feet and bigger and not find enough open space to do a walking lunge or a blank wall that can be used to toss a medicine ball against.

The members are reading these magazines, and watching everything from *The Biggest Loser* or fitness shows on the Golf Channel, and are seeing people get results doing fun and challenging moves that don't involve going around in a circle on a fixed circuit. But most clubs still are reluctant to part with some of this old equipment and create open space, therefore, forcing the members to struggle in any open space (such as the walkways) they can find in the club.

Space is not a luxury; it is required to do most of the current workouts the members are reading about. Good service means you break away from some of your old habits, such as seeking the bragging rights for having the most equipment in your market, which is only important to drunken owners in a bar at an annual convention, and design some space that enhances the workout experience for the members. Following are a few ideas you can easily incorporate into your club.

Add a training lane that is highly visible to all members.

This lane needs to be only about four feet wide and only about 15 lunges long to work. If you have more space, then add two lanes at about three-and-a half feet wide each. Get the right flooring so you can get the members pulling small sleds, which the women love because of the direct feel in the hindquarters. Sleds are fun, but aren't used enough yet in most clubs, although the members love to play with them.

Do not put the training lane directly against a wall. Allow at least a foot of differently marked space between the wall and lane so the members don't slam shoulders while using the track, and so you also have a space for med racks and other equipment that is stored out of the way but easy to use. This does not refer to just training clubs. Every club, even women-only facilities, could benefit from a training lane to do agility and upright movements.

Open up some space in the corners.

Depending on your club, open some space in the corners around the club of about 150 square feet each. These spaces are perfect for the trainers to use with semi-private training (groups up to four people) or for the members who are grasping functional training to have access to kettles and suspension training, which should be part of those areas. The corners work best, especially if you have an outer wall that can be used for medicine-ball training.

Develop a stretching area.

Members love a dedicated stretching area, but most club people deny it to the members because it appears as just open, wasted space. Get some nice mats and keep them clean, get some foam rollers of varying density, and add a few other tools, such as stability balls and bands, and dedicate a quieter space in the club where the members can do a little floor work prior to and after their workouts.

Become very strict about starting and ending classes and services as scheduled.

If the member has a 2:00 training appointment, the trainer has to be there at least 15 minutes prior to that time and ready to go. If the group class starts at 6:00 p.m. and is supposed to end at 7:00, be rigid about keeping exactly to those times. Members plan their day around appointments, and there is very little that shows as much disrespect for another person than to waste their time.

Also be extremely tough on the instructors who always think adding a bonus five minutes at the end of their class is customer service. The people in the class who have to pick up kids, for example, are mad at the instructor, but don't want to show disrespect to the instructor by walking out. And most likely, when that class runs over by five minutes, the next class now starts five minutes late. The classes must start on time and end a few minutes before the hour so the classes can change over and everybody stays on the schedule.

This rule also applies to the big picture of opening and closing on time. Many young morning staff team members simply open the door early because they see a member peering in. Do not, under any circumstances, get into the habit of opening the door prior to your stated opening time. By doing so, you train the members to appear a little earlier each day, winding up with a whole lot of mad members on the day you actually stick to your opening time. If you say you open at 5:00 a.m., open exactly at 5:00 a.m. and not a minute prior or a minute later. There is also a legal issue to consider if the staff lets people in early and then goes and finishes getting the club opened, leaving the members unsupervised. If there is an accident during a time when the club was supposed to be closed, you will have a major issue on your hands.

Take the financial hit, and get hand towels.

Hand towels are a nice service touch in almost any club and are relatively cheap to service each month. Keep stacks around the club and always on the front counter for members to carry while working out. There should also be spray bottles of disinfectant around as well, and since we are in the days of widely spread illnesses, such as the various flu viruses that hit each year, make it a habit to either have dispensers or bottles of hand sanitizer placed throughout the club. Items such as the towels and sprays give the perception that the place is clean since you can see members actually wiping stuff down after they use it. The spray smell also kind of lets members know that this place is constantly being cleaned, as well.

Group rooms become nasty and are often forgotten by everyone but the group instructors.

Group rooms become the private domain of the group people over time and slowly become the most disgusting rooms in the building. Junk starts piling up in the corners, lights start to go out, wires run everywhere left over from old music systems long gone, and the ever-present dirty fan sits in the corner near the front of the room as a status symbol for the hardcore groupies who love the front row. The club's management stops going in these rooms, and eventually the room just becomes a nasty mess.

Customer service dictates that these rooms need their own special routines to keep them acceptable for both members and guests. Each month the rooms should be stripped down to the basics, and anything that hasn't been used during the last 30 days has to go. Be especially aware of the tools that become gross from too much sweat and too much use.

High-volume items, such as bands and the small hand weights, are always the first to become funky and should be replaced completely on a regular basis. There is just something rude about a piece of equipment that has been sweated on by 38 different people a month. You may pretend to clean it, but at some point it just has to go. The staff has to be trained to hit these rooms several times a day, looking for unnecessary clutter and garbage left behind in the corners, such as coffee cups and used towels. People bring a lot of different junk into class, but never carry as much out as they carry in.

Anything with water needs to be inspected more often.

If it has water, it can quickly surprise you with how bad it can get. Shower areas, pools, hot tubs, sinks, toilets, and urinals all need extra attention throughout the day. If you have a dedicated maintenance person who is there throughout the day, that person needs to have a special checklist for these areas.

These are, by the way, the key areas that will cost you female members if they are not kept at a high level of cleanliness. The bad news is that it only takes one questionable experience with any of these areas before the member hits the door. You will not get a second chance to prove that those nasty wet areas were just a fluke of the moment, and that these spots are usually, but not right at the moment, really kept nice and clean.

These areas are also the spots that can quickly cost you new memberships. Potential members judge the cleanliness of your entire facility by these areas, and once the judgment of dirty is passed, then there is not much you can do to change that perception.

Some owners consider the criticism they receive for the occasional dirty club as too harsh, but they forget the term "club blind." This means that most owners and managers are in the club so much that they stop seeing the club as it really is. Once you get used to seeing something almost every day, you actually stop seeing it at all. But a guest who is in the club for the first time is not blinded by familiarity and sees every dust ball, broken light switch, sweat stain, and smear on your mirrors.

Keeping things clean for the members, which will be pounded a little harder in Chapter 18, is another way to show respect for the guests of your house. If you invited your family over for Christmas, you would probably make sure your house is spotless for your very discerning mother, and you would make sure that every guest is treated special. The same is true for your members and your club. It is your house, and these are your guests each day, so make sure you show these guests the respect they deserve by offering a clean house.

Do These Things Now

- Initiate a three-foot contact rule with your staff.

- Start locker-room patrols every 30 minutes.

- Get into the habit of doing club sweeps.

- Consider getting service specialists back on the floor.

- Open up space in the club so members have room to move.

- Stick to rigid times for your training appointments and classes.

- Visit every room in the club every day to check for clutter and dirt.

Customer service is as simple as ...

decent soap.

Buy some quality soap for your locker rooms and showers.

You cannot use those small, fragile, very low-end white dispensers and hope to give anyone the illusion of service. And if the soap is some strange green color, then you purchased an industrial compound better used to clean your SUV because you should not even use that garbage on your dog.

Get nice dispensers, fill them full of high quality soap, and then keep them full. The same goes for toilet paper. If you can use the toilet paper to sand down the rust on your old plates, you have a cheap issue you need to deal with.

Spend a little money where it counts. Buy some nice soap for your members.

18

Your Club Is Never as Clean as You Think

Even the owners with the dirtiest, nastiest clubs always claim the same thing when asked, "How do you stand out from your competitors?" "Why, I have the cleanest club and the best staff in the market," they answer. "All my members tell me that every day."

Every owner claims this, even if his staff is as dumb as a field of bowling balls and his club hasn't been cleaned since his wife left him four years ago. All owners claim that they have the cleanest facility and the best staff because what is the alternative? Admit that they hire stupid relatives and that they are pigs who don't even clean their own homes?

Cleanliness is the direct child of customer service. You can't have a dirty club and have any hope of anyone ever saying you have great service. Imagine walking into a disgustingly dirty restaurant with soiled tablecloths and sickening restrooms, yet would you walk out after your meal and then tell your friends about the wonderful food? No matter how good the food is, if the restaurant is nasty, then there isn't much the staff can do to win you over as a long-term customer.

It is the same in the fitness business. Buying decent equipment and training your staff will only get you so far if your physical plant is so dirty it becomes a distraction to your members. Remember, you may not lose all the guys, but you will probably lose most of the females who try your club. Men, being the socially negligent outcasts that they are, often don't "see" the dirt or clutter that can mar a good facility, unless they are the higher earners in your community or have businesses of their own that demand an awareness of what's clean and what is not.

The women in the club, however, often look for a higher standard than the guys. They ask questions, such as, "Would I shower here myself?" or "How desperate would I have to be to use that restroom?" Their standards are often more directly related to the practical cleanliness of your business, but if you fail the cleanliness test at any level, it will cost you members at retention time, and you would be much less likely to ever get a single referral from your female members.

The women in the club, by the way, are often higher referral sources than the men. If women find something they like, they are much more likely to share that source of something good with a wider range of friends than most guys. Track your referrals closely for a year, and you will validate that the majority of your referrals are from the women in the club, especially if you master group activities of any kind and if you keep your place clean.

Cleanliness is customer service, and neither concept can exist without the other. It is probably a fact for most owners that a dirty club has cost that owner far more members than all the dumb staff he has ever hired combined, or probably more than his competitors have taken away through the years.

The bad news for most owners is that a clean club is not something worth bragging about in the paper or during a membership tour. Having a clean business is a base expectation for your members. This means that they pay each month, and for that payment, they expect certain things to happen in exchange for that money.

For example, if a member gives you $49 a month, he then expects you to know his name, have working equipment, be nice to him when he is in the club, give him enough help to be able to get something out of his membership, and that you will keep a high level of cleanliness as a minimum standard.

Providing these things to your members is not customer service. Customer service only occurs when you exceed base expectations. Meeting all these base expectations just gets you into the game, sort of like putting an ante into a poker game. Putting in an ante gives you a chance to see the cards, but paying an ante does not guarantee you will win.

It is the same with the member and his base expectations. Meeting these gets you a chance to run a business in the marketplace, but meeting these doesn't guarantee anything except that you have a right to chase new members and try to make money, as does every other competitor in the market.

How You Clean the Club Controls the Perception of Whether It Is Clean

There are generally only three ways a club gets cleaned each day. You either use an outside cleaning company, have your own cleaning crew, or you aren't making much money, or are just getting started, and you and the staff try to clean it.

The downside of all three of these cleaning methods is that they all rely on the same technique. No matter who is doing the cleaning in your business, everyone involved in the process only relies on surface wiping instead of practicing deep cleaning.

Surface wiping gives the illusion that everything in the club is clean, but this method doesn't really hold up to much scrutiny under close inspection, such as the prying eyes of the members. In this method, a cleaner walks through the club with a bottle of some type of spray disinfectant in one hand and a paper towel in the other, wiping down everything in her path. It smells clean, and you watched her do it so you know she did clean stuff, but the club really isn't clean.

The problem is that she never really moved anything or went beyond the surfaces of the equipment. Look at a typical fixed bench, for example. Your cleaner walks up to the bench, sprays the seat, and wipes off the vinyl and maybe the edges of the top seat, and moves on. Yes, she did hit the area where most people sit, but the bench is not clean and will still stink and still be dirty.

What she neglected to consider is that the members use that piece of equipment in a variety of ways. They sit on both sides and the end, lay on it for certain exercises, kneel on it for dumbbell movements, and some even step up on it using it as a rigid plyo box. All of these members are leaking sweat like a cheap water balloon.

This also means that the members sweat on this machine from all angles. All manner of body oil, sweat drips, perfume traces, and other things too nasty to mention are all over every part of that bench. If you want to really clean this heavily used piece, then you need to wipe the legs, the base, and probably underneath the seat as well, since sweat will run over the side and then curl under before it drips. Wiping the seat is surface cleaning. Turning it over and wiping down the entire piece, to ensure that it is really, truly clean, is deep cleaning, and you don't get deep cleaning in your club unless you set the standard yourself and then direct the results.

Keeping a clean business, again the foundation of customer service, has to be planned like every other worthwhile activity. Hiring a cleaning company and giving them a list will not get you a clean club. In fact, because these companies only really surface clean, your business will actually get dirtier over time since the neglected areas just get and worse and worse due to accumulation.

Other ideas about deep cleaning include:

- The cardio has to be cleaned down to the floor, and often during the day. Sweat stains on the cardio, even if they were just put there minutes ago, give the perception that they are never cleaned, which is not what you want for a member who just jumps on a piece and says, "Gross" under his breath.

- You also have to clean under the cardio each week. Not only will the cardio last longer with fewer repairs, but the gunk that is under there will escape as members walk by creating swirls of air with their feet.

- Wipe the inside of the lockers daily.

- The floor in front of the toilets needs to be cleaned several times a day.

- Anything that is involved in a group-exercise class needs to be either dipped in a cleaning solution, such as bands and hand weights, or have every surface cleaned weekly in the case of the steps. These are always the nastiest rooms in the club when it comes to accumulated gunk and need special attention daily.

- Clean the corners of every room. This does sound weird, but over time the cleaners (with their mops and floor squeegees) end up pushing cleaning solutions that have mixed with floor grime into the corners of every wet area, where it dries and accumulates. You have to hit the corners with a putty knife several times a month, or that stuff will smell.

- Replace ceiling tiles. Stains on ceiling tiles kind of send that going-out-of-business message. Tiles are cheap, and fresh ones add light and a sense of cleanliness to a room.

- Drinking fountains need to have every inch of surface—top, bottom, and sides—wiped several times a day.

This list could go on and on, but these examples should help you recognize that the members' perception of clean and the standard-issue, underpaid, hating-their-job cleaner never match unless you set the standard of how things are supposed to be cleaned in your house for your guests.

I Know It Is Clean Because I Watched You Clean It

The perception of clean involves all of your senses. You can smell clean, you can feel clean, you can taste clean in a glass, you can hear the vacuum running and know something is being cleaned, and most importantly for many people, you know something is clean because you watched the person actually clean it.

Most club owners could greatly enhance the members' perception as to how clean their club is by actually having people clean it while the members are using it. How clean is this place? It must be really clean because I just watched that old retired guy spend an hour cleaning the cardio while I was doing my workout.

Creating this perception would involve hiring a cleaning person, such as a retired guy or just a regular cleaner, who wears a club uniform and does deep cleaning throughout the club during normal business hours. This is not the same type of cleaning that the crew would do at night, where the showers and locker rooms should be getting torn into, but rather more of spot cleaning designed to keep the club ready for the members and guests throughout the day.

This person can do almost everything but vacuum during the busy hours, which does drive the members insane (a short drive for many, and some have already taken the trip). The goal is to let the members see that you care enough about customer service that you have people constantly keeping the club up to a very high standard of cleanliness. The member's perception becomes their reality over time, as they grow accustomed to seeing your cleaners constantly on the job.

Going for the Big Clean

At least once a year, you have to shut the club down and go for the big clean.

No matter how hard you try, even if you understand the concept of deep cleaning, you can never get enough bodies in place at one time to clean the club deeply if you're restricted by normal business hours.

With this thought in mind, you need to close the club during one of the slower times in your area from Friday at 5:00 p.m. through opening on Monday. It goes without saying here that there will be members who get upset that you closed for a day or two, but when don't they get mad about something?

Understand now that you can never please everyone, so just do what is right for the business. If you wait to make change until all members agree, then you will never make change because you could give the members free money, and someone would complain that you gave them a hundred-dollar bill and they had a hard time getting change.

The Plummer 50/50 Rule

No matter what you do in your business, at least 50 percent of the members will love you for it and the other 50 percent will hate you. Always do what is right for the business, and live with the members who disagree.

In the case of shutting down your business for a couple of days, there will be a small handful of disgruntled members in your face, but the overall effect on the entire membership of having a really cleaned and restored club will far exceed the minor pain of dealing with the ever-constantly complaining few.

Your goal of closing for a few days is to get a large number of people focused on doing nothing but helping you get your club back to what it was the day it was opened. It takes bodies to do this, so you might bribe your kids, pay out-of-work friends or relatives, trade membership time for hours worked for some of the members, or just plain pay people to help. It will take many more people than you think because everything in the club needs to be touched, fixed, painted, oiled, greased, or carried out the door.

Following is a partial list of what you need to try to accomplish during the two-day club closure and makeover:

- Assign someone to check every light bulb and switch in the club. You would be surprised at the number of these that simply don't work after a few years of being busy.

- Get someone else to close every door in the club, including all lockers and stalls, looking for that latch that doesn't work or lock that is broken. While you are it, make sure the inside of every locker is ready for business as well, including hooks and shelves.

- Flush everything at least once to see if it works.

- If you haven't used it in three months, throw it away. Clutter is dirty to the members, and this is your chance to toss it all.

- Clean out all the storage units. That strange smell in the free-weight area isn't that stinky member; it's the spilled drink in the storage closet (if it is a member, he goes, too).

- Move every piece of equipment, and clean under it.

- Wipe down every plate and dumbbell. If it is rusty, paint it, replace it, or lose it.

- Maybe it is time for some new wood in the sauna? Five years of naked butts on those seats might be enough.

- Don't forget to clean all the vents for the heating and air conditioning.

- This is your chance to replace the small things in the group rooms that get the most use and are the nastiest. New bands and hand weights are cheap and easy to replace.

- All clutter must go. Clutter is the equivalent of dirty, and you can't get the perception of a clean club if there is a surface layer of clutter. Do you really need that broken piece of equipment that has been in the corner for a year? Do you really need that box of lost and found under the desk that hasn't ever been cleaned out? Close your eyes and toss, or go get a drink and let some clean freak do it for you while you're gone.

- Consider a new club layout. Things change in the business. Maybe this year you have more functional and need less fixed equipment. Get some of the old stuff out that weekend, and blame the insurance guys, who told you that the neck machine is an issue and you have to get rid of it. Space is valuable, and open up some by eliminating some of the older fixed equipment. Hey, some of the members are already mad at you anyway for closing for a few days, so you might as well go for it all and get rid of some of the clunker pieces, too.

- Clean both sides of the rubber mats, and use a high-grade rubber/vinyl treatment to restore the luster of those mats (if needed).

- Paint something that weekend. Touch up everything if marked or scuffed, but paint at least one wall a new color to give the members the smell of new paint on Monday. New paint means fresh in their minds. You should, in fact, paint a wall a month so you always have that smell in your place.

This list could go on for quite a length. The point is that you can't do all of this if you are restricted by normal business hours. It takes a lot of people to take a club all the way back to the day it was new and fresh, yet this is what help sells memberships and adds to your member retention. Do this at least once a year, and if you have an extremely high volume club, consider twice a year.

Customer-Service Training for a Clean Club

Build cleaning into your service training. Most club staff can't really tell the difference between dirty and clean in a club. If you cringe at the thought that most of your younger staff couldn't tell if something was really clean, try to remember what your level of cleanliness was in your first apartment or in your dorm room at college.

Your standards rise as you age for most people, and if you have your money in it, then you might have even higher standards yet. Following are three simple training games that will help you build staff awareness in learning that cleanliness is customer service.

The white-glove meeting

This is a simple meeting idea. Get a box of cheap, white-cloth gloves, and give every staff person one. Then, tell them to spread out and rub any service in the club they can reach with their gloved hand and then write down what they found in that area on a clipboard. Give one person a ladder so he can do the top of the lockers and fans. If you rub and the glove comes away clean, you have a great club with a perception of service. If the club comes away dirty, you have something to talk about in the meeting, such as how this affects sales and retention, as well as having a complete list of the spots the cleaner needs to go after during his next visit.

Bombing the locker room

This is a little extreme for a staff-training exercise, but if you do it once, you will make a lasting impression with your people. Schedule a staff meeting during a really slow part of the day, or better when you are closed, and then come in early and destroy your locker room.

Take a can of talcum powder, and dump it all over the floor. Open most of the lockers, and throw a few old socks inside. Stuff a toilet with paper and mess up the shower drains. Make it nasty, much like it really looks like after a day of neglect by your staff that avoid the 30-minute walk-throughs they should be doing.

Start your meeting elsewhere in the club, and begin by talking about the effect of a dirty club on new sales and member retention. Take the staff on a tour of the club pointing out the key areas, such as cardio, that always give a bad impression if dirty. End up in the locker room, where they should be appalled as a group.

Tell them that this locker room is the key to creating member service, and the first impression they felt as they walked through the door is greatly amplified by a member who is paying to be at the club. Then, spend the next hour cleaning the room together so you can hammer home the point.

The individual walk-through

As noted earlier, you and your staff spend so much time in the club that you actually stop seeing it for what it really is. Becoming "club blind" is the enemy of customer service because you can never really keep the member's perception of what is acceptable in your mind. You may want to keep the club clean, but you just don't see what needs to be done anymore.

During a slow time of day, just grab a different member of the staff and do a walk-through, looking for cleanliness issues. By forcing yourself to walk and look, you can often lift the blinders that prevent you from seeing what is really there.

As you walk, you can also use that time to show your staff person what you see, and then educate him as to why that is bad for the business. Once the staff starts to see the business through your eyes by learning what is really important, they will start working toward the same goals you are. Most staff want to do a good job, but many just don't have your experience or eye as to what is really important in the business.

Don't Forget That the Club Will Never Really Be Clean

There are varying stages of what constitutes a clean club, ranging from simply disgusting to somewhat nice, but there will never be a perfectly clean club. The club just can't be perfectly clean, due to the constant interaction between people trying to clean it each day, but a much larger number of people trying to make it dirty by working out.

Your goal is to create a perception that your club is indeed the cleanest in town. Cleanliness is service, and service is retention. Most owners place cleaning somewhere on the routine list, when it is actually one of the more important things you can do each day to keep the members you already have, and to make it easier for your sales team to acquire new members.

Do These Things Now

- Ask yourself this question: "Would my mother shower in this club?"

- Learn the difference between surface cleaning and deep cleaning.

- Get someone to clean the club while the members are in the club.

- Close the club down completely two days a year with the goal of making it look as good as it did when you opened.

- Create training games for the staff that highlight keeping the club clean for members.

Customer service is as simple as ...

space to move.

Give the members a little room to breath in your club.

In the 1990s, competition was based upon how big your workout floor was, and then how much equipment you could cram into the space. This started with the Gold's Gym guys from that era who always sought to best each other by having bragging rights to the biggest space and the most stuff.

The situation has changed dramatically in the last several years in the member's head, although the old club owners still keep buying as much as they can afford and then stuff the club. Training now is not based upon one person using one machine at a time and then moving on to the next space. Training in the '90s was very contained. People didn't use or need much space except to walk to the next piece, lock themselves in, and do their thing. Today, people move and want space.

Walking lunges, pulling sleds, farmer's walks, kettlebell swings, and agility work on a floor ladder are now all part of someone's workout choices, and all of these need space for the person to do them. Simply look out at your floor on a Monday night, and see how many of your clients are trying to do lunges with a medicine ball using your walkways.

Even the training clubs need more space. Most of the old-style training clubs were built too small with only about 1,500 square feet, which is fine when you're training one-on-one with someone, but horrible if the members want to use the space as part of a group experience.

Mainstream fitness businesses need training lanes (similar to a single-lane track), open space in the corners where they can do kettles and balance work, space for suspension training, and space around the functional cable equipment so members can use the equipment as it was designed.

You also need socialization space in the club. People don't want to always rush away from the club. If you have nowhere to sit, such as a sports bar/juice bar area, or a stretching area to just sit and wind down before finishing your workout, you force people to just hit the club and leave, which is not what they want from you.

Open up your space a little, and remember to create the entire experience and not just rely on the sheer amount of stuff you can force into a single training space.

19

We Always Dress for the Guests of Our House

It's your house and your guests. You should always dress respectably for the guests of your house.

How you and your staff dress for a day of work at your business is a direct reflection of how you feel about yourself and your members. Most club owners, however, take the low road when it comes to uniforms and dress codes, relying on tee shirts, badly fitting golf shirts, or baggy workout clothes.

Customer service is a perception drawn by the person who is receiving the service at the time. This perception is based upon many factors, but the foundational question all members ask is: "Am I getting the respect I deserve in this transaction?" This perception is also transitional in nature and can vary to extremes during an ongoing transaction, such as a person holding a long-term fitness membership.

The member could be happy for months with the service he is receiving, but it might only take a small incident to instantly change how he feels about his relationship with your business. There is also the factor of the sheer number of members you might have in your business. The more members you have, the harder it becomes to keep everyone feeling like an individual and special during a lengthy relationship. Remember, being taken for granted in a business relationship is a feeling that angers most people and spells the end of the possibility of that relationship continuing into the future.

For example, a member who is in her 40s and who is paying $49 per month arrives at the club and has a small problem with her membership billing that she would like to receive some help with during her visit. The person behind the counter tries to help, but is fumbling a little with the computer. While the member is standing there, she notices that the counter person hasn't shaved in a few days, has a wrinkled tee shirt on and baggy jeans, and looks like he just rolled out of bed about 20 minutes before he came to work.

This guy represents your club at the moment. No matter what you have invested in your business, and no matter how good you think you are in the club market, this guy at that point in time is your business, and you are not looking good. His image lowers the member's expectation that he can help. He doesn't look professional. He obviously is a very low person on the team chart because no real employee would dress that badly, and even if he can help, the member walks away, shaking her head and muttering to herself, "Where do they get these people?"

Creating a Professional Image Is More Important Than You Realize

Staff that is professionally dressed convey an image to your clients that you have the team that can get things done. You simply gain more credibility with a staff that is dressed ready for business compared to a competitor who is lax about what his team wears to work.

Why do you think other professionals—which is the image you have to build within your business—dress well? How believable is a banker dressed in a tee shirt and jeans? Would you trust a doctor in a worn-out golf shirt with a frayed collar? The first impression of your business is formed by, and the ongoing image of your ability to provide service is tied to, the image of those standing behind your front counter.

But in the fitness business, we don't think of the people on our staff as professionals. Your failure to think of your staff as a team of professionals created to support the needs of a paying membership is just plain bad business. The clients who do support your business look at you and your staff as a team of fitness professionals there to service them and to help them reach their fitness goals. The members pay, and they expect you to build a team of people worthy of the money they give you each month.

We should be comparing our businesses to the good service businesses in the world, such as the higher end hotels. At first, this does not seem like a direct comparison, but, in reality, hotels and fitness facilities are very close in their goals. These hotels, for example, cater to people looking for a good experience during their visit, who are willing to pay a reasonable amount of money not to stay at a low-end hotel, and bring the expectation that they will receive excellent service in exchange for the money spent.

In good hotels, everyone on the staff is part of a team dedicated to delivering a complete blanket of service, covering every aspect of the interaction between the guest and the hotel. The kids parking the cars are a vital link in the service chain, as are the front-desk people, the bellmen, the bar workers, housekeeping, and all the others that work in the hotel. If one person lets down and provides bad service, the overall image of the hotel, as perceived by the guest's experience during the stay, is negatively affected.

The fitness business does not use this team approach to service. The front counter people are usually undertrained, underdressed, and throwaways who are simply hired to fill slots and shifts. The trainers do their own thing and operate as a separate unit that usually has little interaction with the rest of the staff.

The group people come in, teach, and leave, having essentially been paid for doing their own workout. The sales department often believes that everyone else on the staff exists to service them and often look down on the rest of the team. Simply put, there is no consistent team delivering service, but rather a bunch of separate departments doing their own work with no relationship to the overall goals of the business.

The hotel staff is dressed in uniforms that convey respect for the guest, demonstrate that they are a team in this together, and most importantly, make a statement that they are all professionals who exist to make your experience better.

The club team, on the other hand, dresses poorly and often dresses differently by department. The counter people wear their street clothes or tee shirts and golf shirts. The trainers, who always fight any type of uniform because it restricts their ability to show their own bodies off a little, usually free style, wearing the hot trend workout clothing that is often too tight and intimidates the very people they are supposed to be serving.

The group people wear virtually anything that they own, and often those clothes are too revealing, conveying everything but a professional look. The salespeople are often workout people who dress with shirts too tight or clothes that are too revealing. The owners and managers start dressing down after working in the club for any length of time, forgetting that it is a business with an image to protect.

What Is a Professional Look for a Fitness Staff?

First of all, it is not about wearing formal business clothes. You do not, nor should you even consider, wearing ties and formal dress clothes to work in a fitness business. But you should on all occasions dress to achieve a professional look.

It is worth noting that most clubs seeking a higher level of customer service adapt a dress-code policy of some sort. Dress codes lay out the restrictions of what a staff can, and cannot, wear before the staff person formally accepts the job. Clubs that add dress codes later after their businesses are up and running often give the employees at least 30 days notice before enforcing the new policy. As always, run the dress code you wish to use by your attorney first to make sure you are not breaking any labor-board rulings in your state.

Dress codes also have to match the type of club you own. For example, if you have a high-energy, serious workout club, you might have a different restriction on facial hair than an owner trying to run an upscale adult club, catering to people in their 40s and 50s. The first club might be okay with a chin piece on the males, but the second club might say no to that look in their club. Remember that if your dress code is in writing, and the staff signs it prior to hire, or as part of an introduction program of a new dress code, you can enforce most of the restrictions you feel are important to building a professionally dressed team.

The following are a few tips that might take your thinking toward a better definition of professional. There is one simple rule of thumb for what is professional: if you have to ask, you probably already know the answer. For example, an owner might ask, "What about a guy with a raging dragon down one arm? Should he cover that up at work?" If you had to ask someone an opinion about the dragon, you already know the answer, which is, "Yes, he should be covering it up at work." If it bothers you enough to ask, then it is already a controversial issue and you need to always err on the conservative side.

- Professional is well-groomed. Hair is neat, you are clean and showered, you are shaved (according to the club type), your teeth are brushed, and you are ready to talk to the members. These points might seem obvious to many people, but too many of you have staff people who sleep late, pick up the golf shirt they had on yesterday off the back of the chair, and show up for work less than 30 minutes after opening their eyes. Remember that customer service is a series of small things all done well. Take no chances when you are building a professional team, and teach your staff exactly what you want and how you want it done, even if it involves teaching your people that they need to get up and shower and put on a clean shirt before work.

- Your uniform, which will be discussed later, is pressed and ready for business. You would not be allowed to wear a uniform top, for example, that is frayed around the collar, stretched out by too many laundry cycles, or is just too old because the staff person only has one shirt.

- You should have shoes that are only worn in the business and are used for work only. Beaten-to-death workout shoes or scuffed dress shoes are not allowed.

- Tattoos and body art is fine, as long as it isn't displayed in the club. Body art is still too controversial for too many members to have a place in your business. If someone has a complete arm sleeve done, that is fine, except he should expect to be wearing a long-sleeve shirt year-round in that club to cover it up.

- Piercings are also controversial, and somewhat of a health risk in the club. Eye piercings, nose studs, and anything on the tongue is just bad for the image of your business, because it is very difficult to maintain a professional image, and to build trust that you can help the client, when you have a spike in your tongue and speak with a lisp or spray saliva every other word. For example, one club owner introduced a dress code as part of his takeover of a club in his market. The club had been flat for several years, and the existing owner wanted out. The new owner came in, met the staff, and warned everyone that a dress code would be coming and would be enforced in 30 days. One aspect of the new code was no piercing except for normal ear wear. One young staff person, who had an eye pin and a nose stud, threw a fit that the club had no right to tell her what she could, or could not, wear on her body. She was right, the owner couldn't tell her what she should and could not wear on her body, but he could tell her that if she wanted to work in that club, then the piercings would have to disappear during normal business hours. You can build and enforce a dress code if you do it legally and enforce it across all employees so you don't discriminate.

- Hats and other props can also become an issue when you are trying to build a professionally dressed staff dedicated to customer service. Wearing hats in a building was once thought of as very bad manners, although that rule seems to be dying with the rest of common courtesy. If you wear hats for a special promotion of some kind, then everyone wears that same hat pointing in the same direction. Hats in the business should be considered props used only on special occasions and not allowed unless they are part of a team look. Next time you are in a nice restaurant or hotel, note how many members of the staff are wearing ball caps backward.

- Almost anything that is too overdone is always bad. Giant, dangly earrings are dangerous in the club and should not be allowed. Too much cologne or too much perfume is irritating to many people and should be restricted on the staff. Shirts that are too tight, bare midriffs that are too revealing, hardcore bodybuilders, and most anything in the club that is extreme or edgy is not usually part of a great customer-service presentation. You can be too big, too smelly, or too tattooed to work in a professional environment.

Many small-club owners think that these rules don't really apply to them because they only have a limited amount of clients. If you only have one client, and that client is paying you, dress as a professional to show respect for the person who is paying your bills. Having only 50 to 100 training clients is not an excuse to disrespect the people who are supporting what you do for a living.

Keep Your Concept of a Uniform Simple

The power of dressing alike as a team is that uniforms build pride in that team. Professional uniforms also unify your people by building the sense that they are all in this together. If everyone wears the same look, and the uniforms are chosen to give a professional edge to what amounts to a lot of inexperienced young people working in a fitness business, then your staff will realize that they are all on the same team, trying to accomplish the same things no matter what type of work they do in this business.

Due to the cost of a uniform, owners and managers should try to shift the cost to the staff for a certain portion of the expense, such as owning their own pants and shoes. The typical club will spend at least $10,000 per year on logoed shirts that still don't convey a professional look.

First of all, you do not need to get your logo embroidered on your uniforms. This is a total waste of money for the club owner, and that money could be better spent in marketing or club upkeep. Your staff members are not billboards for your business; they are a team of people whom you are trying to develop into professionals capable of attracting more members and of keeping the ones you already have in the system.

There is also a legal issue here. If you require logos on your shirts, then you are also required to pay for those shirts. If you require the staff person to just wear black, or black and white, however, you do not have to pay for those clothes, according to the labor boards, but again, run this by your attorney first in your area.

If you don't have uniforms in your business yet, or are trying to upgrade away from tee shirts and badly fitting golf shirts, start with just wearing basic black. Everyone owns something in black, and black clothing often conveys a feeling of dressing up a little. The staff rule would be to dress for success, and no tee shirts or golf shirts would be allowed as part of the work dress code.

Golf shirts have long been the standard for many clubs, having somehow made the transition between what a pro golfer might wear to work to what is acceptable as a uniform in a fitness business. Golf shirts were originally designed for men by men. Traditional golf shirts fit the majority of your staff very badly. Women, for instance, look horrible dressed in a shirt that is almost always too baggy, with sleeves that are not designed for a female body and with a buttoned front area that sags too low.

There are newer model golf shirts that have become available during the last several years that are fitted better, but we are talking about uniform shirts that might cost $40 or more for a single top. The cost for the return just isn't worth the money since outfitting an entire staff could cost thousands of dollars a year. You have to get away from spending so much money on something that gets you so little return as an owner.

Stop paying for your logo on clothing that gets you no return, and just simply require the staff to wear black within certain guidelines. Black gives a professional look, and you are now $10,000 or so ahead in a typical club that could be applied somewhere else where you might get more of a direct return for your investment.

If you are profitable, you can go beyond the basic-black rule. For example, if you want to add some color over the summer, such as a purple shirt; then buy the staff the look you want, and wear them for June through August, but still don't waste the money in getting logos done.

There are a few exceptions to the logo rule. If you are working with a strong clothing provider that can get you fashionable clothing, such as resort-style shirts or mock turtles, then adding the logos is usually done as part of the order and can be done cheaply. But buying a $40 custom shirt and then adding a logo is a worthless waste of your money.

Traditional nametags are also not much use in a club. Most owners put too much information on too small of a space and then have the staff wear it in an area that shouldn't require the member to get that close to read what it says.

Lanyards worn around the neck are a much better choice for nametags and do a lot less damage to the shirts. Lanyards can be made of bright colors, and the nameplate itself can be a plastic disk with the employee's first name on it. Just the first name is all you need. Most owners put the name of the club on it, the employee's full name, and the person's title, all on a few inches of plastic.

First of all, putting the name of the club on the tag doesn't really accomplish anything. If the member doesn't know where he is, putting the club name on the tag really isn't going to help. Secondly, you don't want to put the employee's last name on anything anymore for liability reasons and to protect your staff. If you have someone's last name, you can usually find that person's address. Protect your staff, and keep last names restricted to only the areas of the club, such as sales business cards, that might warrant this usage.

Titles are also not needed. When you build a customer-service team, you want to build that image that we are the same and we all exist to help you get the best experience you can from this business. Titles on nametags send the message to the guest that there are different levels of service available, depending on who you talk to up the food chain. Work toward the image that everyone can help you no matter what you need.

Following are a few uniform ideas that can be applied to all the departments in your club.

The owners and the managers

If you work in the club, or have a presence in the club, you should dress like everyone else, only better. If you interact with the members in any part of the day, you should be wearing the same uniform as the rest of the staff. The emphasis is on team-building, and you are part of the team you are creating.

You should also be the one setting the standard of professionalism in the club. It is hard to hold a young staff accountable when you are the worst-dressed person in the club. If you are holding other people accountable, then you have to hold yourself accountable.

If you are starting with black as your uniform base, get some solid black pants, black socks, and black shoes that are functional, meaning you can wander around the club during the day without killing your feet. You can wear a black mock turtleneck in cooler months, or a black shirt with a square cut bottom and with buttons down the front designed to wear not tucked into your pants. Depending on the region of the country, these might be called resort shirts. If you own the place (or manage it), act like it, and dress as a leader, setting the example for the rest of the team.

Salespeople

Salespeople should dress a lot like the owners and managers by wearing nicer clothing that fits well. The sales team can go with the black pants, or black skirts and a top appropriate for that person. In the cooler months, the women on the staff can wear blazers and feminine tops instead of going for the baggy workout jacket.

IHRSA's *Club Business International* magazine printed an interesting article in late 2009, citing that the potential members touring the club said they would be more comfortable on the tour with a trainer instead of a traditional salesperson. If you are building a career in the fitness business, or if you someday wish to own your own fitness business, getting certified as an ACE-certified trainer, even if you never actually intend to train people in the future, is a solid career-building tool.

All salespeople working full-time in any club should have a training certification and be put through an extended length of personal training in the club as a client. Remember that you are selling the benefits of what fitness can do for you, not a membership, and you can offer much more help and guidance during a sales tour if you also have a training background.

The training department

The training department can, and should, conform to some type of uniform standard in your business. Everyone realizes that trainers have to move for a living, but this doesn't mean that you have wear your favorite training tee shirt from college that has been worn for every workout you've done during the last six years.

Trainer clothing has taken some odd turns during the last few years. Trainers often emulate what is trendy in their field, and if some whacked-out trainer perceived as a guru in a fitness magazine is wearing strange headgear and a shirt so tight it looks painful, then every trainer in the country wants that look. If you doubt this happens, just remember back to the orange work-boot phase in the 1990s or the first generation of Under Armour® that every trainer owned during the early 2000s.

Trainers can wear shorts with pockets and a zipper in the front, such as coaches' shorts, or black pants that are loose enough to allow them to move a little. They can also wear black mock turtles with any sleeve length appropriate for the time of year or other classier versions of the basic tee shirt, such as ones that have banded collars with a neckline and banded sleeves. Trainers also have to be taught that the shirts need to be one size too big. It is not about them and their bodies; it is about the clients they are supposed to help. And too tight is often too intimidating to the client. The lanyard nametags also work for trainers. They can just swing them to the back when demonstrating an exercise or remove them completely when they lead a group training.

The counter team

How the members of the counter team dress is about trying to achieve a positive first impression when a guest or member walks through the front door. Due to the nature of the business, we often hire younger people to work the counter areas, and often these folks don't have any idea as to what proper dress is for a business. If you want to be safe, assume that anyone working the front counter area, no matter what that person's age, needs help getting dressed for work.

Clearly state what is acceptable dress for the counter. You might even do a mini-fashion show during a staff meeting to show what you think is good and what you think is unacceptable.

If you are following the black theme, require that everyone stick to the rules. You don't want your young guys wearing nasty workout shoes with black pants. You also don't want your young female staff wearing clothes more appropriate for a bar instead of a day shift in a fitness business.

If people show up dressed poorly, and you have a dress-code statement they signed and agreed to in their file, then send them home and don't let them work that day. Your members, and member retention, is worth far more than keeping a young staff member on the job who isn't bright enough to dress properly for work. Set the standard, enforce the standard, and have zero tolerance in anything that might cost you a membership or a renewal.

The group-exercise people

They have to dress as part of the team, although they would be the exception to the black uniforms. Many of the national group-exercise companies, such as Body Training Systems, recommend uniforms on a quarterly basis that reflect a professional look and that is also fun.

The thing to control is that many instructors dress to show their bodies too much. If you are in San Francisco, you are probably okay with that, but if you are in more conservative parts of the country, then you need to set some type of minimum standard as to what is acceptable as an instructor. The issue is how far you can go with a bare midriff or how small is small when it comes to workout shorts.

Many group instructors have the same uniform issues as the trainers: they believe that they are role models and that showing off their bodies is what the members want to see. This logic is probably as far from the reality of what the members want as you can get. Group-exercise instructors and the trainers are there to provide a supportive and caring attitude while guiding the members toward achieving a higher level of fitness. Due to their choice of clothing, group people and trainers are often entry barriers to the business, not the role models they often believe themselves to be. These groups need to conform to the same standards as everyone else on your staff.

Childcare people and the maintenance staff

These people are usually neglected when it comes to uniforms, mainly because the current uniforms the club owners are buying are too expensive to give to what is considered "non-vital" staff.

If you are going with the black look, then these people need to be part of the team, as well. The W Hotels, a chain of boutique hotels that tend to offer the guests a unique experience with a top-end flair, dress their janitors and other maintenance people in black jeans with black mock turtles. The staff can move and do their jobs, but when you pass one of them in the hall, they look professional. This type of secondary staff will also bring more pride to their jobs when they are dressed as part of the team.

The basic-black uniform is a good starting point if you are tired of wasting money on expensive logo wear that really has no bearing upon your business. In this system, the staff wears their own clothes, yet you make the decision as to what is acceptable in the business. If you want to go beyond the basic-black look, you can do so by simply adding color. If you get into the solid color scheme, change it quarterly. There was a successful chain in New York that changed the colors of the shirts the staff wore four times a year. It gave the staff a nice change, but it was still somewhat inexpensive for the club's owners since they were buying simple shirts without logos or custom work. The rule for building professionals is to just stay away from cheap uniforms that lower the perception of service in your business.

The Concept of Pride

Many successful businesspeople find it hard to imagine that you would have to actually tell a business owner that he has to dress to go to work. These same businesspeople find it inconceivable that a young owner would invest that much money to open his own business and then wear old jeans and a worn-out golf shirt to work. The question is: where is this guy's pride?

This same question also applies to most of your other staff as well. Should anyone really have to tell a trainer that he is being judged as a professional on how he presents himself and not on just what he knows or how good of shape he is in?

Pride has to be taught by the owners, who have to first find it in themselves. If you want to be successful, start dressing like you are successful now, and don't wait until someday when you might make a little money. If you are a salesperson who wants to someday be an owner, remember that you are judged every day, and judged harshly, by how you present yourself.

You teach pride by setting standards in your business practices, such as how you dress in this company, and then you explain to the staff over and over that customer service is a perception based upon the professional standards this company sets and lives by each day.

Uniforms are just one of the many answers to the question: "Where is your pride in this business?" Dress your team in a manner that shows respect for the people who pay the bills, and you will become a more financially successful company over time.

Do These Things Now

- Create a professional image in your business by dressing your staff at a higher level.

- Learn that there is a look beyond tee shirts and golf shirts.

- Assume that no one has ever shown anyone on your staff how to dress.

- Keep your concept of a uniform simple.

- It is not worth your money to buy uniforms.

Customer service is as simple as ...
good nametags.

Most nametags actually work against the members. The tags are too small, contain too much information, and the staff person's name is so small that a member and staff almost have to be dating before the member can get close enough to read it. And why does every owner dictate that the badge is situated on one side of the staff person's chest, which might be the worst place you could put a tag with so much information on it that the members have to get just inches away to read?

Use lanyards that hang around the staff person's neck instead of traditional nametags. Lanyards can be purchased with bright colored materials, and they hang much more discreetly in the middle of the person's chest. Lanyards also do not damage the shirts as many nametags can.

Just put the staff person's first name in large print on both sides of a plastic disk that attaches to the clip on the lanyard (so in case the disk gets flipped over it can be read from either side). Do not put the staff person's last name on the tags. If the members need to know someone's last name they can ask, and the salespeople can hand out cards with their full name as needed. Protect the safety and privacy of your staff at all opportunities.

The members do not need to be reminded of the name of the club they joined. They do not need to know your title. Good service dictates that everyone on the staff is a team dedicated to helping the members get the most out of their workouts. Titles convey a varying degree of service, meaning the people with the lower titles can't really help you much, so you might as well keep working up the chain until you find a better-sounding title.

Just the first name is all that should be on the tag that can be easily read from a distance with discretion by a member is all that you need. Everyone on the team is equal when it comes to their ability to deliver service, so let your nametags reflect that statement to the members.

20

Love What You Do, and Share the Passion

Fitness is a personal journey. Most people find an aspect of fitness that suits their interest and lifestyle, and that activity becomes the person's primary vehicle to pursue fitness. This activity also can rise to a higher level of importance for many people by becoming something in their life that invokes a great deal of passion.

The negative side of this passion is that once you find your sport, you usually do so to the exclusion of all other activities in the fitness world. Runners are runners, group-exercise people are group people, and the weight lifters remain in a land all their own. If you want to verify this passion in people, try putting a serious runner in a room with a serious lifter and see if they can agree on any common training ideas. What you do becomes the right way—and often the only way—to train, to the exclusion of all other fitness venues.

This linear approach to fitness is also one of the things that can hurt your ability to provide service to and retain members. We know what we know, and we force the members to follow our path. The problem with this is that you have an entire staff all pursuing fitness in their own way, trying to get the members to believe what they believe.

Perhaps among the worst people to have on your staff are a born-again fitness person who is now in sales, coupled with a trainer who enters bodybuilding shows as his hobby. The born-again fitness person has lost big weight working with the trainer, who, because he is extremely linear in his approach to fitness and trains every client as if they too are entering shows, has set a goal for your other staff person to enter her first natural bodybuilding show as a way to increase her motivation.

The salesperson starts every tour with a personal monologue on her fitness journey, how she lost so much weight and what fitness means to her. She often tears up during her story and always shows the picture of her third-place finish in the show in her little bikini thing.

The trainer, on the other hand, takes every client, no matter how they live or what they want from a fitness program, and puts them on a split workout, doing isolation exercises. He trains for show muscles, and all his clients, because they trust his judgment and expertise, follow down that path without realizing that training for bodybuilding really doesn't help your golf swing that much.

Neither one of these people are helping your business. They are passionate, and they probably mean well, but the salesperson is forgetting that it is really about listening to the guests and helping them get what they want, while the trainer fails to understand that just a small percentage of people coming through the door are looking for a 1970s bodybuilding approach to fitness.

Another example might be a person who rotates through trainers based upon who is available. In clubs that don't have a central fitness culture established, this switching amongst your trainers can be a real adventure.

For example, the member trains with Sarah on Monday, who is a vegetarian and who believes in high reps. Wednesday, the member works out with Sam, who is an older trainer who still believes in circuit training and one-set high intensity training. Sam doesn't, by the way, give a damn what you eat because then he would have to explain why he is so fat.

On Friday, the member ends up with Martin, who is a functional freak, and the member finds himself flipping tires in the parking lot and smacking them with a sledgehammer. Martin is a high-protein fanatic, and the member also walks out with several buckets of protein powder he bought from Martin out of the trunk of his car because the club just doesn't sell the stuff Martin believes he should be taking.

All of these people are passionate, but all of them are doing a lot of harm to your business since you, as the club owner, haven't taken the time to establish a consistent approach toward using fitness as the foundational tool of customer service.

The lesson is that many owners create a business, but end up letting the individuals in the business dictate the philosophy of fitness the club will use to help its members. Without a strong owner, coupled with a strong head trainer, the inmates run the asylum and use their personal beliefs and prejudices to train the members you own.

This scenario can obviously affect your level of customer service in the club. As clubs age, most become even more linear in focus, making it even more difficult to attract and retain members. Legendary customer service requires that you first must take your business back to a more balanced approach of management by ensuring that all staff can help and guide the members to not only get signed up easily, but to also get the highest results possible from that membership.

The Holy Trinity of a Fitness Business

Being successful in the fitness business starts with a solid foundation of *all* the things you need to know to make money:

- You have to understand the management/business side, including such items as marketing, staffing, and financial controls.

- You have to master the fitness aspect, which is what the client is seeking from us. This also means that you have to establish a single belief system in the club as to how you are going to approach fitness.

- You have to understand weight management, which is by far the biggest driver of potential members to a typical fitness business.

Most owners are also linear in their approach to business as well as fitness. By nature, most people are strong or passionate about one of these things, but they neglect their education in the other two areas.

It is not uncommon, for example, to see an owner who has been in the business for years still doing the same workout he did when he opened the business. He might have learned how to run a business successfully, but he hasn't learned anything new on how to train people since he was taught his first workout in the first club he worked in 20 years ago.

Another example of this is an owner who started in fitness in the 1980s. This guy built his first club in the '90s, and it looked like an equipment showroom, featuring every brand and type of fixed equipment made. Ten years later, he opens another club and buys the same basic equipment configuration because he hasn't learned anything new in fitness in the entire time he has been an owner. He knows what he knows, and that is the end of that discussion.

> *When was the last time the owners or managers*
> *of your business actually spent time in a training seminar*
> *with some of the good minds in the training end*
> *of the business, learning about all that*
> *has changed during the last few years?*

Many owners forget that we are not membership mills or just plain businesses that exist to sell somebody a product. We sell guidance and leadership to people who are seeking a higher level of fitness in their lives, but we stray from that idea as the day-to-day stress of running a business forces us to lose our way.

Successful Fitness Businesses
Have to Be Balanced Businesses

The people who start training businesses have the right concept in their heads, but they seldom use a sustainable business model to deliver their concept. But most of these trainer-based businesses do know how to get results with their clients.

Your trainer, who is most likely the guy who owns the facility, tells you that if you want to work with him, and if you want results, he will tell you what to do, he will tell you what to eat, and he will tell you that you will be taking supplements. If the training client is willing to listen, he will enter a very structured world where the only intent is to get results.

This system does get the results that many mainstream fitness facilities can't match. These guys have to get results in their business because if they don't, they soon run out of clients. If there are no results, then there are no referrals, which are almost everything in most of these small businesses.

Customer service is often very strong in these businesses as well since the entire process has to be individualized. This doesn't mean that every training facility does only one-on-one workouts, but that most clients are there trying to accomplish a specific goal in their life and are following a total plan to get there. Some of their workouts might be in groups, or even on their own, but they are still following a plan that will lead to their next level of desired fitness.

We Lose the Essence in Mainstream Fitness

What makes these facilities strong is the desire to see every client succeed; yet, this is what most mainstream fitness businesses lack in their plan.

> *The essence of what we do in this business is*
> *to create a business based upon the concept*
> *that everyone who trusts us with his money*
> *has the highest probability of achieving success.*

Where we go wrong is that most fitness businesses are out of balance. The majority of mainstream commercial fitness businesses only exist to sell memberships first with the idea of actually getting someone in shape somewhere down the list. These businesses can get you signed up as a new member, but they can't get you in shape unless you can afford one-on-one, and very few of these businesses have anyone who can discuss what it takes to be successful with personal weight management.

These commercial facilities are just one-dimensional entities; therefore, they are limited in their ability to make money. If you only get the generating-new-money aspect of the club business, then you will be forever chasing new members to replace the ones you lose each month because the existing members fail so often in their quest for fitness.

These members leave you because you simply neglected to learn how to get results with your clients through training, or to be able to guide them through their weight-management needs, which, as stated previously, is the biggest driver of leads to our doors. They trusted these clubs, and these clubs failed them.

Legendary customer service can only be achieved when you develop a staff that can master all three aspects of what it takes to run a financially successful fitness business. You have to be able to run it as a business, you have to be able to create results-driven training, and you have to have a support system in place that can guide people through weight-management issues.

If you have created a business that can apply all three of these concepts to your daily operation, you still might struggle with the delivery system it takes to apply this to your membership. Most clubs run every department as a segregated unit, meaning that the sales team has little interaction with the training department, or that the childcare people are rarely kept informed of what is happening in the rest of the club, or even how things work outside their small, enclosed world.

Owners just don't take the time or make the effort to keep every employee moving in the same direction at the same time. Very few are willing, for example, to block out three hours on a Friday once a month to get the entire staff together to ensure that everyone knows what is happening in the business, get a chance to know each other, and to become a team that is effective as a unit in servicing the membership.

Most owners train the staff from department to department and only give them the information that they need to know to do their job without regard to what is happening elsewhere in the business. This approach leads to territories being drawn between the departments and little, if any, support for what the others in the business are trying to accomplish. Everyone is in it for himself, since this is the model the owner created by isolating each department as a separate entity.

Every Staff Person Has to Master the Basics of the Business and What It Takes to Help Every Single Member in the Club

The role of the entire staff is to guide and support the members on their daily journey of fitness. Your team can do this better if they all have a grasp of the same basic information they can use to answer questions about programs and services, steer members from department to department, and to help the members understand every option the member has for support from the business.

For example, a new member walks up to a staff person on the floor and inquires about the club's cycle classes. The staff person's eyes light up, and a small drool forms at the corner of his mouth because he is so excited. "Our cycle classes are outrageous," he screams. "Sometimes we will go for two hours with the seats off just standing up and gutting it out. Only the strong survive, man; only the strong survive." The new member walked away, shaking his head, very glad he didn't sign up for that class.

This staff person is a cardio freak. He lives for the pain. He was also so excited that he forgot to mention that the class he was referring to was an advanced class that was only offered during the winter for serious bikers looking to enhance their winter training. The club offers a full schedule of cycling classes that were fun and easy to get started in, but the staff guy hadn't been to one of those in years.

The new member stopped and looked at the schedule again on the way to the locker room, noting that there seemed to be other classes on the list where he might not actually die if he took one. He decided to give it one more try so he walked to the front counter and asked the person there if she could give him any information about the cycling classes on the schedule. She looked up, smiled, and said, "I have no idea. I've never been in one" and returned to her work.

In the same club, the member encountered a cardio extremist and full-time staff person working prime hours at the front desk who had never been in a class and knew nothing about one of the club's major offerings. Neither person could provide any member service because neither could answer a basic question about a class posted on a board that was open to all members.

Customer service is the ability to help and provide service, but neither person could help or guide a member to where he wanted to go. How many other members were lost or confused because the staff couldn't help them? Most importantly, how many members does this club lose because the members just get frustrated and quit when their memberships are up? The club can obviously sell new memberships, but it is also obvious to the new member that the club isn't really interested in servicing the client after the sale since the management doesn't put any effort in developing its staff.

The foundation for service in this club would be to get all the staff trained with a basic, shared understanding of what is going on in the business and how to help people with simple questions. Listed in the following sections are a few simple tools and rules you can use to build this service base.

Everyone does everything.

All full-time staff members, including all managers and owners, have to be involved in all activities of the club on a monthly basis. This should not be optional, but required as part of the job of anyone working full time in the business. Part-timers should have special times set aside for them so they too can experience everything the club has to offer.

> *You can't sell the Ferrari if you have*
> *never driven the Ferrari.*

For example, if you have a full-time salesperson, she should be required to take a few group classes a month, work with a trainer (at the club cost) for at least one eight-week sequence, and try any other offerings, such as yoga or boot camp. This salesperson just can't explain the magic in the club if she has never done what the club offers.

Remember the study cited in the IHRSA's *Club Business International* magazine that was mentioned in Chapter 19? The majority of people inquiring about a club membership preferred a trainer to show them around, not a salesperson. If your salesperson has become totally involved in the club, she has a much better chance of establishing a rapport with the potential members since she can now answer questions based upon experience and not sales BS.

If the club offers weight loss, this salesperson should at least go through the first few steps as a real member would, whether she needs it or not, and if the club sells supplements, she should be given a 90-day supply as part of her job at no cost to try for herself. The more she knows, the more members she can help. This applies to all full-time people. If time is an issue, arrange a special class featuring one aspect of your programming.

Owners and managers especially have to be involved in everything the club offers on a regular basis, not just once and they are done with it. The senior management in the club often loses touch with what is really happening because the staff sometimes shields you from the reality of the business.

If you think about it, owners not taking a cycle class once in a while just to see what is being taught, and to get a feel for the upkeep of the room, is much like a restaurant owner not eating in his own place. The chef could be doing drugs and serving truly lousy food, but the owner will be the last to know since he will only know the truth when he hears it from disgruntled guests, which by then is too late.

Develop a common sales talk.

Sales talk means that each member of the staff explains everything in the club exactly the same way each time. All employees, whether new or old, develop their own terms and language to explain programming and services. This leads to incomplete information, or just plain wrong information, being given to potential members and to regular members, who might be inquiring about services the club offers.

Each component of the business should be explained exactly the same way each time, and the manager or owner should control what is being said. This common language, or sales talk, ensures that the important information is given the same way to anyone who is asking. This information can be given to each employee as single sheets in a notebook (one for each component) or printed on oversized index cards (5x7).

Keeping in mind the previous example about the two staff people who couldn't help the new member find out about a cycle class, following is a sample copy explaining a standard cycle class that both employees should have had memorized and been able to paraphrase for the inquiring member. This copy would have been on the back of a 5x7 card with the words "cycle classes" on the front:

> *Many of our members consider our cycling classes as the most fun and exciting cardio you can do anywhere. We offer six to eight classes a week led by a certified instructor who takes the class, each working at their own level, through about 45 minutes of a high-energy workout with great music. Working out in a small group like that brings out the best in you, and everyone who takes the class claims they get their best workout of the week, and have the best time, pedaling with their friends a few nights per week. And don't forget that all cycle classes are included in your membership.*

The staff should have a matching card for every program and service in the club. Keep the copy simple, and always cite the benefit (what's in it for the consumer) in each description. The staff may not get each word exactly right, but if they memorize and practice the scripts, over time everyone will start to get the key concepts presented correctly to the members and guests.

The Index-Card Training System

This system adds another layer on top of the sales-talk card system. Many owners balk at doing staff training because it seems so time-consuming. Spot training, on the hand, is a simple way to get a lot of training into your people in a very short period of time.

Spot training revolves around the idea that every staff person carries a stack of index cards that lists the programming, service, and all products on the front of the card with a list of the benefits or recommended explanation on the back of the card.

The manager can then just walk up to an employee during a slow time of day and say, "Get your cards out. Let's do five minutes of training." The owner can say the keyword on the front of the card and then check for understanding as the staff person either recites the description or benefits that are on the back. This allows the owner to get a feel of what the staff person really does know, and if he is starting to understand the total business and how it applies to all the members.

One of the problems you will encounter when you first create your cards is that everyone wants to list all the features of the club rather than answering the key question of what is in it for the members.

- A *benefit* is what is in it for the consumer.

- *Features* are the individual things that comprise the club, such as the number of classes or number of treadmills.

- Benefits sell memberships. Features don't sell anybody anything.

Most new salespeople have a hard time getting past the feature trap. "Here on the left we have 50 new treadmills. And here is our group room where we have 60 classes a week. We also offer personal training at $50 per hour."

If the consumer believes that what you are selling is good for him, and will benefit him in some way, he will buy it, but most club staff never get to the point of explaining what all this stuff really means to them. What the club contains is far less important than how you can use all this stuff to help the person get the help they came in for in the first place.

The index-card system is a starting point to get everyone on your team to start thinking about how to apply all the wonderful tools you have to an individual member. At some point, you can get these cards printed, but when you first begin, you can practice by just writing the cards by hand. Following is a sample front and back of a card, explaining training.

Front of the cards (Keywords used to cue the staff)

One-on-one personal training

Back of the cards (Explanations of the benefits of all the club's services, programming, and products)

- One-on-one personal training appeals to those members who want to have someone design a personalized workout for them and then to ensure that they always get the best workout possible through personal supervision and guidance.

- Some of our members find that having a set appointment with someone gives them that extra reason to come to the club that night rather than skipping their workout.

- This type of training is also for those members who are seeking specific fitness goals, but would rather have a professional design a program that is personalized just for the type of shape they are currently in or for their personal goals, such as improving in golf or losing 10 pounds.

Don't forget to create a card for each product you sell as well. If you offer supplements, for example, you would want a card for each product. The simplified version is: who should use this product, and what would that person get out of it if he did? If you answer that question and can put it on cards, you will ultimately sell more of everything in your club because the staff will become more successful in translating all that you sell to the people who ultimately buy.

The Club Worksheet

Every staff person must be able to explain all of the basic club components before he is allowed to work a single shift. Everyone on the staff should have a mastery of everything the club does and offers and be able to explain the other club service issues, such as how to get billing help or where to park on a busy night.

The club worksheet might be anywhere from 3 to 10 pages when completed, depending on the size of the club and its offerings. You can use these sheets as a training tool as well since everything a member needs to be successful should be covered on these pages.

Don't forget the small things, such as the cost of a shake, how to sign up for a special class, who to call if you need help, or even what days the club is closed throughout the year. The entire staff needs to know all the basics because you never want to tell a member you don't know an answer to a basic question if you can help it. The staff is there to support the members, and part of that support is the ability to keep the members informed. The following is just a rough guide to get you started. Use it to build a complete set for your club.

Services

- Sports bar prices and benefits

- Childcare hours, restrictions, and cost

- Spa services, and how to get information and an appointment

- Extra offerings, such as boot camps or specialty classes

Programming

- Group schedule, types of classes, extra costs, and instructors

- Cycle-class restrictions, and how to reserve a bike

- Lifestyle enhancement (personal training) costs, individual trainers, the differences between one-on-one and semi-private, specialty classes, and other offerings from the training department

Club basics

- Hours

- Days when the club is closed

- Who to call for membership payment information

- Parking issues and solutions

- The management team and their roles

- Current marketing

- How to answer the phone

Sales

- How to fill out a contract

- How to fill out a renewal

- How to check people in, use the computer system, and work with the club's third-party financial company

- How to fill out an inquiry sheet

- Following up

- Using the Welcome Guides

Personal

- The proper uniform

- Personal sales tools, such as sales notebooks

Other Methods You Can Use to Keep Everyone Informed

People who don't have real information tend to make things up to fill the gap, especially your members. Most people don't mind a little inconvenience once in awhile, but they do get angry when no one is telling them what is going on in the club. Following are two additional tools you can use to enhance your customer service and to keep the members informed in the club.

Member information boards

Anytime there is a new project going on in the club, such as a locker-room remodel, set up an information board near the project, and change it daily, telling the members what is going on, when things might be done, and any issues that might be causing problems. For example, if a construction guy didn't show, tell the members that someone was set for today but didn't show up, and that you are as frustrated as they are with the problem.

You can also use the member information boards to inform the members about new staff hires, maternity leaves, staff that has moved on to other jobs, or just about anything that affects them. Most of this stuff is suited for posting on your website, and some of the important stuff is worth posting on the social sites, but there is something immediate, and yes a little retro, about an owner taking the time to keep the members informed daily by simply creating a talk format on the board.

Continuity books

There are a lot of things that can really make your members mad, but nothing really sets them on fire like having a conversation with a staff person and then walking into the club an hour or two later and that person is gone, and no one is left who knows anything about what you are talking about.

Continuity books are simple tools that the staff uses to make sure that each shift change gently flows into the next. For example, a staff person might take a call from a member who wants to stop by the club that evening to meet with the head trainer to discuss workout options.

The member spends 10 minutes or so explaining what she wants, but the staff person just writes down an appointment with the trainer at 7:00 p.m. The member comes in to have the meeting and the trainer says, "So, how can I help you?" The member becomes frustrated because she has already covered that, but the staff person didn't leave any notes or do anything beyond just scribbling in the time and name.

If you were using the continuity books, the staff person would have had a place to write notes to the trainer, who came on shift later. Every employee reporting for duty starts his day with the book to see if there are any notes for him about issues he might have to deal with during his shift.

In this example, the trainer would have found a note that said something such as, "Nathan, Trish Miller has a 7:00 appointment with you. She is interested in training for a race later this summer and wants to see if you can train her. She has been in training with us since last year."

Nathan can now start his appointment with an idea of what is going on, which makes the member feel that she wasn't lost or taken for granted by the staff. In this case, the continuity book allowed the team to provide a higher level of service beyond just writing a name and a time in the book or on the computer.

Knowledge Is Service

Being able to answer someone's question with solid information might be the simplest form of great customer service. Your members should be able to approach any staff person and be able to ask basic questions concerning the operation of the facility. If you visit a Disney park, for example, even the people cleaning up the park can tell you where the gates are, where the restrooms are located, and how to get the help you need. No one works in the parks unless he can help you have a better guest experience, which is what we need to learn and emulate in our own businesses.

Do These Things Now

- If you want to be successful over time, you need to master management, how we train people, and weight management.

- Remember that the essence of what we do is helping people get success in fitness.

- Everyone on the staff has to master the basics of everything we do in the club.

- Every full-time staff person has to be involved in all the club's offerings and programming.

- Develop a common sales talk so that every person can explain the club's offerings professionally.

- Learn to keep the members informed about everything that affects them in the club.

Customer service is as simple as ...
removing the idiots.

One of the lessons learned by many owners too late in their careers is that sometimes you need to fire a few of your members.

Anytime you have hundreds of people or more all using the same club, the chances are very high that you will get your token fools, idiots, and socially incompetent and just plain mean people who should never be allowed to be part of a large social group.

Working out is an intimate activity, even in the largest of clubs, which seems to amplify the social issues some members carry with them in their lives. Members are casually dressed, everything is somewhat informal, and that seems to give certain people permission to do stupid things.

These people are also the ones who can lower the perception of customer service in your business, as well as your retention rate. People don't like to hang out with people who are loud, rude, or mean, and the good members will leave the club if you as the owner don't deal with the situation.

For example, all of these people should be tossed out of your club the minute you finish this page:

- *The guy who puts all the weights on the leg machine and then leaves them there after his set of moving the weight all of a foot for three reps*
- *The guy in the locker room who insists on getting on the scale right out of the shower leaving a puddle of water for the next guy to stand in to weigh*
- *The woman who bad-mouths everyone—and everything—in the club because she needs the attention*
- *Anyone who spits in a drinking fountain*
- *Anyone who sexually harasses another human being*
- *Anyone who continually drops weights or screams during a lift*
- *Anyone too stupid to flush a toilet*
- *Anyone who abuses a staff person over something minor in front of the members*
- *Anyone who chews your butt for closing on Christmas, Thanksgiving, or Easter*
- *Any member you can't stand to see in your business*

This list could keep going, but the point is that if someone is a distraction to you, they might be hurting your other members. Life is too short to hang out with idiots.

You should incorporate a "three strikes, and you are out" rule, which states that a member will be politely warned once about something, warned and threatened to be removed with the second violation, and then tossed with the third strike. Make sure you have a check in hand for any money you might owe against his membership so he has no reason to chase you for that issue.

21

The Magic of Common Courtesy

We often overthink customer service, believing that it is something only truly great service companies, such as Nordstrom or Disney can figure out how to build. Because of this belief, most owners really never try to instill a sense of service beyond the old "just smile" and "just be nice" training.

Service is a lost art in this industry, and you don't have to do a whole lot to make a difference in your business compared to your competition. Service training can be made easy, and it is often the simplest things that substantially raise the perception of good service in your business.

There are three basic assumptions you can use when you initiate a customer-service training program:

- Assume that none of your employees have ever had any common-courtesy training in business or from their parents, which means that this is the first place to start.

- Assume that none of your employees have ever had anyone coach them on acceptable business dress and developing a professional look.

- Assume that your team really wants to do the right things with the members and guests, but no one has ever taken the time to show them the right things to do.

You can't build legendary service unless you lay the first brick. This foundation is nothing more than the rules of common courtesy, which have faded and have become almost meaningless to many people.

In a service business, however, we need to rediscover this lost art because the essence of service is being polite to the people who are supporting our business through their memberships.

We will list the rules of common courtesy. You might want to modify these rules according to your own business, or your own training and upbringing.

Keep the list short, publish it as part of your employee manual, and teach it in your meetings at least once a month for as long as you own your business. You may smile at the simplicity of these, but sometimes implementing the old rules is still the most effective way to make money.

The Rules of Common Courtesy in a Fitness Business

- *Say "Please" and "Thank you"*: When you say "Please," you are acknowledging that the other person will have to go to some trouble in your behalf. When you say "Thank you," you are now acknowledging that someone did something in your behalf, or in the behalf of the company, and saying "Thank you" shows appreciation for that effort.

- *Be polite*: Polite is another word for being a professional. "Please," "Thank you," "You are welcome," and "Excuse me" are all words that demonstrate your ability to act like a professional while at work and in your life.

- *Be punctual*: Being punctual shows respect for the other person. Being late insults the other person because you are demonstrating that their time, and the person himself, are not worth your respect.

- *Never complain about any club problem, or about any person, to the guests of this house*: Gossiping makes you look foolish and hurts the image of the club. Everyone, no matter who they are or what they do, deserves a little respect.

iStockphoto/Thinkstock

- *Never swear in the club in front of a member or guest*: Many people find that swearing is offensive. Be respectful of the guests of this house, and do not swear while at work.

- *Switch off your cell phone as you walk through the front door*: You are hired to take care of the guests and to do your job. Cell phones interrupt your ability to do both. Cell phones are to be used on your breaks only and are to be turned off during your shift.

- *Do not chew gum in the club*: Smacking gum while you are talking to someone in person or on the phone is very unprofessional. You are a human being; you are not a cud-chomping bovine.

- *If you have forgotten someone's name, ask again politely by saying that you are sorry but you can't remember his name*: Use member names whenever possible, and ask if you forget. Each member is an individual, and using his name shows respect for who he is as a person.

- *Hold the door for the person coming through behind you*: Be polite, be courteous, and help everyone equally.

- *Greet all members in the club if you come within three feet of them*: We are the best part of the day for the members every day. If you walk within three feet of someone, stop and acknowledge that person, and thank him for coming to the club today.

These are the 10 basics of common courtesy and a good place to start your service training. Teach these in a one-hour staff meeting, and then repeat monthly as needed. If your staff can at least master these things, you are ahead of most of your competitors and are well on your way of establishing a customer-service-based club.

Other Important Courtesy Considerations

These aren't necessarily rules, but each item on the list is also a good thing to teach and review with your staff. All of these could also be added to your employee manuals and should be reviewed with all new hires.

- *Always introduce people who might not know each other*: If two members are in a group training, for example, make sure everyone is introduced to each other.

- *Use the magic words*: A flat "no" can quickly end any perceived customer service by the member. Teach the magic words that the staff can use whenever a member or guests asks a question:

   ✓ Of course.

   ✓ Absolutely.

✓ Yes, I can do that.

✓ I would love to help you with that.

✓ I will be happy to get that for you.

- *Never assume that the male is one you have to deal with in a couple*: This is rude. Treat both parts of the couple as equals, and explain everything to both of them at the same time.

- *Learn how to shake hands*: When you meet someone, male or female, offer a handshake. It is professional and conveys respect for the person you are meeting.

- *If a person has a title with his name, use it unless he instructs you otherwise*: For example, if a person is a doctor, then use "Dr. Kincaid" as the appropriate reference unless he asks you to call him something else.

- *Remove your hat indoors*: There are courtesy rules that seem loose in the fitness world but become more important as you progress in the real world. Removing your hat when you enter a building, especially in a restaurant, is a code that will serve you well in years to come as you build your career.

- *Don't pick at anything on your body in public*: Picking your teeth, or nose, or belly button isn't acceptable unless you are alone in your room.

- *If you are working out during off hours, you still need to respect the members*: If you are on a treadmill after your shift and a member walks up and has to wait because all the cardio is full, get off, and give the person your machine. It is all about him as a member instead of you as a workout person.

- *Use the corner of your arm when you sneeze or cough*: Sneezing into space is nasty. Sneezing into your hands is even nastier.

- *Wash your hands after every restroom break*: Do we have to explain this one?

- *Remember texting at work is the same as cell phones*: Turn your phones off completely as you start your shift.

- *Learn basic table manners*: If you progress into management at your club, you will occasionally be faced with a business luncheon or dinner. Avoid opening your mouth while chewing, learn to use a fork and knife, never place your napkin on your plate after you're finished, drink within reason, and dress appropriately for where you are going. Remember: the hat is off.

- *Dress for success*: Have pride, and dress like the professional you want to be.

- *Don't interrupt others when they are talking*: Stepping on others while they are talking to you is rude. Let the person finish, and then respond.

- *Respect your fellow workers*: Sexual harassment is not funny, may cost you your job, and is damaging to other people. Sexual talk, innuendo, hugging members, and other forms of harassment dramatically affect the image of the business, and most fitness businesses now have zero tolerance for any behavior deemed unsatisfactory.

This list is just a partial accounting of the things the staff needs to know. Some of these are discussed in other parts of the book but are also listed here as part of a complete list.

It's been said in this book before, but legendary service is nothing more than a lot of little things done well in a business. Having a staff that is polite and courteous to the guests and members is so much more service than most people find anywhere in their daily life and will quickly separate you from the others in your market.

Train your staff on the basics of courtesy, and then layer up on service from there. Common courtesy is the foundation you need to train a staff that can get and keep the members.

Do These Things Now

- Teach your staff the rules of common courtesy.

- Build courtesy into all staff training.

- Remember that being polite to people is the simplest, and strongest, form of customer service.

Customer service is as easy as ...
the owner in the club.

There is always something special about meeting the owner of any business.

You are in a restaurant enjoying your meal, and the owner walks up to your table, introduces himself, and thanks you for coming in tonight, giving the experience an added touch of service. There is nothing that can raise your perception of personalized service quite like an owner or manager who still cares enough to meet the customers of their business.

One of the biggest mistakes an owner will make early in his career is that he will start going home at five o'clock. At that point, he stopped being a club person, and he became a weak impression of a 1950s banker.

Money is made in the club in the evenings during the first four days of the week and Saturday morning up till about 1:00. This changes a little from market to market, but there is always a prime time in every club where most of the members show up, and where most of the money is made. Why do owners forget this and head home during the most important hours of the business?

It is interesting to see the habits of different owners throughout the years. You might find an independent who complains about the revenue in his single club, and who is out of there by 6:00 every night, or you might find an owner of 25 clubs who still visits a club each night of the week during prime time just so he doesn't lose touch with his members.

There is a correlation between the success of the owner and his willingness to stay involved in the business. Do you have to be there every night until closing? Of course not. But you do have to have a presence in the club and occasionally give the members a chance to see you standing behind that counter on a regular basis so they believe that you still care and are still willing to work your own business.

Even if you are old and jaded, or own too many clubs to matter, stand behind the counter once in a while during prime hours and shake hands, thank the members for being part of your dream, and stay in touch with what you built and own.

22

Handling
Member Complaints

Good owners seek complaints from their members. Listening to the people who know the working side of your business well, and who are interested enough to let you know when something is wrong, might tell you everything you need to know to be successful in that market. Sadly, we usually end up hating the members who complain the most, who in many ways might be the best members you have.

Complaining members are your best members. This group of in-your-face individuals cares enough about "their club" and their membership that they insist everything to be right and don't hesitate to point the things that aren't.

Complaining members are like the concerned spouse who tells her husband to sit up a little straighter, fight harder for that promotion at work, and to stop wearing that old tee shirt out in public. He is getting corrected for the same reason your members correct you: because both parties have a vested interest in you or their spouse, and because all of them care enough to take the time to try to make things better.

You will get complaints in the club business, and often more than you want. The skill of handling these complaints is another thing you can learn in your continued search for legendary service that will set you apart from your competitors in the market. Every club has members that complain every day. How you handle those complaints can establish your customer-service image in your market.

How to Handle Customer Complaints

There are three easy steps you can learn that will help you immediately raise your club's image of service:

- Establish a set procedure as to how you want your staff to handle each complaint.

- Develop a customer-service card that is filled out by the member for each individual complaint he might voice.

- Post these complaints on a common member service board to show the entire membership how quickly you reacted to the problem.

The Procedures Your Staff Needs to Learn

Your staff can learn this procedure in about an hour staff meeting. Every new person you hire that will be in direct contact with the membership needs to learn these steps and use them every time a member presents a complaint.

These steps can also be introduced as a training card for use in your index-card training system for spot training the staff. Make sure you teach the staff to follow every step every time, no matter what the circumstance or complaint.

Stop what you are doing, and listen to what the person offering you the complaint is saying.

Multitasking is the wrong move. If you continue to keep working on that computer, or shuffling paper, while the member is trying to share something that he thinks is important with you and you are not giving him your undivided attention, you will make him mad, and most importantly, you are being disrespectful to a paying member. Stop what you are doing, turn and face the member, and pay attention to what is being said.

Never argue with a member.

Arguing with a member solves nothing. For example, if a member complains about a certain instructor she doesn't like, there is often nothing you can do but listen. Firing back that everyone else likes that instructor, or that she is your most popular, doesn't help the situation at all. Be respectful and listen, and maybe the member has a valid point about something he noticed in particular that will help the club.

Don't let the member get you mad.

Many of the young staff get defensive and often feel that the members are personally attacking the club or a certain staff person, and they feel the need to defend. Your job is to listen and handle the complaint. If you feel the issue is personal, take the information the member is offering, but make sure a supervisor is informed about this particular issue if it seems like a personal attack.

Listen patiently while the member describes the entire situation/problem.

Sometimes the complaint is one you have heard before. For instance, a favorite treadmill might break, and five different members feel the need to complain at the front counter. Even if you have heard the complaint earlier, let the person finish the entire story. Just the act of venting frustration is helpful to the member and eases a lot of the stress. Resist cutting the person off early, and patiently let him finish the story even though it isn't your first time through it.

Let the member know that you are on their side, and that you are there to make the experience a good one.

Words such as "I completely understand your frustration" are powerful and let the member know that you care and that you are on their side. Thanking the person for taking the time to come and see you at the front counter is also important because some people do feel bad about sharing bad news with you. For instance, any conversation that begins with "You're not going to want to hear this but..." is probably about something broken in the club that is not only going to inconvenience the members, but cost the owner money as well.

Ask the member to please fill out a customer-service card.

Filling out a card is an action step that demonstrates that you are serious about listening and responding to any problem the members might share. Without the card, the member walks away mumbling, "Yeah, that was a waste of time. She didn't even write it down."

Keep the cards simple and easy to access behind the counter. The cards should be 5x7 inches and have the following headers, followed by sufficient space to write after each head, for the member to fill out on each card:

- The date

- The member's name

- The issue

- What needs to be done (from the member's viewpoint)

- Other suggestions for improving that section of the club (from the member's viewpoint)

- Taken by (the staff person's name that took the complaint)

- Action taken

The action section is for use by the club management. The club should write how it handled the problem, and when, and place it on the member service board that will be discussed later.

If you can fix it now, or solve it now, then do it now. If not now, then react to it within 24 hours.

In many cases, someone on the staff can fix the problem immediately, such as a toilet that is overflowing or a treadmill that simply needs to be reset. If you can fix it now, do it now, while the member is still in the club. Nothing conveys service to a member like complaining about something and five minutes later the staff is on it. If you can't fix it now, then respond within 24 hours. Complaints that aren't responded to in that time period frustrate the members who feel you are ignoring them and the issue at hand.

Follow up with the person who offered the complaint by sending a note thanking him for his concern. Reward him for his effort.

The member who offered the complaint should receive a hand-addressed thank-you card sent the next day, thanking him for taking the time to address the issue. You should also include a $5 gift card for use in the club as a way of thanking him for his time. The member took the time to help your business, and he should be rewarded for that extra effort.

Any members who take the time to complain are on your side and are usually doing the right thing for the business. Thank them for their time because they just might find something that is important to your business that you might have missed on your own. You want these bird dogs sniffing everything that is wrong because they are often the first ones to find things that can do you damage if left untended, and they should be rewarded.

If you have the crazy member who complains because he just wants the $5, then handle him separately, but don't crush a good system because one or two people might try to misuse it.

Use the Member Service Board to Demonstrate Your Service

The member service board is a very retro tool that still gets the job done in the club. This board is used by the management team to post the customer-service cards it collects as members complain, with the action taken by the club at the bottom of each card. The action taken should be written in red ink and dated with the day you fixed or responded to the problem.

For example, if a member complained about a piece of equipment that was broken and you managed to repair it the same day, the card would have the date taken at the top with "Fixed" at the bottom in the action section with the same date.

Using these cards and posting the action taken demonstrates a commitment to service. Many owners do things for the members, but feel a little frustrated when the members don't really notice that the management team is on top of things. This is your opportunity to get the sales kick you should have when you react quickly to their issues and complaints. It is good for the member and it is good for the club when you post these cards on a board visible to all the members during each visit.

You can hang this board outside the locker rooms for maximum exposure. You should also have a "We care" button on your Web page that lists the complaints and your action taken. Get the mileage out of doing the right thing for your members.

This board should have a large sign on the top, stating:

Member Service Board
We listen, and we respond to your suggestions.

Seek complaints; they are good for your business. Members who take the time to complain are your best members because they are vested in your club. Club owners with a lot of membership base can get worn out due to the intensity and sheer number of members who have something to say, but developing a good system will help you service these members without feeling you are getting beaten to death.

The final note about handling complaints is to do everything possible to avoid taking what the member says as personal. Complaints always feel personal because someone is telling you that what you own and care about is somehow not right.

Hearing four or five members a day tell you that your business has issues will almost kill any owner or manager, no matter how tough, but that complaining member who found the backed-up toilet might have saved you a new sale that day if it had been a guest who discovered the issue instead of a caring member.

Do These Things Now

- Set up a procedure to handle all member complaints.

- Teach this procedure to all employees with an emphasis on the counter staff.

- Develop a customer-service card for the members to use for their complaints.

- Create a member service board in the club.

YOUR BUSINESS IS A DIRECT REFLECTION OF WHAT YOU BELIEVE

Jupiterimages

Section Three

Customer service is as simple as …

VIP members.

We often lose our perspective the longer we are in business.

Take for example an owner who has been in business for 10 years and still has a number of members with him who signed up during his first year in business.

Over time, these members too often become perceived as a liability to the business. We get mad at them just because we know them too well, and that they most likely pay a lower rate than today's members.

Most owners can't stand this. One of the most often asked questions is whether an owner should ever raise the rates of the existing members. Let's see if we understand that question correctly. You as an owner want to raise an old member's monthly payment by a few dollars: this same member who has been with you for 10 years and who has never missed a payment. This is the guy you want to punish for his loyalty by raising his rate.

The comeback is always that it costs more money to run a club and that everyone's rates should go up. Yes, it does cost more money each year to run a fitness business, but the only ones who should be getting raises are the new members just coming in to the club. Pass the increased cost of doing business to the new members, but reward the existing members for their loyalty by not raising their dues.

There is another business issue that occurs when you raise existing dues as well. It seems that every time you raise the existing member's dues, the fallout from members who walk away from the club will cancel out the total gain you would have gotten from the raise; plus now you have a lot of members unhappy that you raised a rate they have had for 10 years.

The other way to look at this is that anyone who has supported your business for three years or longer should have VIP status in the club and should be rewarded for that loyalty, not penalized. He should receive a special membership card, receive special privileges and discounts not available to the regulars, and he should receive increasing status as he progresses through the years.

We sometimes get greedy and go after the old members because we don't like the payment amount, a membership that we were desperate to sell them 10 years ago. People who are loyal to you deserve respect and loyalty extended back to them. Honor your VIPs, and protect their rates rather than trying to make a small amount of money off the people who have been with you for so long.

23

Your Business Is a Direct Reflection of Your Personal Values

Imagine you have 10 staff people sitting in a room and waiting for you to begin your first training session about customer service. Also imagine that this is your first attempt at teaching customer service to your team. Where would you begin their education?

Before you begin the meeting, take a few minutes and think about why you got into this business in the first place. What made you open a fitness business when you could have done so many other things with your life?

The answer for most owners, if they were truthful, is that they have a deep love of fitness, and their initial motivation was to change lives through sharing their passion. There are also an increasing number of owners who might have gained a little more business sophistication through the years. This new generation of business person/fitness expert would couple this drive to change lives with the reality that a fitness business done correctly can make a great deal of money. This is what makes the fitness business so unique in the world of small business: you can change someone's life, and you can still make a lot of money doing it.

This owner has two choices when he begins this meeting. One choice might be to start with a simplistic list of actions he has gathered by sifting through all the classic, but generic, customer-service books lined up on the shelf at his local bookstore.

These books all elaborate on the need for service in a business, and most can tell you why good service is important to the survival of your business, but how to actually get it done is usually left to the overused niceties, such as smile, be nice to people, learn names, send professional emails, or any of the other simple actions we associate with simplistic customer service in the real world.

All these things are just the superficial trappings of customer service, and while each one is important, they are hard to inflict on a staff that feels that these requirements are a little too much fluff that gets in the way of actually doing any real work in the club.

Your best choice to begin your staff's customer-service education, however, would be to spend the first hour of every new hire's training teaching your staff about how you feel about the value of the customer in this business. Most staff will do anything you ask of them for a while, but customer service is about more than getting a few staff people to smile more at the desk. Before anyone works in your club, and comes near your paying members, they should be solidly anchored to what you believe and how you feel your members should be treated in your business.

Real customer service, meaning the kind that gets the members to bring their friends and to stay longer and pay longer at your club, has to be based upon creating a culture in the club that places a high value on the member and guests and how they are to be treated every day in the business.

Most staff people want to do the right thing, but there are very few people you hire who won't have their own interpretation about what is right and wrong when it comes to how to treat people. But when that person on your team brings his own belief system with him to work about how he feels people should be treated, his personal ideas may not reflect the way you want your paying members and guests to be valued.

Any staff person can learn to smile and say "Thank you," but if this is all you teach them, then you have missed the most important part of their training in customer service.

*True customer service is based upon core values
that guide the staff as to how we value
the people who support this business.*

In other words, you have to teach the people on your team what you believe and how you feel the members and guests have to be treated in your business before you can teach them the actions they need to implement service.

Always Do the Right Thing

If all else fails, always do the right thing. These are simple words, but these are also the first words you need to teach your staff. You can teach someone how to do a basic job and how to carry out a hundred different procedures, covering various situations that occur in your business, but none of the procedures teach the staff how to treat the large number of people they must interact with daily.

For example, a client walked into the club who was obviously stressed. He had a training appointment at the club scheduled, and he showed up with grease on his hands and a small tear on his dress shirt about an hour after his appointment was supposed to take place. He was on his way to the club when he passed a little old man along the side of the road, attempting to change a flat tire on his car.

The club's member stopped to help and realized that the man's spare tire was also flat. He put the old guy in his car, drove him to a station, had the tire repaired, and then took him back to his car and changed the tire. All of this had taken over an hour, and the member had completely missed his training time.

The club's procedure manual clearly stated that if any client missed an appointment, and did not give the club 24-hour notice, the member would be charged for the hour anyway. The member was clearly late, did not call as the policy dictated, and was now standing in the club in front of a young counter person who had to deal with this situation.

The club's owner had one set rule for everyone who worked in the club:

Always Do the Right Thing
*If, as part of your job, you have to make a decision
that conflicts with the club's procedures, always err
on the side of not hurting anyone, and we'll deal
with what should have happened later. You will
not be punished for taking care of the members.*

The counter person listened to the story and noticed the grease and torn shirt. She reminded the member about the club's policy, but told him not to worry, she could fix this situation. She found a trainer who would be free in 30 minutes, made the decision to let the member train with no penalty, set him at the counter, and bought him a bottle of water to help him settle down a little before his workout.

She could have been a robot and blindly stuck to the policy, which many owners would have been thrilled with. But in this case, she made a judgment call. Her decision, which was based upon her training that reflected how the owner felt about the value of his members, allowed her to handle the situation as she felt the owner would have wanted her to act.

Most staff instinctively wants to do the right thing if they know what the right thing is from your point of view. The staff in your club simply mirrors your belief system, but if you don't share what your core values are, then the staff will rely on their own values, which can often be in conflict with those of the owners.

Since most owners don't share their values as to how a member should be treated in the club, the staff is always in trouble and appearing to do the wrong things, because they make decisions based upon what they believe personally, which is often out of line with the owner, who never bothered to give them any guidance.

Customer Service Has to Be Built Upon Your Core Values

Your business is a direct reflection of what you believe, whether you consciously guide the staff or not. The staff is a lot like a four-year-old. Small kids miss nothing in the house. If you swear in front of your child, then your kid will wait for the opportune moment, such as when you have guests, and then start shrieking swear words over and over again until you have to lock him in the bathroom.

Your staff is just like this. For example, you are in your office at the club, and a counter person sticks her head in the door, "Sorry to bother you, but we just got a complaint about…" The first thing out of your mouth, after putting in a full day of frustration, is, "What did the animals tear up this time?"

Whether you realized it or not, you just did a little staff training there. You showed a total disrespect for your members in front of your staff person, and she will reflect that in every interaction she has in the business until she is taught differently. When you're out of the club, her decision-making is based upon the fact that your members are considered "animals" and that you don't really respect them that much, which must be how things are around this business.

The 1980s and '90s were not our best years in the fitness industry. Many of the big chains were tearing up the market with extremely aggressive sales and business practices. One of the biggest chain organizations at the time even received newspaper coverage detailing how the sales teams were writing memberships out of the phone book to make their numbers, or using guest sheets from potential members who visited but didn't buy to fake memberships and then forging the person's signature.

The belief system that came from the top in this organization was that these things weren't really that bad and were just the result of a good staff trying to make their numbers. The sales culture in the company was simple: sign them up, but don't let a potential member leave the office unless he was crying. The culture of the clubs was that this was the normal way to do business. The staff people working in these places had to either mirror this abusive system or walk away from their jobs.

Obviously, there was no customer service in these clubs. How can you help members when the overall culture clearly states that everything we do in these clubs is not in the best interest of the people we trick into signing memberships? Getting the new sale was far more important than keeping the members you already had.

The fitness industry has matured, and club owners are positioning themselves for the next era in the business. These owners realize that the competition for new members is extremely competitive, and that the business has shifted from just new sales at any cost, to the combination of the ethical acquisition of new members, coupled with keeping the ones you already have in the system longer. Customer service will be the major differentiator in the next era of the club business, and this service has to be based upon the direct application of your core values.

Establishing Your First Set of Core Values

Core values, which are the core beliefs we use to guide how we choose to live our own life, are built upon the combination of all these guiding questions that follow.

Examples of core values that you might adapt in your own life are honesty, respect, integrity, compassion, courage, and fairness. You might apply a single value, such as honesty, by consistently seeking and speaking the truth and by living a lifestyle without lying, cheating, stealing, or other forms of deception.

If you believe in honesty, and this is one of your personal core values, then you would choose to live your life by this rule without exception. Core values are who you are as a person, and reflect how you live your life and treat the people around you.

When you start to reflect on what you personally believe in, and how you want your business to be run, you have to first answer these questions as a guide to keep you focused. Remember, you can't lead a staff and create a culture of customer service if you don't or can't express what you believe and how you feel people you do business with should be treated.

- What core values do you believe in personally?

- How do you feel the members should be treated?

- How do you feel the guests who wish to become a part of your business should be treated?

- Are ethics, honesty, and professionalism part of what you teach the people who work for you?

- Are your values part of your hiring process to ensure that everyone who works in your business brings the same high standards you have to their job?

Core values can be also called a *code of ethics*, since a system of core values gives a person a sense of what to base their daily actions upon. *The 20 Laws of Customer Service in a Fitness Business*—which was mentioned in Chapter 10, and that will be described in detail later in this one—is a tool that defines the actions you take and the behaviors you exhibit as you carry out your duties in the club.

Many owners learn best when they have a model in front of them. The core values listed in this chapter are derived from many years in business and reflect the belief that the paying member deserves more respect than he is ever given in most clubs.

> *Members are doing us a favor when*
> *they choose us, and the people who support*
> *the clubs through their monthly payments should be*
> *given the respect they have earned and deserved.*

At no time in the history of the industry has learning to value the members you already have been more important. There are so many competitors who still believe that the members are expendable commodities, and that have little value beyond the initial sales number they represent. Learning to value these members is customer service, and customer service cannot begin unless you have a base of core values upon which to build.

Core Values Upon Which You Can Build a Business

Your goal in your club is to achieve legendary service, every time, with every guest, and with every member. These core values are your basis to start creating that plan. Action steps for many of these values have been blended throughout the rest of the book. Following are eight essential values you can adopt today in your life and business.

Guests first: Help every guest and every member feel that coming to the club is like coming home.

The "My house, my guests" analogy that started this book best reflects this particular value. We strive to create an environment where the customer is part of a mutual relationship where he is valued for his contribution to the business. Building a customer-service business means that you have to break away from the old culture of failure that has permeated the industry for so many years. The members are not expendable nor easily replaceable and have to be valued for their support of your dream.

Members have choices in today's market. They are people, not sales numbers. These people probably chose your business out of many other choices in your market.

We also strive to become the third leg in the member's life behind his home and his work. We want to be that third place that he values and protects, and is not willing to give up easily, due to his relationship with the club's owner, staff, and other members, and because he is respected for his contribution and support.

When the member walks through that door, we should be thrilled to see a paying customer arrive. Sadly, many clubs have so many members that the sense of the individual is lost. We can teach our staffs, however, to warmly greet each and every member coming through the door as if they were truly welcome guests to our home.

Show your caring attitude: Take the time to show sincere interest. Be involved, show that you care, and be sincere.

Good customer service is the ability to make a person believe, even if he is one of many, that he is a valued individual in your business. We do that by learning his name, greeting him at the door, thanking him each time he leaves the club for his business, and perhaps recognizing him occasionally with a birthday card.

Stated throughout this book is a very clear and simple statement:

Customer service is doing a lot of small things well.

Don't overthink service. Relationships can be cemented with a simple statement such as, "It is good to see you today, Kevin. Thank you for stopping by."

The core value is that you remember and teach that all the members are individuals and that each one is worthy of us knowing their name and recognizing them in the club as individuals.

Be knowledgeable: Love what you do, and share that passion with all who trust us to provide leadership.

People join clubs for a number of reasons. The main one, however, is that most are looking for leadership during their fitness journey.

Fitness is very confusing for most people and is becoming more so every day. Your members don't want to have to figure out fitness on their own; they want you to guide them in the process.

Most clubs simply can't do this because of the business system they have chosen. Their system is based upon the concept that only the elite few have enough money to buy leadership.

This also means that in most clubs the members never had a chance to succeed. No money, no help beyond a stupid workout that won't last more than a few weeks for the person. These clubs are in the membership sales business, where there are always more new members coming next week, and not in the business of taking care of the customers you already have.

Customer service is retention:

*If you can keep people in your club who pay longer
and stay longer, you have a huge advantage
over your competitors that still believe the
only good member is the new member.*

Your members will stay if they get results and will continue to pay for as long as they keep moving further down the fitness path. These people will leave early and often, however, if they don't get anywhere. Why would anyone keep paying for something that isn't working for him? That is sort of like going to a restaurant each week and paying the bill without getting any food. It is that simple in the member's mind, yet most club business plans are based upon a completely opposite system where you are expected to keep paying even though you don't get what you paid for in the transaction.

The core value is that we have the knowledge to get results for our members, but most club owners refuse to share that information because they feel it is too expensive to get to the customers, which is in essence lying to our members since they join thinking they are going to get help.

We claim we can help them when we take their money in the sales office, but once they are members, there is no help available because help is too expensive for most clubs to deliver due to their dependence on the traditional one-on-one model.

Delivering this core value means you have to create a system based upon cost-effective group dynamics that allows you to help the most people you can in your club and still be profitable. Everyone who signs up with you is looking for leadership and guidance, and it is up to you to create a system that allows that to happen.

Strive for profitability: Being profitable allows us to continue our mission into the future.

Very few people you will ever hire understand how money works. In fact, many of the staff that will come through your organization will have a very nasty view about money, believing that making money is bad, and that you can only make money if you somehow hurt people. This is why so many staff people always believe that customer service should be just giving the members things for free.

You have to teach people about money, how it is made, and especially that if you make money you can continue to help people in your community into the future. Get your staff involved in the money side of your business by showing them what things cost. Letting your team know, for instance, that your new heating and air-conditioning unit cost the same price as most of the cars they drive is not a bad thing for them to understand.

Show the team the little things of being profitable, such as turning off the lights in storerooms, getting better control of the utilities, not wasting supplies, and other tips that they can be aware of that affect your bottom line. Awareness is the first step toward understanding for many of the staff, but most of your people just don't realize the relationship between ethically generating money and the often huge cost of staying in business.

Have pride: Show pride in who you are and the company that employs you.

Pride in your staff can be created through leadership. No one really wants a routine job that is just one of many he might go through in his life. Employees who are happy at work are the ones who feel that what they are doing is important, and that their work is part of a much larger picture of making a difference.

Teaching to value the members, talking about changing lives, sharing testimonial success stories with your team, and teaching them pride in how they look and dress is all part of this core belief.

Pride can be instilled. Staff people dressed in nice clothes feel much better about themselves than kids dressed in tee shirts and jeans. Professionalism has to be taught, and you have to lead by example in a business full of younger people looking for value and meaning in their jobs.

Owners can also instill pride relating to the company itself. Teach your staff why you are different than the competitors and how your members are more valued and appreciated compared to every other club, but never bad-mouth anyone in your market since that often ends up devaluing what you are trying to accomplish.

Show respect: Respect and support those you work with, the community you live in, and yourself.

Your club has a shift change at 5:00 p.m. One of your counter people runs out of the back, heading home, and passes by the front counter. He notices that the team is getting slammed. He also notices that the trashcan is overflowing and that the blenders are both dirty. He jumps behind the counter, cleans the blenders, and then empties the trash. He yells, "You owe me" with a laugh, and then leaves. This is showing respect for the other members of the team, and this can be taught.

This is also a key area where the staff learns the most often by mirroring you and the other members of the management team. Your staff will mimic what they see each day through your example. If you demonstrate respect for your team, rather than taking a "Do as I say, or you will be fired" stance, the staff will respond and show you, and each other, respect.

Staff also learns well when you use strong examples, such as helping the team at the counter, that clearly illustrate the right thing to do. Again, most people want to do the right thing if they only knew what the right thing was. In your own life, did you ever have a teacher, strong parent, or coach who influenced your life and whom you still imitate through your own actions? Well, you, and your management team, are these people now. You are the ones that others are looking to as role models in your business.

Most owners fall short on showing respect for the communities in which they live and work. You want, you want, you want from the community, but you rarely give anything back, which shows a lack of respect for the people who you expect to support you in your business.

Every club owner needs to get involved in the community, and then get his staff involved as well. For example, an owner might get involved in a charity that he strongly believes in, such as the American Cancer Society. This owner should be on the board, contribute time and money to this organization, and get his staff involved as well.

If the local chapter has a walk to raise money, the owner can advertise heavily with his members, put teams together, and maybe run a volunteer booth that day to support the walkers. He can bring his staff as well, for pay or as volunteers, but never forced to go for free.

This charity can become the club's special commitment to the community, therefore, showing respect for the people in the area that support the business. It is also a great chance to spread the word about the club, and that type of PR does not hurt your business either. The old adage that you get out what you put into it is still true, but you can't take unless you give, which is illustrated by the core belief of respect for the community.

Many of your staff also needs help from time to time with learning how to respect themselves. Everyone stumbles at some point in his life and needs to be reminded that taking care of yourself starts with learning to respect yourself.

Working out is a form of showing respect for one's self. Eating healthy is another form. Beating smoking, staying away from drugs, and avoiding other high-risk activities are all part of leading a life that is based upon personal respect for who you are as a person.

Being an owner is often a form of being a role model. The people who work for you will look up to you. How you live and act is also something the staff will mirror. This core value teaches your staff lessons that will stay with them forever.

Change lives: Always remember that every member and every guest represents a chance to change a life.

There isn't another business like the fitness business when it comes to the effect we have on such a large number of people. If you own a fitness business, you have the opportunity to change many people for the better, helping them live more healthful and productive lives.

For example, if you have 500 members through your club on a Monday, that is 500 chances you had that day to make a positive difference in those people. Police and firemen, two of the hardest jobs in the world with very little pay in return, might have a chance to affect a few hundred lives a year. Fitness people, on the other hand, have the power to change thousands of lives throughout a typical business year.

Most owners, however, forget this over time. The dark side of the fitness business is that it is so customer-service intensive. There will always be a certain percentage of your membership that is high maintenance and who have the need to express their feelings daily. Sometimes they are right, and the things they find do need attention. At other times, they are wrong, and it is really about them seeking attention for themselves.

Over time, this constant criticism can wear you down and you can lose sight of this core value completely. *We exist to change lives.* That is why your business was built. That is why you exist, and that is why the fitness business will be even more important in the future.

Teach your staff that you are doing the right thing, and that your business does matter, and is far more important in the community than the endless fast-food restaurants and other businesses that don't always do the right things for their customers.

Bring it all: At the end of your day, can you truly say this was your best work?

Learning to manage people is a game of trial and error, especially for a young manager. Perhaps one of the biggest breakthroughs you can have is when you start learning to ask the right questions to your staff each day. They want guidance, but we often fail to lead because we fail to inquire.

Most owners and managers at some point begin to realize the typical questions they use to get information from their people are somewhat worthless. For example, the answers to these types of questions, such as "How did we do today?" or "How was it today?" tells you nothing about what happened in the business, and more importantly, does not really give you any idea as to what that person contributed to your business during his last eight hours of work. You asked a generic question, and probably received the usual generic answer: "It was a good day. We had a lot of business."

Change your questions, and you can change your results, especially if you are trying to be the leader and role model the team wants and needs. A question that you could be asking that would lead to better information might be, "You just finished an eight-hour shift working for me. Was that truly the best work you are capable of in this job?" Ask this question, and things will start to change in your business.

The usual answer to this when you first use it to challenge your staff, once they get up the courage to actually answer, is, "I'd say it was about 80 percent."

Another way to ask this question is, "Did you really bring it all today?" Anything less than a 100-percent response means that the staff person wasted a day of his life, and had a less-than-effective day in your business. The core value is that you have to teach your staff to strive for a 100-percent day every day, because everything else is a waste of the most valuable thing you own, and something once wasted can never be regained. As you age, have children, and take on responsibilities in your own life, you come to realize that there is nothing more important than a day well lived, but your young staff hasn't learned that lesson yet, and it is your job to start the learning process.

You can't change lives by living an 80-percent day. You can't be the best part of a member's day, every day, if you can't learn to reach your own potential each day.

You do not have to be a motivational guru to adopt this as a core value in your business. Merely asking the question, "Did you bring it all today?" or "Was it a bring-it-all day?" will change how your team thinks about what they are trying to accomplish while they spend a day at your business. Leadership is asking the right questions, and this is a powerful question that can get some good discussions going in your business.

You might also want to introduce this saying into the culture of your club. Have signs made with "Bring it all" on the front, and hang them in the staff rooms, in your office, and wherever else the staff might spend time. Challenge them by using the question often as part of your daily routine.

This is also a good personal value to make part of your own life if you haven't done so yet. Many owners get into the routine of being very busy, but we lose the skill of being effective. There is a big difference in the business world between being busy all the time and running a financially successful business. Busy is busy, but effective is something totally different. Ask yourself this question every day, and hang a small sign on your computer: "Did you bring it all today?" If you can answer yes to that more than occasionally, you are on track to becoming a legendary owner—and perhaps living a legendary life as well.

Core Beliefs Define the Motivation

Core beliefs define the motivation behind the action. The simple tools of customer service become much more important to the staff when they understand that what they are doing is part of a larger concept based upon the premise that everything they do is part of showing value and respect for the members through your beliefs.

Once you establish your core beliefs, you can then add another layer on top. This layer takes the "why we do things" to the next level, which is "how we do things" in the business. We call this level of action *The 20 Laws of Customer Service in a Fitness Business*, which is a tool that defines the actions and behaviors employees take in the day-to-day operation of the club.

In other words, core beliefs are things we believe in and who define who we are, and the code is how we carry those things out in our interaction with others in the club. These should be added to the employee manual and reviewed during their first three hours as a new hire or during their initial training.

The 20 Laws of Customer Service in a Fitness Business also makes a great one- to two-hour staff training since each point is designed to raise a discussion with the staff as to how to apply these things in your business.

The 20 Laws of Customer Service in a Fitness Business

1. Always remember that those who are paying to belong to this club are people who we consider guests and are not account numbers or just another member.

2. Do exactly what you promise when you promise.

3. Always show the proper respect for our guests by being on time, prepared, properly dressed, and ready to take care of their needs.

4. Answer the phone within three rings, using a positive welcoming statement.

5. Greet our members at the door as if they are coming home.

6. Know everything about what we offer, and be prepared always to answer questions and help our guests get what they are looking for in our club.

7. Thank every single member every single time they leave the business and whenever they make any additional transaction with our business.

8. All managers will be available at anytime while on duty to help solve a guest's problem.

9. Keep the guests informed about every change or issue in the club immediately if it affects the quality of their visit.

10. We promise to be the best part of the guest's day, every day. Always remember that we work so our guests can enjoy their time with us.

11. We are here to make things easier for our guests.

12. Always be courteous, and always be smiling.

13. Never complain about any club problem to our guests.

14. Use the guest's name every chance you get.

15. Any questions from our guests? You find the answers.

16. If you can, handle it yourself instead of passing it along to someone else.

17. Strive for profitability. The profitability of our company creates opportunity for everyone who works here and a better experience for our guests.

18. Do everything in your power to make this the cleanest facility in town.

19. The safety of our guests is the most important thing in this business.

20. Take this job seriously, but not yourself. Remember, we are the best part of their day every day, so make it fun.

These seem like very simplistic guidelines for an employee, but if you look more closely, the laws are really a detailed set of rules that govern the day-to-day behavior of all the people that work in the clubs.

This code should also become the core of the culture of service you are trying to build in your business. Changing the culture in most clubs is mostly getting everyone armed with a common set of beliefs and actions and then using those to run your business every day.

For example, if you have 20 employees in your business, and all of them are coached weekly to live and work by the code of conduct, then a rule such as "Use the guest's name every chance you get" becomes an action statement carried out daily by your entire staff. Twenty people all learning and using the member's names each day becomes a powerful customer-service tool that most other clubs can't match.

Another way to state this is that we plan the staff person's day based upon what he will be assigned to do for work, but we neglect to teach this employee how to act during his day.

*Ninety percent of what we teach the staff is
what to do, and 10 percent or less is how to
interact with our paying customers.*

The core values are nothing more than a tool to teach your staff how you feel about the members and guests who support your business and how they should be treated. The Code of Conduct tells the staff how to translate those values into concrete action steps they can use every day they are at work to dictate how they interact with the most important people in your business, the paying guests.

Do These Things Now

- Think about, and then write out, your personal core values.

- Teach every staff person to always do the right thing by the member, and they will not be punished.

- Your staff mirrors how you act in your business. Be aware that everything you do is a form of staff training, whether you realize it or not.

- Teach the eight core values in a staff meeting.

- Teach *The 20 Laws of Customer Service in a Fitness Business* to all staff during their first day and base the service culture of your club on these action steps.

- You have to teach what to do in their jobs, but you also have to teach your team how to respect and value the people they interact with in your business.

About the Author

Thomas Plummer has been working in the fitness business for over 30 years. He is the founder of the Thomas Plummer Company, as well as the National Fitness Business Alliance (NFBA), a group of industry vendors and suppliers who have banded together to provide education and tradeshows to the independent club owner. Currently, the NFBA offers over 20 seminars a year across the country.

Plummer is in front of more than 5,000 people a year, through numerous speaking engagements as a keynote speaker and event host, and he also gives lectures and workshops worldwide. He has authored five books on the business of fitness, which have remained the bestselling books in the industry for over 10 years, and several of the books are currently used as textbooks in numerous college programs.

Due to the over 50,000 people who attended his seminars during the past decade, coupled with the continuing popularity of his books, many industry experts feel that Plummer is the most influential person working in the fitness industry today.

In the early 1980s, he was the vice president of marketing for American Service Finance, the largest third-party financial-service provider in the industry. Soon afterward, he became the executive director of the National Health Club Association, which was founded by the owner of American Service Finance to capture the independent market.

He created Thomas Plummer and Associates in 1991, and started a small, limited tour with industry sponsorship. In 2003, he reformed the company and moved it to Cape Cod, Massachusetts. The NFBA, which was founded in 2006, is currently the largest provider of education for the independent owner in the world.

Plummer attended Western Illinois University and then attended graduate school at the University of Arkansas. He started working in the martial arts (Taekwondo) in 1976. He worked as a ski instructor in Colorado for 10 years, raced bicycles in the 1970s, reached a third-degree black belt in the 1980s, and loves music, books, and the water. He currently lives on Cape Cod with his family, travels extensively, and is presently working on his next book project.